D1541716

SEWING THE EASY WAY

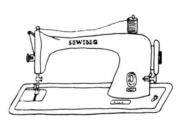

Books by Mary Johnson

SEWING THE EASY WAY

New, Completely Revised
and Enlarged Edition

MARY JOHNSON

NEW ILLUSTRATIONS BY MARY JOHNSON
RENDERED BY JEANETTE FOLETAR

E. P. DUTTON & CO., INC.
NEW YORK   1966

TT518
.J6
1966
Copy 2

Copyright, ©, 1958, by E. P. Dutton & Co., Inc.

Revised Edition Copyright, ©, 1966, by Mary Johnson

All rights reserved.   Printed in the U.S.A.

No part of this book may be reproduced in any form without
permission in writing from the publisher, except by a reviewer who
wishes to quote brief passages in connection with a review written
for inclusion in a magazine, newspaper or broadcast.

Published simultaneously in Canada by
Clarke, Irwin & Company Limited, Toronto and Vancouver

Library of Congress Catalog Card Number: 66–13657

To My Students Who Have Taught Me So Much

CONTENTS

PREFACE

This book has been written at the suggestion of many, many women who have enjoyed learning to sew the modern way in my classrooms. Sewing should be fun. It should be a delightful relaxation that is gratifying both financially and creatively. It will be, if it is done in the modern way. The new methods outlined in this book have benefited women who have had vast sewing experience, as well as those who were just starting out on their first sewing ventures.

These modern techniques in sewing are designed for the busy woman of today, who, with all her other activities, desires to pursue the art of sewing beautiful clothing for herself and her family. Many time-consuming steps, long associated with sewing, have been eliminated as unnecessary. Modern construction procedures and short-cut techniques have been substituted instead, not only to cut time down to a minimum, but also to give better results. These methods have proved invaluable to women who sew professionally, because by saving time, they can reap greater reward from their work.

With attractive dress playing such an important role in life, making your own clothes is a wonderful hobby. Besides enabling you to dress distinctively at a minimum cost, sewing gives you a feeling of satisfaction comparable to the elation an artist feels when exhibiting a masterpiece. The beautiful colors and textures of modern fabrics, the endless variety of patterns and trimmings, will put your imagination to work and bring out the true artist in you.

Treat your sewing and styling ventures as an enjoyable diversion. Remember, the modern woman need not sew for herself or her family unless she really wants to, as her clothing needs can be met most satisfactorily by a gigantic clothing industry. Mass-produced fashions at popular prices have earned the American woman the reputation of being the best dressed in the world. All types of clothing are available at prices within the reach of every clothing budget. Quite frequently, the popular-priced models are copies of more exclusive designs, with slight changes made in fabric, cut, and trimming, in order to cut down the expense of manufacture.

The woman who is not too concerned with individuality in her wearing apparel is quite happy with these fashions and looks very smart in them if she chooses with an eye toward becomingness and suitability. On the other hand, the woman who feels that absolute exclusiveness is of prime importance in her wardrobe must pay for this distinction. She is most gratified by the material advantages of making her own clothes, as home-sewn clothes can be produced at about one third the cost of ready-mades.

The sewing techniques set forth in this text will enable you to produce any type of wearing apparel with the utmost confidence. You will be able to add attractive details to your costumes, whether or not they are featured on your pattern. "Driving" the sleeves into the armholes and "walking" the linings into your coats and jackets will be a joy. These foolproof techniques are the result of the author's many years of experience in the field of sewing and styling, both as designer and teacher.

It should be the aim of all women who sew to produce clothing comparable in appearance to fine ready-made designs, or, better still, with those made for the individual by an expert craftsman. These professional results can be achieved by any woman, whether her experience in sewing is vast or nonexistent. Frequently the person sewing for the first time, who knows only enough to thread the sewing machine properly, does a better job than an experienced sewer. She does not have old-fashioned habits to "unlearn," but faithfully follows the instructions set forth for her, not knowing how to deviate from them in any way.

Some women who sew very well always seem to miss the mark of smartness in their finished work because they put too much time and effort into it. If you are one of these people, you'll find it to your advantage to proceed with the steps in the exact order and method in which they are presented in this text, as if you were sewing for the first time. You will be pleased with your results, and will surely adopt these new methods in your future work.

The art of sewing has been handed down from generation to generation, and many women are still using the methods used by their ancestors. These women would be horrified at the thought of heating a flatiron on top of the coal stove in order to press the seams of their sewing projects. Yet they sew just as their grandmothers did, with endless pinning, basting, and fitting. No wonder they think of sewing as a chore. The modern sewing machine is geared for speedy, easy work. The sewing techniques used here will give you sewing methods just as easy and up-to-date as your new machine.

To get the most out of this book, use it as you do your cookbook. It isn't necessary to remember from one sewing session to another how a certain operation is done any more than it is important to remember what ingredients go into an unusual dessert that you make only for special occasions. Sew with the sewing book at your elbow and refer to it as you proceed, so that you can refresh your mind as you go along. Don't close the book until the last stitch has been taken. Isn't that what you do with your cookbook?

MARY JOHNSON

SEWING THE EASY WAY

INTRODUCTION:
THE ART OF DRESSING
ATTRACTIVELY

Attractive dress has been the desire of the human race since the first primitive man adorned himself with leaves, shells, and bones to gain admiration and praise from other members of his tribe. Even today, the tribal chief in remote parts of the world displays his rank and commands respect with an ornate and impressive appearance.

The civilized world is not too different. Society first judges us not by what we are, but by how we look to others. Our impressions of other people are influenced by the clothes they wear, and we, in turn, are judged in the same way. Your true value as a person will eventually be recognized, but this recognition comes sooner if your appearance is pleasing.

To look smart is to feel smart. Because clothes have a psychological effect on the wearer, they can very easily affect your success or failure in your job and in your social life. Every woman knows what a new hat or a new dress can do to bolster her confidence and self-esteem.

Your clothes, therefore, besides protecting you from the icy winds of winter and the scorching heat of summer, should flatter you in every possible way. Your figure faults should be minimized; your good points should be highlighted. Your clothes should be becoming in color, and their style should be suited to your age, type, and personality. Let your way of life determine the kind of wardrobe you wear. Too many cocktail dresses are a waste unless you attend many cocktail parties.

Choosing the right styles for *you*

A really glamorous woman is not just born that way. Rather, she cleverly creates the illusion of a perfect face and figure. Some women have a natural flair for choosing costumes that are right for them in every respect, but most of us must acquire this aptitude. The best way to do this is to learn a few basic principles. Once learned, apply them unfailingly to yourself and all your clothes.

19

A well-dressed woman combines good taste and fashion sense with a dash of imagination and foresight. She is analytical in her selection of wearing apparel, not only from the angle of becomingness and suitability, but also from the standpoint of the possible lifetime of her styles. She chooses the important items of her wardrobe—her coats, suits, and fine basic dresses—in designs that will keep her smartly and fashionably dressed for several seasons.

It is not unusual to hear someone say, when complimented on a costume, "Oh, I've had this for at least three years." Trends in fashions come and go, but a good style goes on indefinitely. Extremely high-fashioned or dramatic clothes do not always express good taste, but those chosen with an aim toward loveliness, simplicity, and suitability to the wearer always do. Good clothes have a subtle elegance about them, rarely extreme either in design or color.

Just as dramatic designs soon become outmoded, exotic colors are big news for one short season before being replaced by other colors equally as exciting. Include these colors in your wardrobe by all means, as they will add new interest to your clothes, but choose them only for your "little things." A scarf, belt, or costume pin will give you an up-to-the-minute look without breaking your piggy bank. Blouses, sweaters, and skirts, even an extra dress, will help to establish your reputation as a smart dresser without involving major investments. But the basic items in your wardrobe should be chosen for several seasons of wear. A gray worsted suit with simple lines will fit into many more roles in your daily activities than would one of more dramatic design or color.

You will surely be admired for your good taste in dress if you give thought to the important matter of selecting wearing apparel suited to your age. All things in life eventually come to an end, and so it is with your youth. At about the middle thirties you should face the stark fact that most girlish fashions won't be so becoming to you as they were in the past.

Many women cling to the idea that if they cover up a mature mind with a girlish hairdo, and continue to wear fashions meant for a high-school junior, they will remain young looking forever. This is a mistake. Clothes that are too juvenile in style tend to make the mature woman look older; the contrast between adolescent attire and the skin, hair, eyes, and figure of an older woman is too great for pleasing effect. You can remain distinctively dressed, regardless of your age, with styles that have a certain timeless quality about them, neither too young nor too old.

The transition from girlhood to a more perennial smartness need not cause you to change your mode of dress too drastically. Although a junior miss might wear your timeless fashions becomingly, your sophistication and charm would be obviated by most of her clothes. In other words, Daughter should be able to wear most of Mother's selections, but Mother should not wear some of Daughter's.

Try to picture in your mind how the outfit of your choice would look on someone ten or fifteen years younger than you. How would it look on a person ten years older? Chances are that if you keep in mind the quality of agelessness when choosing your ensemble it would be equally becoming to them both, just as it will be to you.

How to dress to suit your figure type

A woman's size or age has never been detrimental to her attractiveness, as long as she is clever in emphasizing her good features and camouflaging the bad ones. Certain basic principles make some designs do more for you than others, and although fashions constantly change, these principles remain the same. Line is one of the elements of dress design that should always govern your choice of styles. Depending upon your individual figure, emphasis on vertical lines, horizontal lines, or diagonal lines will have a magical influence on the all-over looks of your garment.

It does not matter how small or large you are, or how wide or narrow. The important thing is that you must have an appearance of good proportion. The feminine figure is pleasing to the eye when the shoulders and hips are equal in width. For example, if yardsticks were placed against the right and the left sides of a well-proportioned figure, touching the hip line and shoulders, they would form two vertical lines. But if the figure were larger at the hips, the yardsticks would project ungracefully outward at the hips and tilt inward at the top, making the shoulders look small by comparison.

Many women believe that their figure fault lies in narrow shoulders. Since it is easy to make an object look larger than its actual size, this situation is easily remedied: their clothes should feature details above the waist with lines to give the appearance of width. Styling lines can be just as effective with other figure problems.

Remember that lines are produced not only by the construction seams of the garment, but also by the soft, flowing ripples of the fabric in the skirt and bodice, the placement of the tucks and darts, the spacing of the pleats, width of gores, the angle of pockets, and other details, as well as the general outline of the silhouette.

Getting acquainted with a few basic principles on the subject of line and its wonderful merits will soon put you on the right track toward making parallel lines out of those imaginary yardsticks, no matter what your figure. Just remember, actual size doesn't matter. It is only im-

21

portant that you appear proportionate. Clothing designed with the right lines for you will do the trick.

It will be to your advantage to study each of the figure types described on the following pages. They represent five basic figure problems. The manner in which the element of line is applied to each of them will help you solve your own problems. The matter of choosing flattering pattern fashions for your newest undertaking will be simplified greatly if you know which lines to look for and which to avoid.

True, there are many more figure types than can be analyzed here, but too many examples would only tend to confuse. Get acquainted with these fundamental types, and you won't go wrong.

THE HIP-HEAVY TYPE   If you have a hip-heavy figure, you will achieve an appearance of good proportion with designs that place interesting details above the waistline, keeping the styling of the skirt unobtrusive. In this way the eye is directed away from the faulty area of the figure. The hips will take on a slimmer appearance when the lines of the skirt have an up-and-down movement, produced by vertical stripes, gores, pleats, or rippling fullness in the lower section of the skirt. These ripples form up-and-down lines, and thus create the illusion of length, slimness, and better proportion.

The flare of the skirt should start from the largest part of the hips and drape becomingly from there. If the fullness started higher, the effect would be one of bulk. Skirt fullness should be restrained, but a too narrow skirt would also call attention to the size of the hips, thighs, and derrière. If a skirt needs to be slim in order to do justice to the upper section of the design, make sure that the line falling from the largest part of the hips to the hem line is straight, without the slightest slope inward toward the legs. This would only emphasize the bulge of the hips. Any such inward slope can be remedied easily when you cut the skirt. This will be fully explained farther along in the text.

Many women with this figure problem also need to minimize the size of their legs. The first consideration for a slimming effect here is the length of the skirt. This matter, of course, is determined by fashion changes, and is not a hard-and-fast rule. When the legs are heavier than average, it is smart to wear the skirt slightly longer than the popular length while still maintaining a stylish appearance. This will also improve the general silhouette of the figure. An inch in either direction from that decreed by fashion will not throw you out of focus in the fashion picture. But don't go too far—a skirt worn too long may call attention to the fact that you are concealing something.

The upper section of the garment should carry the interest of the design. Dramatic detail will hold the eye where it should be held and keep it away from the faulty area. For instance, the pockets on a suit jacket should be located above the waistline instead of in the hip area. A jacket with lapels, instead of the cardigan type, will emphasize the upper part of the figure. The shoulders will appear broader, and thus make the lower section of the figure seem slimmer in comparison.

Sleeves, too, play an important part in your appearance. If long sleeves are full or the cuffs are wide and bulky, the hips are doubly emphasized when the arms are in a downward position. Sleeves that are smooth and trim below the elbows are far more becoming to the hip-heavy figure. Short sleeves, however, are a different story, since the upper part of the figure can stand any width that wide cuffs or dramatic treatment can give.

Wide or colorful belts should not be worn, even when the waist measurement is small, since they would only point up the difference between the hips and the waist. Narrow, self-colored belts are much more satisfactory. If a contrasting belt is worn, it must be of the narrowest type possible.

Proper choice of fabric is also important in minimizing the size of your hips. The cloth should be smooth and light in weight, since heavy materials will add to the over-all bulk. Dull finishes are the best, because lustrous surfaces such as satins, polished cottons, and iridescents, would highlight the large parts of the figure.

THE BUST-HEAVY TYPE A woman with this type of figure gives an illusion of roundness even when she is of normal weight, owing to the fact that she carries most of her weight above the waistline. Curved lines create illusions of softness and fullness, so this type of figure should avoid them in styling lines and in printed fabrics. Collars and lapels should be pointed, to make the natural figure less round-looking.

A top-heavy appearance is minimized when the interest of the design is concentrated on the lower section of the garment, below the waist instead of above it. If the suit jacket features pockets, they should be placed below the waistline to draw attention away from the upper part of the figure. Disguise the upper figure with simplicity, softness, and a beautiful fit. Moderation is the keynote here, so simplicity should not be carried to the extent of plainness, any more than softness should be full and blousy. Too close a fit would only call attention to the size of the bust.

The imaginary yardsticks when placed on each side of this type of figure would tilt outward at the shoulders and inward toward the legs. The thing to do, then, is to straighten them out with fuller skirts. Pencil-slim skirts would make the bust look heavy, but a slight flare will balance the figure.

Sleeves should be trim and smooth above the elbows. When a short sleeve is desired, a much more pleasing effect is achieved when the length is extended to just above the elbows, instead of stopping directly in line with the heavy part of the bust line. More liberties can be taken with long sleeves, where wide cuffs and fullness below the elbow will create a flattering balance.

Necklines are important focal points and should be chosen to enhance the facial features. For example, a long, thin face can be widened by a neckline that features soft, rounded edges. A round face would look better with a low V neck, or a square one. The bust-heavy figure type must be extra careful in the selection of necklines, because the neckline must flatter her figure as well as her face. This type generally has a short neck. Large collars, high trimming, or heavy jewelry would only call attention to this fault. Collars should be small and pointed. They should lie flat rather than roll up onto the neck. Collarless necklines are also good, as these show the entire length of the neck to full advantage. Lapels should be kept narrow, long, and pointed, never round.

Ornaments such as brooches, bows, and flowers are more flattering when placed to one side, instead of in the middle of the chest. At the side, they create a diagonal line that is a most effective camouflage for a large bust.

Fabric textures should be confined to the medium and light weights, to keep the figure from looking heavier than it is. Fabrics with dull finishes are better than those with lustrous surfaces. Clinging fabrics, such as glove jersey, are not so good as those with firmer textures. Transparent chiffons and organzas are not so suitable as fabrics that are opaque.

Belts should be kept inconspicuous, so that the eye is not attracted to the great difference between the bust line and the hips. Too wide a belt will accentuate the bust line.

THE HALF-SIZE OR DIMINUTIVE TYPE At one period of her life the half-size figure wore a junior size, but extra weight gained along the way has placed her in the half-size category. If she is smart, she will not stay in that class any longer than it takes to wake up to the fact that, although she has a short neck, waist, legs, and arms, she can look smart, trim, and "diminutive" instead of short, dumpy, and half-size.

This type is very apt to make herself look older, unless she steers clear of the fashions that are aimed for the half-size mature figure. You do not have to look frumpy or middle-aged, no matter what age group you're in, especially when you can choose your own styles and make your own clothes.

Half-size patterns are made in limited numbers with little choice of styles. Although this individual may be shorter than average, she should always select pattern designs as though she were of average

24

height, choosing lines that would give slimness and length to the average figure. The illusion of extra heights thus gained will make up for the limitations of her own short stature. Choosing her patterns in this manner will give her a much wider selection of styles than afforded by the half-size patterns.

Fabric selections should be confined to smooth, lightweight textures for a more streamlined appearance. Bulky fabrics add weight and reduce the height. Accessories should be in keeping with this woman's size. She should not carry oversized handbags, nor should she wear wide-brimmed hats. Hats with an upswept look will do more flattering things to the silhouette than those that seem to swoop downward to the shoulders. Jewelry, too, should be in proportion. Although it need not be so tiny as to appear insignificant, it should not be overpowering in size, either.

Point upward in every way you can, with the lines of your design, the points of your lapels, the tilt of your hat, and the style of your coiffure. All these will make you appear taller, more slender, and better proportioned.

THE TUMMY-BULGE TYPE For some unknown reason, more button-down-the-front dresses are made for the larger woman than any other style. Unfortunately, this is not the most flattering design for the woman with a prominent tummy. To be sure, a dress that opens from top to bottom is an easy one to get in and out of. But how much better this woman would look without those buttons in the dead center of the styling area, accentuating her figure fault.

She could have her cake and eat it, too, if the buttons were brought over to the side front instead of the center. This would give the garment a diagonal feeling, which is flattering to every figure and especially to this type. Belt buckles and ties should be brought over to the side of the front, also. These should be in tone with the garment, not in contrasting colors. Belts should be narrow.

Eye-catching details placed on the upper part of the garment will keep the eye away from the faulty area. Too much fullness in the skirt is not recommended for the larger woman, although there should be enough to avoid cupping underneath the stomach and the derrière. Confined fullness is better than complete flares. Pleats, either pressed or unpressed, will give the necessary ease and comfort in wearing but will maintain a slimmer appearance because the fullness is controlled. If the skirt is not sufficiently roomy, it will crawl up unbecomingly when she sits down.

If the skirt is designed to flare, let the fullness start at the fullest part of the tummy, gradually tapering outward toward the bottom of the skirt. Fullness that starts too high will make the figure look larger.

There should be no indication of where the tummy ends and the flare begins as you look down on the garment. Check the side view in a mirror to be sure of this.

Fabric selections should be subtle in color as well as in texture. Shiny or bulky fabric should not be worn. Prints with subdued tones and figures are much better than those with outstanding lines and startling contrasts. The designs in printed fabrics do not have to be tiny, but neither should they be giant-sized.

Because this woman has a round, full appearance, she should avoid curved lines, such as round collars and necklines. Pointed collars and square necklines are far better and will give a less round appearance to her whole figure. Accessories, too, will do much toward achieving a pleasing proportion if they are in keeping with the size of the individual. The large woman should wear hats, jewelry, and handbags in proportion to herself. Tiny accessories would only call attention to the size of her figure. Remember, size is not so important as a look of good proportion. That's what counts.

THE THIN, ANGULAR TYPE Every woman's first duty to herself is to use all her know-how to achieve a feminine appearance. Her height or lack of it is secondary. The thin girl has greater advantage than her more buxom sisters in creating pleasing lines, because it's lots easier to add something that isn't there than it is to conceal an overabundance of it.

The thin girl will take on an appearance of well-proportioned slenderness if she chooses semi-tailored suits and coats instead of severely man-tailored designs. The dressmaker suit with softness in detail will create a rounded appearance. Her suits do not have to drip with peplums or cape collars, but they should avoid pointed lapels and mannish collars.

Her suit and coat fabric textures should be soft and feminine rather than men's-wear worsted types. Her tweeds should be in gayer colors and softer textures than the subdued tones seen in men's wear. In fact, a man wouldn't want to be caught dead wearing the kind of tweeds that this girl should choose. The proper fabrics will give softness not only to her figure but to her face as well. Warm tones emphasize; therefore, they should be chosen in preference to the cooler colors. If you are thin and angular, you can wear all the styles that the other figure types can't touch. The fully gathered, pleated, or flared skirt will do wonders for your silhouette and make the lower part of your figure appear faultless. Padding the bust line slightly will add those few needed curves. No one needs to know. You are just making up for what nature left unfinished, in the same manner as you use lipstick to make your lips more luscious.

Perfectly straight up-and-down lines are not so flattering as those that slant flamboyantly outward, especially when these lines radiate from the waistline. These outward lines create the illusion of feminine curves. Wide belts and cummerbunds look very well on this type. Curved yokes can be worn on the upper section of the garment or on the hip section, as long as the skirt is kept full. Peplums are also flattering.

The texture of fabrics used in your wearing apparel may be either light in weight or bulky, depending upon the garment. If lightweight fabric is used, it must be used in quantity. If the texture is heavy, it need not be quite so generously designed. When stripes are worn, they can run either vertically or horizontally. Just be sure that there is plenty of fullness when they run up and down, to avoid a look of skimpiness. All your clothes should emphasize a look of sylphlike slenderness, not one of angles and flatness.

FABRIC FACTS

When planning your sewing project, you should give first consideration to the selection of the fabric because it is, after all, your largest financial investment. But don't let your clothing budget worry you: good quality materials come in all price ranges. So be open-minded when shopping to be sure that you do not miss the exciting new weaves, textures, and colors. Do bear in mind that the same time and effort will go into the sewing, whether the garment is of plain "yard goods" or the nicest quality fabrics; why not make the hours spent on your project pay high dividends? Furthermore, when you are working with a good quality fabric in an attractive color, you will find yourself more eager to produce the best job possible. And if you decide that for a classic suit or coat or special dress, you want a more expensive fabric, you may find that you can afford to splurge because of all the money you are saving by the very process of making your own clothes. On the other hand, if you want to be the first to wear the "newest look" in your community, you can pick less expensive fabrics and thereby not feel you have lost too much if the fashion becomes outdated.

Working with fabrics

Let your imagination help you visualize how the fabric of your choice will look when made up into a garment. Give yourself a color test by draping the cloth across your shoulders and letting the mirror show what the color does for your eyes and complexion. Some tones of a color will be much more becoming than others, and the only way you can judge the best one for you is by looking into a mirror.

Even though you choose the fabric first, don't actually buy it until you've selected your pattern design, too. Otherwise, you will have no way of judging the amount of yardage required for your project. The envelope of your pattern design not only tells you the yardage needed, but also lists various materials suitable for this particular design.

Consult this list if there is any doubt in your mind as to whether or not the fabric you have selected is right for the style. Only when the texture and the design are suited to each other will the final results of your work meet with your utmost approval.

Not all fabrics are suitable for all styles. Tailored effects can be produced only when the texture of the cloth is firm enough to lend itself to tailoring, just as soft, flowing lines can be created only when the material is soft enough to ripple into beautiful draping effects. The ability to coordinate fabric and design, so important in creating lovely fashions, will develop quite readily as you gain sewing experience. While this flair is being cultivated, however, it would be wise to consult the list of suitable fabrics on the pattern envelope just to be sure that you are starting out on the right foot.

WOOLEN FLANNELS AND SOFT TEXTURED TWEEDS are particularly good fabrics for you if your sewing experience is somewhat limited, since their pliable nature makes them so easy to handle that they will help foster your confidence. Most domestic woolens are woven 54 inches wide, although it is not unusual to find worsted suitings anywhere between 50 and 60 inches wide. Imported woolens also differ in widths. This matter of width should be kept in mind when buying yardage, as the requirements specified on the pattern envelope are usually based on the average widths in which the suggested fabrics are woven: 54 inches for wools, 42 to 50 inches for miracle fabrics, 39 inches for silks and rayons, 36 inches for cottons, and 35- and 36-inch widths for linen.

Pattern manufacturers make allowances for slight differences in fabric width, so if your fabric choice is an inch or two narrower than that specified on the pattern, you need not purchase extra yardage. But if the difference in width is greater, play safe by buying a little more than the specified amount to be sure of having enough. Trying to squeeze all the parts of a garment from a limited amount of cloth can be a very exasperating experience. It is seldom worth the extra time and effort involved in laying the pattern pieces first one way and then another, to fit them all in correctly. The time and energy saved by purchasing a few more inches of cloth will more than make up for the extra money you spend. Sales clerks are usually very willing to help you determine the correct yardage when there is any question.

COTTON is another wonderful easy-to-work-with material. This fabric takes a deservedly prominent place in the modern woman's wardrobe because of its year-round wearability and around-the-clock usefulness. Regardless of the occasion, cotton fits in everywhere, every time. Small wonder that it has become a fashion favorite! There are endless textures and finishes from which to choose, ranging from the sheerest voiles for evening gowns to heavy tweeds for tailored clothes. Some cottons have even been polished to the rich luster and sheen of

29

luxurious silks. Many cotton mills process their fabrics so that little or no ironing is needed after washing.

LINEN is one of the all-time favorites. Now that it has a crease-resistant quality, it remains fresh-looking from morning till night. Linen comes in a variety of weights and textures—some smooth, others quite rough, some richly embroidered. It can be used for everything from a beautifully tailored suit to a dress for the most gala of affairs. No wardrobe should be without a few garments made from this lovely and versatile fabric, and it, too, is easy enough to handle for even the beginner. Press the seams and darts with a steam iron or wipe the fabric with a moist sponge (from the bottoms of the seams upward to prevent the yarns from fraying); the iron can be placed directly on the linen: no press cloth is needed.

For suits, linen should be handled as though it were fine wool. It will retain its original shape better if it is dry-cleaned rather than washed. Linen dresses can be washed with better results, but even then dry cleaning is recommended to keep the colors new-looking longer.

SILKS AND RAYONS will present few problems, if any, once you have gained experience and confidence by working with the fabrics already mentioned. Both of these materials come in a great variety of weaves, textures, and weights.

In their manufacture silks and rayons are usually treated with special dressings to give weight and added richness of texture, and this effect is best preserved if the garment is dry-cleaned: laundering can remove some of the dressing and make even a washable silk or rayon limp.

If you are making something that you wish to be able to launder, get a scrap of the silk or rayon and test it with soap and water. Some of these fabrics take to water quite well, some not at all. So it pays to find out about your fabric before you purchase it. Don't take chances.

When you are working with these materials, press with a steam iron on the wrong side of the garment. If you use a dry iron, wipe the seams with a slightly damp sponge or cloth—not wet enough to spot. Set the temperature of the iron to "silk" or "rayon," or if your dial indicates only "cool," "warm," and "hot," experiment with a scrap of the cloth to find the right temperature to prevent scorching. Use a press cloth, if you wish, to prevent any possibility of iron marking. But you can press directly if you keep your touch light.

MIRACLE FABRICS come in weights and textures of wool, silk, cotton, and linen, and are, as you know, extremely good imitations of their natural cousins. They are distinguished as well for their ease of care. These man-made materials may be laundered at home and require little or no ironing—of adult garments or children's. Men's suits in this category are made completely of the synthetic fabric—inside as well as out—so that they will be washable. A bathing suit of miracle velvet will look just as new and fresh after a swim as before, once it has dried.

Note, however, that the fabrics made from the miracle yarns do not have the suppleness of those made from natural fibers. It is advisable, therefore, to choose styles that do not require "ease" in certain areas, because those parts of a garment would look wrinkled. If, for example, you choose patterns featuring kimono and raglan sleeves rather than set-in ones, you'll avoid disappointments and make your work easier at the same time.

STRETCH MATERIALS are the result of added special textured yarns which allow the finished product not only to expand but to return to its original size and shape upon release. The physical appearance of the fabric as a whole (whether it is natural or synthetic) is not changed by this extra element in it. These materials are now available not only for sportswear and foundation garments but for more dressy wearing apparel too. Even velvets and elaborate brocades are now being made with stretch yarns in them.

There are different types of stretch fabrics: some pull from side to side, others up and down, while still others pull in all directions. You will not need to buy a special pattern. Just remember that material should be used in whichever way the stretching is most beneficial. For example, ski pants or long tapered pants with a strap around the instep should have an up-and-down stretch so that the pants will fit smoothly whether you are standing, sitting, or stooping. For skirts and jackets, a side-to-side stretch is better. If you pick a cloth which looks the same whether used up and down or crossweave, you can pin the pattern to it so that the stretch will be as you want it. If, however, you choose a stretch fabric in a woven or printed design, remember that you will have to use it as the design itself indicates. But you can make your garments as close-fitting as you like: you'll still have room to sit down or move around in them.

Coats and jackets should be lined in the usual way, but skirts—whether separate or part of a dress—require no lining to hold their shape.

Use nylon thread for stitching stretch seams, because it, too, "gives" and bounces back when released. If you own an automatic sewing machine, use zigzag stitching both to join the garment parts and to finish the raw edges. Otherwise, overcast or pink for your finish. Press like any other fabric on the wrong side.

WOOL JERSEYS have a natural stretch of their own even when made without the stretch yarns: check the manufacturer's label for contents. Use mercerized thread rather than nylon if the jersey is made completely of nonstretch yarns.

31

Some jerseys are underlined completely to hold the garments in shape; others are underlined only in part. If your pattern calls for complete underlining, you need give no special treatment to the seams: just pin the underlining and the jersey parts to each other on all edges, sew through all the layers at once, and then press the seams apart.

Stretch the vertical seams of the garment slightly with your hand when you are sewing to give extra "play" to the stitching line, so that seams will not be strained—and threads broken—when the garment is worn. Reinforce the horizontal seams at waistlines and shoulders with strips of straight seam tape, rather than the bias kind, to prevent stretching and to give them the support needed to hold them in shape. Sew the tape right into these seams. Interface both collarless necklines and collars with a lightweight but firmly woven material like lawn.

JERSEYS MADE OF MIRACLE YARNS, such as Orlon, Dacron, and Acrilan, are specially popular. They are washable and require very little, if any, ironing. They don't wrinkle or stretch out of shape—even though unlined—when used in easy-fitting styles. The fabrics breathe and so are comfortable to wear in all sorts of weather at any time of the year.

If the style dictates that a lining is necessary—for example, if a dress is not to drape softly but to stand away in a fuller silhouette—be sure to choose a lining fabric that has the same virtues as the jersey so that it will not require different care: otherwise, you'll spend more time taking care of the fabric that doesn't show than of the one that does! If you can't use a lining material of miracle yarn, keep the garment and lining separate by not joining them at each seam and dart: join them only at necklines and waists, so that they can be pressed individually, and hem them separately too.

For machine-seaming synthetic jerseys, nylon thread may prove better than mercerized: the mercerized thread, because it has less give, may produce irregular and giant-sized stitches.

DOUBLE AND TRIPLE KNITS are newly available for home sewing, but they have been used in ready-mades for a long time. These materials are knit from woolen yarns, cottons, synthetics, and blends of more than one yarn. These fabrics have a minimum amount of stretch, so little that they handle almost as easily as any woven cloth with good body. You need not, then, hesitate to use these knits once you have worked with woven fabrics.

Double or triple jersey garments will expand somewhat when worn but will snap back into shape almost like the stretch fabrics do. As a matter of fact, some of these knits do have stretch yarns in them: check the manufacturer's label on the bolt or tube on which the cloth was rolled.

Press the seams and darts of these knits in the ordinary way—with moisture if the cloth is wool, and with great care if it is made of a synthetic, setting the dial of the iron on the right heat. Do find out when you purchase the fabric whether or not it was preshrunk; and if in doubt, shrink it yourself or have it done before you cut the cloth, to be sure that your garment will not shrink after it is finished (see page 38). Many knits come tubular; some come flat. If you wish, you can cut the cloth through one of the folds in the tubular material to make it easier to lay pattern pieces. Note, though, that tubular knit fabrics are apt to come with the right side out: look the cloth over carefully to be sure that you use the right side for the outside of the garment.

LACY KNITS with openwork designs that look like hand crocheting are popular for daytime wear. These fabrics, which come in tubular and flat forms, are made from woolens, cottons, and synthetics, as well as from blends of different yarns. Choose a simple style for this attractive material, because it is decorative enough in itself.

Because of the loose yarns that produce the openwork design in this fabric, it is very stretchy and so must be handled with special care. When you spread it on the cutting table, make sure that the fabric is completely relaxed—test it by patting it—before you pin the pattern to it: any strain either lengthwise or crosswise will make the cut parts of the garment come out too short or narrow. Do not allow the end of the material to hang off the edge of the cutting table: roll it up and rest it on the table so that there is no strain on the length.

If you pick a horizontal design in tubular form, you will have to cut through one of the folds, so that the lines of the design can be matched in the seams of the garment.

All the garment parts made from lacy knits must be underlined separately. The underlining will provide not only support but opaqueness, so that the seam edges and darts will not show through to the outside of the finished garment. The material used for underlining is determined by the style and type of garment. If the garment is meant to drape softly, choose a fabric with a weight comparable to cotton batiste, though the fiber content can be whatever you wish: cotton, silk, or synthetic. It is the draping quality that is important. If the silhouette of the design calls for crisp and tailored lines, use a firmer material for the underlining, like taffeta, linen, shantung, or cotton broadcloth, in the color of the knit.

Cut the knit and the underlining exactly alike. Place the lining pieces on the wrong side of the knit fabric pieces and run a line of machine stitching all around each piece ¼ inch away from the raw edges, holding the lining layer on top during the stitching so that the presser foot does not stretch the knit edges. The supporting fabric must be sewn to the knit at each seam and dart.

Press woolen lace fabric with a dry iron: any moisture will shrink

33

the yarn even though the garment parts have been lined. Similarly, preshrinking this or any lacy knit fabric before cutting is not recommended: the lacy designs will be distorted. In pressing the seams, set the dial of your dry iron on "wool" regardless of what underlining material is being used, as it is the wool which comes in direct contact with the iron; any different setting may scorch the lace.

Regardless of the fiber content of your lacy knit, it should be dry cleaned only by a very reliable tailor or cleaner to make sure that the knit neither shrinks nor stretches in the process. (Woolen lace does not stretch, but it will, as noted, shrink if a dry iron is not used for pressing.)

LAMINATED FABRICS are those materials—woolens, wool imitations, and knits—that have a layer of foam backing to give body to the loosely woven textures and to eliminate the need for interlining cold-weather outdoor wear. Frequently, the foam in turn is covered by a thin layer of cotton so that the fabric can be sewn easily on the machine, but sometimes the foam is exposed. When working with materials with exposed foam, sandwich the fabrics between strips of tissue paper to prevent the foam from catching onto the metal parts of the sewing machine and thereby not going under the presser foot. The tissues will rip off the stitching line easily enough.

It is not necessary to use interfacings in the fronts and collars of laminates, as they have firmness of their own. Even bound buttonholes can be built into these materials without an extra layer of fabric, since the foam provides the support.

Lining materials for outdoor garments also come with foam backing made of single layers of cloth. Such linings provide the required warmth and again make an interlining unnecessary.

BONDED MATERIALS have a nylon tricot backing which serves as a finishing lining and also adds support to the outer cloth. All sorts of materials are now made with this built-in feature, from heavy coatings and suitings to the sheerest laces. All fabrics benefit from such backings, as they give firmness where it is needed, keep knits from curling on the edges, prevent stretching, give body to limp materials, and act as underlining for openwork laces. They allow material to be adapted for more styles, and they provide greater ease of handling, thereby saving time and labor. Furthermore, the tricot backing makes it possible for those allergic to wool to wear woolens: the inside seams of the wool garment can be prevented from coming in direct contact with the skin. You may pink the seam edges on this type of material because the bonding prevents its fraying. Hem stitching will not show on the outside, for the stitches are attached to the tricot, not to the outside cloth.

NAP MATERIALS are those with a definite one-way directional weave. They have a surface finish which is rough to the touch when stroked against the nap and smooth the opposite way. When you use such fabrics, you must cut every part of the garment so that the nap goes in the same direction; otherwise, the finished product will not be uniform in color. The color tone is lighter when the nap smoothness runs downward on the garment, darker when the nap runs upward.

In which direction the nap should run depends upon the fiber content of the material. If it is wool, the smoothness should be downward, but if the material is made from plant fibers, like cotton, the nap is usually made to flow upward, in the direction of the growing plant. Fabrics made from synthetic fibers should have the nap directed the same as it would be if the natural fibers they imitate had been used.

CAMELS' HAIR, VICUNA, CASHMERE, WOOLEN BROADCLOTH, MOHAIR and any other material with a fleecy surface nap should be used with the smoothness of the nap flowing downward on the garment, just as the fur of the animal does. They will look rich and lustrous that way and will show wear less, thus seeming new longer.

VELVETEENS AND CORDUROYS also have surface nap. Garments of these fabrics generally have the smooth flow of the nap going in an upward direction because the yarn from which the cloth is made is cotton. This is particularly important with dark-colored fabrics, as their rich jewel tones show up more clearly when the upward direction is maintained. On the other hand, they will look dusty if the nap goes down. Light-colored velveteens and corduroys will acquire a pleasing frosty look if their nap's smoothness is aimed downward.

To decide which tone of color is the most pleasing to you when working with medium- or light-colored napped cotton, drape the fabric around your shoulders like a scarf and allow the ends to drape across your front so you can look down on them or inspect them in the mirror. Wear marks will show up more quickly on fabrics made of plant fibers when the nap is running smooth in a downward direction, but the light colors are not as noticeably affected as the dark ones.

Patternmakers generally show a layout diagram when a napped fabric is suggested as suitable for the design. Once you detect the proper direction for placing the pieces, you will be sure to come out right. Let's assume that a six-gored skirt is going to be made from cotton corduroy. The center front panel has been placed on the fold of the cloth with the top toward the left end of the fabric, because you've decided that the nap brushes smoothly in that direction. The side front panels are also placed with their tops toward the left end of the cloth. The back sections are all placed with their tops in the same direction as the fronts. In this way the natural upward direction of the nap is maintained in all the panels.

Here is a bit of good advice: If, when cutting napped fabric, you discover that you have cut the first piece or two with the nap directed in the wrong way, then cut ALL the pieces in the wrong direction. Whether the fibers are animal or vegetable, the garment will at least be wearable because each piece will have the same tone of color. If you corrected the position of the other pieces after you discovered your error, the colors would be so entirely different in the switched sections that the garment would be a total loss.

Cutting prints and plaids

Some printed fabrics have a one-way direction in design. Frequently, flowered prints have blossoms or foliage growing in one direction. If this is the case, the cloth must be cut so that all the blossoms grow upward toward the top of the garment. But when the motif runs in both directions, you needn't worry. When selecting a pattern design for printed material, try to choose a style with few seams, so that the print won't look "chopped up" in the finished garment. This is especially true for large, splashy prints, where the cloth itself is an important factor in the style. Tiny prints, however, can be treated as plain fabric.

Certain plaids that are made with an uneven design must also be cut in a one-way direction, just as if there were a nap. On these you must see that all the pieces of the pattern are placed with the bottoms in the same direction. The notches located at the seam edges will make easy work of matching the horizontal lines which comprise the plaid design.

Plaids with an even design do not have a definite up and down, and can be cut with the pattern pieces staggered toward either end of the cloth. They will match perfectly in the seams as long as the corresponding notches are placed on a similar horizontal line of the plaid design. Plaids are much more flattering to the figure when cut with the darkest part of the plaid, or the more predominant horizontal lines, toward the bottom of the garment.

Less material is usually required for even plaid than for uneven plaid, especially when the skirt has flared fullness. On the other hand, in a straight sheath you may need the same amount of cloth for either type of plaid. If the plaid design is a large one, it is a good idea to buy a quarter of a yard more of 54-inch width, or a half yard of narrower material, since a large design doesn't repeat itself so often in a yard of cloth as a small one does. Therefore, you may be able to do a better matching job with a little extra cloth, especially if you are working with a one-directional plaid.

Many good effects can be created with plaids. For instance, when diagonally cut plaid pockets are placed on a dress that is cut with the plaid on the straight, the effect can be very interesting, especially if the collar and cuffs also are cut diagonally. You do not have to be a designer to create special effects with cloth. Your imagination will help you a lot in this direction.

Horizontal stripes and large checks must also be matched in the seams to be pleasing to the eye. You rarely need extra yardage for either one of these, unless the width of the stripes or the size of the checks is unusually large. If checks are minute in size, they may be cut without any regard to matching, because they can be pinned to match when you assemble the garment parts.

FAKE FURS have been made to look so much like real ones that you have to touch some of them to know the difference. When the imitation fabric is dense and heavy, it is best to avoid bulky seams by cutting it as actual fur pelts are cut—to the exact shape, with no seam allowance. Remove the seam allowance from the pattern pieces by cutting through the stitching line; then draw the shape of the pattern onto the wrong side of the fur cloth with chalk or pencil. Use a sharp razor blade—not scissors—to cut through the fabric. Scissors will shear the outside pile and therefore spoil the seamed and darted areas of the garment. When working with furry material, remember to maintain a one-way direction of nap: the smoothness should flow downward as in a real fur.

To sew the garment parts together, place the two furry sides of the fabric against each other and hand-sew the raw edges of the backing. Use close overhand or overcasting or buttonhole stitches; take ⅛ inch or less of each layer on the needle so that when the seam is finished the raw edges of each piece of cloth will butt together and the seams will be invisible. Run a thumbnail over the finished seam to help make it flat. Use an iron to complete the job. Stand the iron on its heel; drape a moist cloth over it so that it will steam; then move the seams back and forth a few times crosswise on the flat side of the iron.

Fake furs make very attractive linings for cloth coats. The sleeves of the lining are not of fur—that would be too cumbersome—but of a durable lustrous rayon or other synthetic.

GENUINE SUEDE SKINS AND SOFT LEATHER PELTS for casual wear have become available to the home sewer at last. You can handle these after you have had some experience with woven and knitted materials. These skins are sewn on regular sewing machines with regulation seam allowances because they are not bulky like fur pelts. Be sure to cut the garments to exactly the right size so that alterations are not necessary during the construction, for the needle marks will remain if you rip stitches.

Place the pattern pieces with the tops toward the head of the skins and the bottoms toward the tail so that the color will be alike in every

37

part of the finished garment, as suedes do have a directional surface, like nap. With smooth leathers, you need not worry about nap. In either case, the size of the skins determines what styles are best to use for them.

IMITATION SUEDE AND LEATHER FABRICS are treated in the same way as any yard goods of similar weight. Naps should be directed as for the real thing, and the same precaution should be used in cutting, as needle marks will mar the plastic top finish.

How to shrink fabric if necessary

Gone are the days when it was a "must" to shrink every piece of cloth before attempting to use it. Today all fine woolen and cotton mills pre-shrink their products before they are distributed. When a brand fabric is purchased, you do not need to take precautionary measures against future shrinking. Most fabrics have a printed statement either on a tag or on the bolt on which the cloth is rolled, to the effect that the cloth was shrunk before it left the mill. There are many trade names for the shrinking process, but all mean the same thing. These fabrics can be used with utmost confidence, as they will not change in size in any way either in working with the fabric or in wearing it. Sometimes the tag specifies that a certain percentage of shrinkage may be expected, but the amount is so little, usually about 1 per cent, that you'd never know the difference in the fit of your garment. Save yourself time and effort by avoiding unnecessary work, and trust the manufacturer's label. It is a guarantee.

But if the woolen material you want to use has been in your possession for a long time, or if you received it as a gift and have no idea whether it has been shrunk, don't take chances. Remember, the woolen and cotton mills did not always preshrink their wares as they do today. Be on the safe side, and either shrink it yourself, or send it out to the neighboring tailor or cleaner, and have him do it for you.

Here's how to shrink wool yourself. Thoroughly moisten a crash or linen dish towel and wring out the excess moisture. Place the wet towel on the woolen material, which is left folded wrong side out, just as it arrived from the store. Set the dial on your iron at "wool" and steam the cloth underneath the towel by running the iron back and forth until all the towel has been covered by the iron. Don't skip around, but cover all the moisture, so that the material underneath the towel will shrink evenly; otherwise it will look puckered and uneven on the surface. If the cloth does not look smooth after the shrinking operation, repeat the process, since unevenness indicates that some parts were steamed while others remained dry. The entire fabric must come in contact with the heat of the iron and the moisture in the pressing cloth. Many woolens will shrink in spots the first time, but a second shrinking job will flatten them out nicely.

Because the cloth is kept folded, it is necessary to do the underlayer of the cloth in the same way as the top one. The steam of the moistened cloth does not penetrate completely through to the under section, especially when the texture is closely woven. A special word of advice: even when a steam iron is available, do the shrinking with a wet cloth. There is not enough steam in the iron, no matter how adequate it is for pressing purposes, to do a thorough job without the pressing cloth.

To shrink cotton fabrics that you are not sure of, just dip them into lukewarm water, wring out the excess moisture, and hang to dry or put into your automatic dryer. Iron the wrinkles out of the fabric, and it is ready to use. It is sometimes advisable to replace some of the dressing that is lost in the dipping process. Use a bit of starch in the lukewarm water, so that when the finished cotton is ready, it will have the same firmness and body that it had before.

Reblocking

If the advice, "Don't buy cloth you must reblock!" could be broadcast from the housetops, perhaps manufacturers would pay heed and not ship fabrics which need reblocking. It is most amazing that a matter so important as proper blocking of fabric yarns is left to the inexperienced hands of the home sewer: even professional tailors and cleaners do not like to bother reblocking a customer's yardage because the work is so time-consuming. To have to immerse a perfectly beautiful new piece of linen or cotton in a basin of water and then iron the wrinkles out of it is enough to cool anyone's enthusiasm. But it is necessary if the cloth is faulty, for otherwise the garment will end as a disappointment.

Off-grain yarns are found not only in inexpensive fabrics but in some of the expensive ones also, and in fabrics made of all sorts of fibers. In heavy-textured materials and distinctly woven designs such as ottoman and basket weave, any fault in the yarn is clearly noticeable. For example, checks and plaids may look as though they were diagonal instead of straight across from one selvage edge to another: if so, the lines must be straightened before the fabric pieces can be matched at the seams. Otherwise, the tilted lines of the unblocked material will make the garment resemble the floor of the fun house at an amusement park.

In draperies, curtains, and slip covers, the weaves of solid colors should run straight across. But some materials, both for garments and decorating purposes, have printed designs which bear no relation to the

39

fabric weave: if the straight weave of the cloth were followed in cutting, the design would become distorted. In such fabrics you must give priority to the printed design and forget the grain of the cloth. Please the eye at all times whether the weave is right or not, or avoid buying off-grain prints: the ones that are not off-grain hang far better, and may not even be more costly.

TO TEST SUSPICIOUS FABRICS, first cut the ends of the cloth in a straight line: follow one of the yarns from selvage to selvage. When both ends are trimmed, fold the fabric lengthwise through the middle and see that the selvage edges are flush with each other and that there is no twisting at the center fold. If twisting does occur at the fold area when the ends are lying evenly, the material needs to be reblocked.

TO REBLOCK WOOLENS, use a friend's help if possible. Each of you should take one end of the unfolded cloth. Pull the selvage back and forth between you diagonally, repeating this effort several times until the twisting is eliminated: test by refolding and checking ends and selvage edges. When the cloth is in shape, refold it, wrong side out, match edges and ends, put a moist press cloth on it, and press it with a hot iron, steaming it slowly so that it will stay blocked. After doing one side of the folded cloth, turn it over so that you can treat the under layer in the same manner. The steam is needed to block the cloth permanently. Just pulling is not enough, as the yarns will go back to their original direction eventually.

Another way to block woolens is to open them up and spread them on a wet sheet, then roll them up in it and leave them that way overnight. The next day, fold the woolen material together to match at the ends and at the selvages; the cloth can be pressed easily because it is supple from being dampened through. You will not even need a press cloth as long as the material is folded wrong side out—the usual way woolens come.

The first method is quicker but both are equally effective.

MATCHING PLAIDS FOR REBLOCKING necessitates that each horizontal line of the plaid design be matched accurately at selvage edges and pinned together at 2- or 3-inch intervals. If twisting occurs at the folded area, unpin the cloth and pull as for the plain fabric. Steam press only when the twisting has been eliminated. Then repin the cloth and steam again.

Plaid wool, too, can be spread out on a wet sheet, rolled up overnight, pinned to match at the selvages, then pressed into shape.

THE BEST WAY TO REBLOCK COTTONS AND LINENS is to dip them and hang them up until they are partially dry. It is easier to press them if they are not completely dry. Fold them through the middle, and make sure the selvage edges and ends are flush with each other; otherwise, the garment will not drape properly.

If some of the dressing has been lost in the dipping, use a little starch to give the cloth body.

BLOCKING SILKS AND RAYONS is done by wiping the wrong side of them with a moistened household sponge and pressing them into shape on the ironing board until twisting is eliminated in the fold area at center. Cut the ends evenly first, as you would for other materials. Do not bear heavily on the fold with the iron because the crease may be hard to remove.

LET'S MAKE A SUIT FIRST!

Don't be surprised! Actually, making a suit will start you off with the easiest sewing project first. The order of construction and the work entailed in making a suit are fundamentally basic, rarely deviating much from the usual order of procedure. On the other hand, the high-fashion touches which are found on some dresses may involve intricate workmanship for which you won't be prepared if your basic sewing knowledge is at all limited. Such complicated details, which you may never encounter again in your sewing experience, can give you the discouraging feeling that sewing, as far as you are concerned, is only for the gifted few.

Coats and suits are not affected too drastically by changing fashions. The changes that do occur are usually in silhouette, color, or fabric texture; construction procedure and workmanship remain pretty much the same. Tailoring a suit first will, then, give you sound, basic sewing experience and send you confidently on your way toward making whatever your heart desires.

The pattern

Major pattern companies leave little to be desired in up-to-the-minute fashions for the woman who wants to keep abreast of the times. Just as soon as a new look appears on the fashion horizon, these manufacturers introduce pattern designs featuring adaptations of the trend. Your garment could easily be the creation of a well-known personality in the fashion world, as many fine designers contribute their talents to the pattern industry.

We have already stressed the importance of knowing your type and analyzing your figure problems so that you can call attention only to your good features. One safe rule to follow whenever you are in doubt about your choice of pattern is: avoid anything that is extreme in design, especially if you have a figure problem. Subtle elegance will outlive high fashion every time. As we noted, you can create your dramatic effects with accessories.

If you choose a suit that is not too intricate in design for your first tailoring job, it will be to your advantage in more ways than one. In the first place, it will remain fashionable for many more seasons than a suit that is highly styled. Of course, you need not choose one that is labeled "easy to make" either, since the instructions in this book will enable you to cope with most tailoring problems.

For learning purposes, a jacket with set-in sleeves and a collar is preferable to one without a collar or with any other type of sleeve, as the experience of inserting the collar and "driving" the sleeves into the armholes will simplify your more intricate future sewing undertakings. True, a garment with kimono, dolman, or raglan type sleeves is both stylish and easy to make, but the basic knowledge gained in inserting set-in sleeves is so important that you should have it at an early stage. Furthermore, set-in sleeves are flattering to every figure type, while the other sleeves generally look best on women who are fairly slim and tall.

HOW TO CHOOSE THE RIGHT PATTERN SIZE   Women who can sew and tailor beautifully sometimes get bad results because they can't seem to choose the pattern size that fits them. The most common cause for failure in home sewing is the fear of cutting things too small. It may be logical to assume that when an object is cut large enough, it can be easily reduced in size, but this theory does not hold for sewing. One alteration only leads to another and then another, ending in complications, discouragement, and a frumpy-looking garment—if the garment is completed at all.

Certain areas govern a perfect fit. Alterations should not be made in these important "styling areas," the parts that are seen when the garment is viewed directly front and back, for they are the focal points of the design. Surprisingly enough, the proper execution of the design is governed almost entirely by the accurate fit of the shoulders, the neckline, and the upper chest areas above the bust line. So this is the sovereign rule for well-fitting clothes: buy the pattern size that fits your shoulders well. Don't worry if your other dimensions vary considerably from the standard measurements printed on your pattern envelope. It is easy to make alterations in the "hidden areas," the sides of the garment that are covered when the arms are down, as you will see later.

The important thing is that when the pattern size is right, the darts, tucks, and styling lines will fall on the body where the designer intended them to be. After all, darts and tucks are placed where they are for a special purpose. They are devices for fitting the fabric to the contours of the figure, releasing fullness of cloth to conform to curves,

43

and disposing of excess material in the narrower sections. The designer places the darts and tucks with an eye for style and comfortable fit and for producing flattering effects even on the figure which lacks good proportion. For instance, bodice darts on a dress usually point to the fullest part of the bust so that the cloth will drape becomingly there and at the same time produce smoothness in the smaller area of the waistline.

If the pattern size is too large, the darts will not dovetail properly with the body contours. Instead of fullness draping the bust, it goes outside that area and forms wrinkles. The shoulders will be too broad, the neckline too loose, and the garment will look as though it needs to be lifted at the shoulders.

Though it is hard to believe, garments cut from pattern sizes that are too large are often quite confining in the armholes, not only when you reach forward but when you raise your arms over your head, for the overly big armholes pull on the whole garment.

If the shoulders droop, the cause is probably an oversized neckline, cut from too large a pattern. For while the shoulder itself as measured from the neckline hardly varies from one size to the next, the neck widths are quite different, thus adding to the breadth of the shoulder.

As pattern sizes get larger, they reflect expansion through the centers of the back and front units as well as at the sides. Length is added in proportion to the width, so that armholes and necklines are in a wider size. And, as we noted, as the necklines widen, the shoulders are affected. The front and back darts also become farther apart on the left and right sides of the garments. Panels and gores of princess styles become wider.

If you have to guess at where darts should go, work to reduce the width of a neck, wonder what to do about armholes that are too deep and about excess material in front and back, you may find yourself awake nights and having nightmares besides—or else abandoning the project. It is certainly far easier to start with the right pattern size and thereby avoid these difficulties.

Use your best-fitting ready-made dresses and suits as guides in the important matter of determining your accurate pattern size. Even though there is a difference in some of the measurements between ready-mades and standard patterns, the shoulders, necklines, upper chest, and shoulder-blade areas are cut the same, so you can pick the pattern in the same size as your ready-mades.

I realize that women are often confused about size when purchasing ready-made apparel. It is not unusual to hear someone say, "When I buy a good dress, I fit into a size sixteen, but in a cheaper model I need an eighteen or twenty." Or, "I buy an eighteen because of my hips and then have to take it up in the shoulders." Or occasionally, "I buy a sixteen and have the seams let out to fit my waist and hips." If you look at these comments carefully, you will see that all of them indicate that a size-sixteen pattern would be the most satisfactory. The shoulder, neckline, and chest areas would fit well, and the other sections could be altered at the sides.

Seldom will one size be exactly right everywhere for you, in ready-mades or in patterns. Alterations will be needed at one place or another no matter what size you wear. After all, sizes are drafted for the average figure, and you are an individual with personal figure measurements which vary from these averages. So again I repeat: buy the size pattern that fits your shoulders and you will be on the road to success.

All the major pattern companies cut their sizes in accordance with the government Bureau of Standards to assure you of a good fit every time, subject, of course, to side alterations. Any slight gain or loss of weight will not affect your pattern size, since the shoulders and the upper parts of your body do not change noticeably unless your weight variation exceeds ten or twelve pounds. If it does, pick a pattern one size larger or smaller as the need may be. Even if you are smaller than the smallest size offered, you can cut the garment exactly like the pattern and make alterations on the "hidden areas," taking in as much as needed.

A WORD ABOUT THE INDEPENDENT PATTERNMAKERS Along with the standard-measurement patterns produced by the major companies, there are other patterns which resemble the ready-mades even more closely, because they are more generously cut throughout the body areas while using the same shoulder, upper chest, and neckline measurements as the standardized patterns. Unfortunately, these special patterns are not available in stores, but they are featured in syndicated newspapers throughout the country, and they can be ordered by mail by you or by the stores which carry their catalogues. A great many of these very smart designs are the creations of famous designers.

Even with these patterns, it is still important to understand how to cut clothes to personal measurements, but when using these special ones the "hidden area" alterations are not as great. Furthermore, the tiny woman will probably have no trouble finding small sizes among these patterns, as she may among the standard ones if she wears size nine or smaller, for the special patterns are sized like store clothes.

Under no circumstances should fullness be removed from a pattern piece—whether special or standard—by creasing the pattern vertically, as the chances of ruining the lines of the design are great. But if the skirt pattern is too long, the extra may be folded out of the way, at the bottom. By the same token, the skirt bottom may be added to by the tall woman who takes a small size.

PATTERN SIZES FOR "SEPARATES" No matter which type of pattern you use, there will be times when you may have to choose two separate ones to complete your suit to your entire satisfaction, one for the jacket and another for the skirt, as both items of an ensemble are not always equally pleasing. In such instances, it is the jacket style that should get first consideration, as it requires the most time and effort to complete. After all, there are many more skirt than jacket styles to choose from and so substituting another skirt pattern for the original one will be no problem.

The substitute skirt can be picked from another suit or dress or it can be chosen from the "separates" section of the pattern catalogue. Though patterns for separate skirts are sold by waist measurement, remember that it is necessary to use the same pattern size for the substitute skirt as the one that came with the jacket so that the lines of the skirt will be in proportion with those of the jacket. For example, if you have a size twelve top but a waist measurement comparable to a size eighteen pattern (30 inches), strive to look as much like a twelve all over as you possibly can, and this you will accomplish if the skirt pattern is right and you make the necessary adjustments to the side seams.

The only styles that should be made from patterns in the size of the individual's waist measurement are those for which the rest of the body dimensions are not important considerations, since the garment is full enough—as in a gathered or unpressed pleated design. When it comes to streamlined fashions, you must match the sizes of tops and bottoms to look streamlined yourself.

STYLES OF SKIRTS WITHOUT SIDE SEAMS Occasionally skirt patterns have large darts at the sides instead of seams; it is impossible to add to these sides without distorting the styling area at least somewhat. Granted, a little taking in or letting out of the side darts will not affect the general shape of the garment. But a woman with waistline or hip problems should choose a pattern that does have side seams so that alterations can be made in cutting the skirt to her own measurements, with the freedom the side seams allow.

What you need before you start

One important bit of equipment required to start your sewing project, aside from your sewing machine, is a sharp pair of scissors about 7 or 8 inches long from end to end, with handles roomy enough so that you can use them comfortably. If you need to buy a pair, it would be a good idea to take a piece of cloth with you to the store so that you can try them out. They should work easily, not require too much effort for cutting. If they are too tightly adjusted, they will not only tire your hand, but may cause you to snip suddenly where you have no intention of snipping. Tightness does not always diminish with use, so if the salesperson cannot adjust the scissors to your satisfaction, select another pair and be safe. If the scissors have sharp points instead of rounded ends, they will take care of all your cutting needs, including buttonholes and set-in pockets.

Don't buy too much equipment. In the beginning you are better off with only a few necessities. As you keep sewing, you will know better what other equipment you may want to own.

Other things you must have in order to get a good start are as follows: A tape measure and one or two pieces of regular blackboard chalk, one piece in white for marking dark fabrics and light pastel for lighter colors. Blackboard chalk is preferred to tailor's chalk, which is apt to leave grease spots on your cloth. A small box of dressmaker's pins is also required. The other things you'll need are regular household equipment: an ironing board and iron, either steam or dry, and an old crash or linen dish towel for a pressing cloth.

All about dress forms, or dummies

A dress form, or dummy, is excess baggage for the home sewer. It is practical only for the woman who designs professionally, so that she can drape the cloth on a form to see what effects can be achieved with various textures, designs, and weaves. A dress form is not so practical a fitting device as you might imagine. Fitting your own individual figure gives much better results, so you should learn to do this for yourself. Your body changes from time to time, even when your weight is not affected, and you must allow for these changes when making new wearing apparel.

New foundation garments will often cause your shape to change from one season to the next because these products are designed with an eye on current fashions. The cut of a new girdle may distribute the poundage differently from your last one, so that the new dress fashions will look well on you. Brassières, too, constantly change in line. Keep up-to-date by becoming an expert in self-fitting. It's simple to do, as you will see in the fitting instructions when you make your suit and your dress.

Your measurements

Take a few simple measurements before starting to work with your pattern and cloth. The best way to do this is over a lightweight dress or slip, wearing the foundation garment that you wear every day, and not the special one that you keep for special occasions. You can have someone measure you, although it is simple to measure yourself quite accurately. Check your measurements from time to time, especially if you haven't been sewing for a while, to see if there have been any of the slight changes we discussed in the last section.

The following measurements are needed:

Bust	Waist Length
Waist	Skirt Length
Hips	Sleeve Length

Measure the bust by placing the tape measure squarely around the fullest part of the bosom. Hold the tape measure firmly, so that it will not slip off the curve of the bust, but do not draw it tightly.

Your waistline is located at the hollow between the lower rib and the hipbone, so place the tape measure around you in that area and draw it in as firmly as you like your skirt bands to fit. Some people like their waistbands tighter than others, so measure exactly the way you like yours to fit.

Some women never know where to measure their hips. The answer depends strictly upon your figure type. It is important to measure the largest part of the lower section of the figure, wherever it happens to be. A specific distance down from the waistline is not a practical way to get an accurate measurement, because of differing figure types.

Compare your figure from the waistline down with either an apple or a pear, and you will have no trouble finding the area that should be measured on you. Which one of these fruits does your figure resemble more? The "apple" type has a short body and longer legs. The curve of the hips starts directly below the waistline, and the area to be measured is a shorter distance away from the waist section than the other type. The pear-shaped figure has a long body and shorter legs. The large part of the hips is farther away from the waistline than the first type, and the curve of the hip is longer and more gradual. Measure either the largest part of the "apple" or the largest part of the "pear" in order to be accurately fitted into your fashions.

Of course there are women who can't make up their minds what shape they're in because the large parts are rather spread around. They should place the tape measure first around one part and then another. Whichever comes up with the greatest number of inches should be used for the hip dimension.

The waist length is measured from the collarbone, the place on the base of the back of your neck where your necklace locates itself, to the natural waistline. If you have difficulty locating this bump, put a string of beads around your neck, and it will show you where to start your measuring.

Skirt length is measured from the natural waistline to approximately where you wear your daytime clothes. This length is flexible, depending on the changing fashions, and must be checked from time to time to keep it up-to-date. When making something that needs to be floor length, of course, the measurement is taken from the waistline to the floor.

Sleeves are measured from the armpit to the bend of the wrist, with the arm extended horizontally out to the side. Because sleeve patterns are usually shaped at the bottom, to take care of changes in length when the arms are bent, you need take arm measurements only in the extended position. This retains the shaping at the bottom of the sleeve.

These are the measurements that will assure you of a good fit when the proper provisions are made for them in cutting your garments. Some sewing courses and pattern instruction sheets stress other measurements. But these are truly sufficient. Too many measurements only tend to confuse.

Here's a final word of advice before you start to work on your suit. It is very important that you should have confidence in yourself, in your pattern, and in the instructions which you have set out to follow. With this positive approach you will be able to achieve more than you dreamed would be possible. Don't rush yourself. Work along slowly and easily, and your speed will develop with your experience. Remember, the ability to sew well is not a gift that is bestowed on a chosen few. It's a talent many women possess without even being aware of it. Once this talent is brought to the fore, you will be surprised at the heights it can reach.

Preparing the fabric and pattern pieces

With your cloth and pattern chosen, you are now ready to start on your tailoring venture. First, separate the pattern pieces that are going to be used on the suit material from those intended for the interfacing and lining. On one side of the pattern instruction sheet you will find layout diagrams that illustrate how to place the pattern pieces on cloth of all widths. Since these diagrams look very much alike at a quick glance, it would be wise to circle the one that represents the width of your cloth and pattern size, so that you can recognize it immediately each time you need to refer to it. If there is a slight difference between the width of your cloth and those shown on the diagrams, you can be sure of satisfactory results if you follow the one closest to the width of your fabric. An inch or two won't matter.

It should be mentioned here that, although it is recommended that you follow the instruction sheet diagram for placing the pattern on the fabric, the simplified tailoring methods you will learn in this book are considerably different from those given in the pattern instructions. You can simply ignore the other pattern instructions, and follow the easier methods shown here.

Pattern pieces are generally placed on the WRONG side of the cloth, so that the markings for darts and other fitting devices can be accurately transferred to the wrong side of the material for stitching. When darts and tucks are meant for fitting purposes only, and not for ornamentation, they are marked and stitched on the wrong side. On the rare occasions when they are intended to be part of the styling, they are marked and stitched on the right side of the cloth. A little study of the illustration on the pattern envelope will help you to decide which way is right for your suit.

Woolen materials usually are, as noted, folded wrong side out before they leave the mill. This leaves them clean and lint free. They should be left folded this way when the pattern is pinned, unless the pattern pieces are so large that the full width of the cloth must be opened up in order to fit that part of the pattern completely on the fabric. Full circular skirts and sleeves cut all in one with the front and back of the garment are examples of styles with extra-large pattern pieces.

Cottons are usually folded with the right side out and must be reversed before starting to place the pattern, so that the marking and stitching can be properly done on the wrong side. This, of course, is necessary only if the cloth has a definite right and wrong side, as in a print or a sateen. If the cloth is reversible, as in the case of gingham or chambray, either side can be used as the right side.

Silks and rayons are generally rolled full width on tubes and should be folded with the right sides together before pinning the pattern pieces. Like cottons, many silks and rayons have no right or wrong side.

Each pattern piece bears a symbol signifying the "straight of the goods," the indicator that will guide you in placing the pattern pieces accurately on the fabric weave. These indicators should be placed in a position parallel to the threads that run the whole length of the material, or, to be technical, on the warp. Occasionally the pattern pieces are placed on the horizontal weave of the cloth, or the woof. This is done when interesting or unusual effects are desired with stripes or bordered fabrics.

50

Remember that only when true lengthwise or crosswise weave of the material is retained in every part of the garment will the results of your labor be gratifying. Otherwise there will be wrinkling where smoothness should be, and seams which should fall into straight, flowing lines will shoot over to one side. Sleeves would twist in a peculiar fashion and collars would be practically impossible to finish properly.

STEP ONE

Laying the pattern

Your dining table makes an ideal surface on which to pin your pattern pieces to the fabric. Place a pad on the table to keep it from getting scratched. If you do not have a large enough table, two card tables put together make a good substitute. You can even put your card table up against your kichen table and see how that works out. The larger the cutting surface, the better and easier it will be for you. A bed, while large enough, is not a firm enough background for the pinning and marking you will have to do.

Remember to pin the pattern pieces on the wrong side of the cloth, and follow the layout diagram in your pattern as closely as possible. See Fig. 1 for a typical layout. There is no special way that the pins should be inserted into the work, just so that the pattern pieces are held firmly in place on the fabric. A pin in each corner of the small pattern pieces is sufficient. Pins placed about a foot apart on the outer edges of the larger pieces will be close enough to secure the pattern to the cloth while cutting. Be sure to insert the pins inside the stitching margin, so that the pattern remains pinned to the cloth after cutting.

Make certain that the cloth is perfectly smooth under the pattern. It is a good idea to get all the pieces properly placed on the cloth before doing any marking, just in case you have to shift any of the pieces for one reason or another. Even though you follow the layout diagram closely, you may need to move some of the pieces slightly to provide a little extra margin for the increases which will be made to fit your measurements. This extra amount is added to the side edges of the garment.

Before leaving this part of the first step, check back to be sure that you are starting right: Are the straight-of-the-goods symbols on the true lengthwise or crosswise weave of the cloth on every piece? Does your material have a nap, and, if so, did you lay the pattern with the nap running in the correct direction on all parts of the garment? If your material is plaid, did you match the plaid perfectly on all joining parts? Look on page 36 for this information before you go further. Are all the pieces that represent the units of your suit placed on the cloth? Are you sure that you do not have a piece of your lining or interfacing on your suit material? Incidentally, don't place the pattern of the waistband at this time. Since patterns for waistbands seldom insure a proper fit, we make a special waistband later on. If everything else checks properly, you are ready to go further.

If the fronts of your garment are meant to be placed on the absolutely straight weave of the cloth, without any allowance for shaping of lapels, you will probably be able to cut the front and facing materials in one piece instead of separately as the pattern indicated. This is certainly desirable when possible—especially for heavy-textured materials

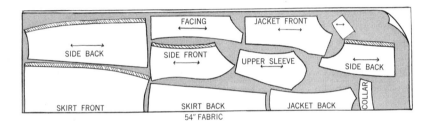

Figure 1

but also for very fine silks—because you will then eliminate a seam down the front. All you do at this stage is pin the front and facing pattern pieces together through their seamlines and then pin the combined pattern to the cloth. Later, when you have finished cutting, you will mark the fabric to show where the facing folds to the inside of the garment. The fold is then carefully pressed so it can be used as a guide when the interfacing gets attached to the inside of the front.

Chalking the adjustments

Very few women can cut the cloth exactly to the pattern and achieve a garment that fits properly everywhere, except when making loose-fitting coats and very full skirts. When the garment is meant to fit the figure closely, provisions must be made for variation between personal measurements and those specified on the pattern. As explained previously,

53

this can be done without distorting the style of the garment in the least, if alterations are made in the "hidden area" at the sides.

Although pattern sizes are marked with specific bust, waist, and hip measurements, this does not mean that the pattern contains only the specific number of inches in these areas. A certain amount of leeway, or "plus," is included in the cutting of the pattern to insure a good fit and to give the effect intended by the designer. A form-fitting design will allow only enough "plus" to make the garment comfortable, whereas a style with lots of softness and swing will have more leeway.

As there is no satisfactory way to measure this "plus," you must trust your pattern. If you add the difference between your personal measurements and those specified on the pattern, in the proper places and in the right way, just as you will be instructed to do here, you will end up with a style that exactly duplicates the original.

Let us suppose that your recommended size is twelve, since that size fits your shoulders perfectly and is the size of your ready-made clothes. The standard pattern specifications for this size are 32-inch bust and 35-inch hips. (We are ignoring the waist purposely at this time and will discuss it later, when it will mean more to you.) Your own personal measurements, however, are 35-inch bust and 37-inch hips. The difference of 3 inches in the bust and 2 inches in the hips must be provided for when cutting the garment, so that you may retain the style and have the same amount of "plus" as was originally intended.

The provisions for your variations are made in the "hidden area" of the garment, the direct side seams. As there are four edges of cloth located at the side sections of the garment, a right and left front seam edge, and a right and left back seam edge, the difference between you and the pattern should be divided into four equal portions and added to each one of these seam edges, just like this:

With the pattern properly pinned to the wrong side of the folded material, we will now add the required 3 inches to the bust line and 2 inches to the lower section of the jacket, if the jacket is long enough to reach the hips. The 3 inches is divided into four equal ¾-inch parts. Therefore, an extra ¾-inch width should be sketched in with chalk alongside the seam edges of both the front and back of the garment in the area of the bust line. The 2 inches required for the hips should be broken up into four ½-inch shares and added on to the seam edges at the hip location. Make the additions on the front of the jacket first with a sharpened piece of blackboard chalk, handled lightly. Use white chalk if your fabric is dark, and a light pastel color if your fabric is a light tone on which the white would not show.

Put a chalk mark at the top of the underarm section of the jacket, on a level with the bottom of the armhole, ¾ inch away from the seam edge of the pattern. Put another mark at the bottom of the jacket side seam, ½ inch away from the seam edge of the pattern. Now draw a continuous line from the top mark, following the outer edges of the pattern, until you reach the mark at the bottom of the pattern. Note that you started with an increase of ¾ inch at the top, and naturally reduced the increase to ½ inch by the time the line joins the mark at the bottom of the jacket. You have now provided half of the required increase in the areas where they are needed: 1½ inches at the bust and 1 inch at the hips.

The same procedure is followed on the back of the jacket for the other half of the needed increase. Whatever amount is added to the front must also be added at the back, so that the side seams remain where they were intended to be. You should never add more to one than to the other, even if you feel that yours is an exceptional case. Because these additions are made in the "hidden area" of the garment, the appearance of the design is not altered in the least. Adding on in this manner will take care of considerable differences, up to 6 or 7 inches.

Did you notice that we disregarded the location and size of the waistline in chalking the side seams? We would do this even if your waistline measured exactly the same as the pattern. By so doing, greater accuracy in fitting will be achieved later on.

Be assured that the location of your individual waistline will be accurately established in your garment if you proceed in this way. It is not recommended that the pattern pieces be folded above the waist to shorten, or slashed and separated to lengthen the waist. Just cut the pieces as they are to retain the original lines of the design. It is a different story when there is a horizontal seam around the waist where bodice and skirt units are joined to each other; for such dresses, added length is allowed at the bottom of the bodice units when needed. But when the garment has an unbroken line from the shoulders to the bottom, the waistline location is flexible. Raising or dropping it is no problem. It is easily taken care of at the time of fitting.

Even though the increase has been made in the side seams of the jacket, thereby increasing the armhole 3 inches, the sleeves do not need to be increased in width if your arms are of normal size. The sleeves will fit into the armholes beautifully. If, on the other hand, your upper arms are larger than average, provisions must be made by adding on to the edges of the seams. There should always be at least 1½ inches more width in the upper section of the sleeve than the arm measures. When the lower section of the arm is also heavy, the increase should be made continuously from the top of the underarm section of the sleeve to the bottom.

An increase in the hip section of the skirt is made in the same manner as in the jacket. The 2 inches that need to be provided for are divided into four sections and added to the side edges of the "hidden area." Start the chalking at the very top of the skirt, even if your waistline measures the same as the pattern. Continue the line along the pattern edge and gradually taper it into the original side seams about midway between the top and the bottom of the skirt. The increase can be carried completely down to the bottom of the skirt if so desired. This may be an especially good idea if the calves of your legs are large and need to look slimmer. The original silhouette of the skirt design will not be altered in the least by providing this extra width.

Note that the increase is started at the top of the skirt, even if no increase is needed there. This makes for easier handling of materials in fitting the curved part of the figure. When the cloth edges are too curved, as they would be if the increase was started at the hips, these edges would be difficult to manipulate, especially on a rounded figure.

When lengths need to be adjusted in a garment, it is more satisfactory to make these adjustments at the bottom. If extra length is required, chalk in the necessary amount at the bottom of the pattern pieces, and include the addition in cutting the garment.

When shortening is necessary, the extra length of the pattern should be folded out of the way at the bottom and the article cut to the adjusted length. True, some of the fullness of a flared or circular skirt may be lost by disposing of the excess length in this way. But if you are short enough to need this adjustment, you will be just as well off without that fullness. Pleats, on the other hand, can always be extended a little higher than marked on the pattern, so that they will not come too low and interfere with the hem line.

This manner of making length adjustments is far more satisfactory than slashing and separating or folding the pattern pieces at specified places, as is usually suggested in pattern instructions. In this way the originality of the design is retained. Finding the right length in any other way might entail making drastic changes in the appearance of your finished garment.

HINTS FOR THE SQUARE SHOULDERED PERSON If your shoulders are squarer than average, make a slight change before cutting the cloth to avoid wrinkles at the back neckline of your garment. After you have pinned the pattern pieces to the cloth, raise the outer end of the shoulder line ⅜ inch above the cutting line. Mark the position with a dot and then rule a straight line from that shoulder and dot to the cutting line at the neck end of the shoulder. Unpin the pattern piece and move it up so that the top of the armhole is at the new line you have just drawn. You will clip in the notches exactly where the pattern shows them to be. To compensate for the raising of the pattern, bring the side seam up higher so that the armhole will not be any deeper than designed. Treat the front the same way. But cut the sleeves according to the pattern. (Fig. 2a.)

HINTS FOR WIDENING THE SHOULDER-BLADE AREA If you require additional leeway across the shoulder blades, you can obtain it in the following manner: before cutting the back of any garment—not just a suit

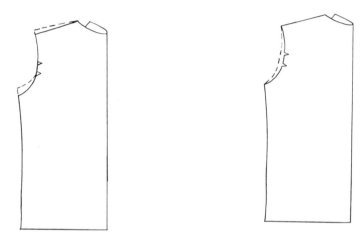

Figure 2a   Figure 2b

or coat—draw a crescent-shaped chalk line around the back armhole. Start the line at the pattern's cutting edge at the top of the armhole and then taper away from that edge as you proceed downward; you should be ½ inch or ⅜ inch away from the cutting edge by the middle of the armhole. Then taper back toward the original cutting edge so that you meet it at the base of the armhole. You will be surprised at the amount of ease this back addition—the front is not adjusted at all— will give without changing the appearance of the garment. Clip the notches where they would have been had you not built out the armhole edge. Shape the sleeves according to the pattern; they will fit in without any problem. (Fig. 2b.)

ADDING TO "HIDDEN AREAS" OF KIMONO STYLES When additions need to be made to styles featuring kimono sleeves, draw them on the fabric with chalk before cutting, the same as you would for set-in styles, starting at the base of the sleeves at the top of the sides. Remember that you need add to the sleeves themselves only if your arms are heavier than average; otherwise, the side edges alone are altered. (Fig. 3a.)

TO ADD TO KIMONO STYLES WITH GUSSETS, use the same method as for the regular kimono. Start the addition as shown in Fig. 3b. Do not increase the gusset; make it only as deep as the original line on the pattern. After you have cut the garment parts, you will place the pattern piece back on the cut material at the edge that has been added to the sides, so that the gusset slash will be the right length.

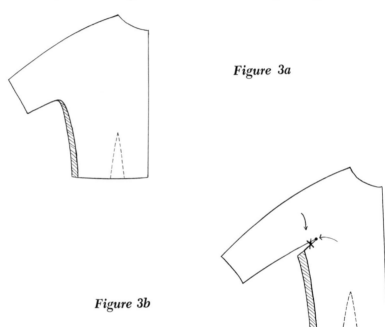

Figure 3a

Figure 3b

Cutting and marking the cloth

You are now ready to start cutting the garment, but first a few things should be checked: Did you divide the difference between you and the pattern by four, because you have to add on to four edges? The more accurate these additions at the sides, the more beautifully your garment will fit. Did you add to the bottom of the skirt if you are tall? Did you take off a little if you are short? How about your sleeves? Are your arms unusually long? It won't matter if you cut sleeves longer than you need, but never cut them too short if they are intended to be full length.

Today all the major standard pattern manufacturers print their pat-

58

terns. You will have no trouble getting acquainted with the pieces, as each one is clearly marked to show what part of the garment it represents. All the printed patterns are easy to work with and, as noted, can be relied upon for accuracy in size.

The cutting is done through the darkest line, the one which borders the printed part of the pattern pieces. Naturally, you should cut along the chalk lines where increases have been made. The irregular outer margin will fall away from the pattern the first time it is used, so it need not be trimmed off prior to laying the pattern on the cloth. Be sure that the chalking is obvious enough so that it will not be overlooked when cutting.

Cut with long, even strokes, with one hand kept on the cloth while the other hand does the cutting. It is more satisfactory to walk around the table instead of drawing the cloth over to you when the large pieces are being cut, since the weave of the cloth may slip out of line in the shifting process. The work should be kept flat on the surface of the table and not raised to be cut.

On the edges of the pattern pieces there are notches that will enable you to assemble the different units of the garment with the proper pieces matching each other. These notches are illustrated on the printed patterns in the shape of triangles or diamonds.

Notches are very important, and should not be overlooked when cutting, especially in the armholes and sleeves. All you do is clip ¼-inch deep into the edge of the cloth wherever a notch occurs. You do not have to cut out a piece of the cloth to form the notch, but don't snip deeper than ¼ inch, either. This straight clipping is quick, and the ¼-inch slits are easy to find when you need them. You can make the notches in each piece as the garment is being cut, or do them all at one time afterward.

On the very peak of set-in sleeves there is an indicator that is marked with either a dot, a perforation, or a notch. Make a habit of always clipping a notch ¼-inch deep at this point, to help match this part of the sleeve with the shoulder seam of the garment when the sleeves are being inserted.

The nonstandardized patterns are made of plain tissue paper and have perforations instead of printing to show where the darts are and what seam allowance to take in joining the seams. These patterns provide the same seam allowance as the others, ⅝ inch, but they omit the blank margin: the pattern pieces are the exact shape and size of the garment parts, and so the cutting is done by following the edges of each piece, except where additions have to be made for personal requirements. There is a printed chart listing all the garment parts so that you can identify each of the pattern pieces as you proceed to put them together. The darts are marked through the holes in the tissues.

MARKING THE DARTS You now transfer the darts as accurately and as easily as you can from the pattern to the cloth. These darts will line up properly on your figure just as they are shown, so leave them where the pattern features them.

There are different types of darts, each serving a good purpose. The "V"-shaped darts are found at the top of skirts, at the waist, in shoulder seams, at underarm sections near the bust line, and at the elbows of some sleeves. There are also long point-to-point darts, sometimes called diamond darts, which are usually found in the midsections of garments that do not feature a definite waistline seam, as in the princess line, or in jackets and coats.

On the standard printed patterns, puncture holes with a pencil point to outline the markings of the darts and other features which are to be transferred to the fabric. Then chalk through the holes. The non-standardized plain tissue patterns already have perforations, and so you need only chalk through them.

Usually the left and right sections of a garment are cut at once, so that there are two pieces of cloth to mark exactly alike. When the piece that is directly under the pattern has been chalked, you can remove the pattern, pin it on the wrong side of the under piece, and mark it the same as you did the first piece. However, there are a few other methods of marking the under fabric. One which is a terrific timesaver, and very accurate, too, uses the sense of touch. After the top piece of cloth has been chalked, remove the pattern and move the material over to the edge of the table, so that the part where chalking is necessary hangs over the edge. Place the tip of your thumb on the chalk dots on the upper piece and twist the pointed chalk on the under section directly under the thumb. Do this to each dot. You will be surprised at the ease and accuracy of this method.

Although chalk marks are not permanent, they will last long enough for the time they are needed. Where more lasting marking is necessary, we do something else, as you will soon see.

When darts are to be sewn from the wrong side of the cloth because they are strictly for fitting purposes, the marking is done on the wrong side of the garment just the way the pattern was pinned to the cloth. If the darts are part of the styling design and are meant to show, the pattern must be removed from the wrong side of the cloth and re-pinned to the right side for marking. The sewing will then be done on the right side also.

Occasionally pleats must be sewn on the right side of the garment, as a special feature of a style. When this is the case, mark the stitching line on the right side of the fabric, so that it can be seen for accurate sewing. Study the pattern design to decide when to do one thing and when to do the other. You personally might prefer one way over another because of the type of cloth you are using. Express your own taste in such matters.

The placement of pockets, as well as other ornamental devices, should now be marked on the right side of the cloth, so that you will know where to put them when the time comes to sew them to the garment. For these markings, it is wise to use brightly colored basting stitches immediately after the chalking is done, to keep the proper placements. Otherwise the chalk marks will disappear because of handling before you are ready to do this part of the sewing. This marking should be done on the right side of the garment.

The marking for buttonholes should be left until further progress has been made in the construction of the garment. At that time they can be lined up more accurately.

In some types of materials it is almost impossible to distinguish the right side from the wrong side once the pattern pieces have been removed and the parts of the garment are separated. Even when there is absolutely no difference in the right and wrong side of the cloth, it is a good idea to pick one of the sides as the right one, to avoid ending up with two sleeves from one arm, or two left fronts on your garment. If you chalk some large crosses on the wrong side of the pieces before you separate them, you'll never have this trouble.

Before going on, check yourself again: Did you cut through the chalk line where you needed to increase? Did you put in all the important notches, especially the ones in the armholes and sleeves? Did you notch the peak of the sleeve so that you can match this part to the shoulder seam? Are all the darts transferred to the cloth? Did you use bright thread to mark where the pockets will be placed?

STEP TWO

Working with your sewing machine

Mercerized thread is the most satisfactory for most fabrics. It blends in with most fibers, and sewing machines perform better with it than with silk thread. Seams often pucker when stitched with silk, and plain cotton thread is apt to give your work a "thready," nonprofessional appearance. Mercerized thread is available in every imaginable color, and its weight is designed for general clothes-making. You need only concern yourself with matching the color to that of the fabric. If you have to choose between a thread that is a little too light and one a little too dark, choose the darker shade, as thread has a tendency to appear lighter in stitching than it does on the spool.

Remember, though, that you should use nylon thread for stretch fabrics and some of the special synthetics.

Sewing-machine needles come in different sizes, from the heaviest to the finest. Heavy-duty needles are practical for slip-cover work, or for sewing on heavy, hard-finished materials, such as canvas or drill cloth, where heavy-duty thread is also a necessity for extra strength.

A medium-sized needle is best for general clothes-making, as it is suited for all types of materials from coatings to sheerest chiffons. You needn't change the size of your needle each time you change from one fabric to another, as long as you use the medium-sized needle and mercerized thread and keep the length of your stitches neither too long nor too short. Once in a while you may use a fine machine needle for sewing a sheer fabric such as chiffon or tulle. Even here, though, a medium-sized needle would do a good job, especially if the sheer fabric is to be lined or superimposed on a foundation of some firmer fabric.

The stitches should be a good average length, about twelve or fourteen stitches to the inch for general clothes construction. With sheer fabric used by itself, as in blouses or lingerie, the stitches should be finer, about eighteen to the inch. An easy way to arrive at the desired stitch length is to sew a short seam, mark off an inch on its length, and then count the number of stitches in the inch.

Every sewing machine has a stitch regulator in the form of a knob, lever, or dial, which is located at the right-hand side of the machine near the handwheel. It faces you as you sit at the machine. By experimenting a little with this device, you will have no problem in learning to regulate the length of the stitches to suit your work.

Your sewing machine is a precision-built mechanism, and is geared to give you fine service when properly handled. It will give you pleasing results if you are familiar with necessary things such as the right way to insert needles, how to wind and insert the bobbin, and the correct way to thread the machine. This knowledge is really all that is necessary to do a good sewing job.

If your machine functions properly, if the stitching is right for the work you are doing, and it looks good on both the upper and under side of the seam, *leave it alone!* Refrain from tinkering unnecessarily with your machine! Some frustrated female mechanics, as soon as they sit down to a sewing machine, adjust everything that will turn or slide, whether it needs it or not. Avoid this habit, because trying to "fix" anything that you do not understand will only lead to real trouble.

On the other hand, if your sewing machine doesn't seem to work properly, even though you have done nothing wrong, it may be that it needs lubrication, especially if it hasn't been used for some time. When sewing machines stand idle for a long time, the oil in the working parts becomes heavy and dried out, full of lint and dust. This causes loss of power as well as speed. Squirt a tiny drop of oil into the holes that are located here and there on the base and head of your machine. They are there for just that purpose.

A good-quality sewing-machine oil should be used, purchased either from the sewing-machine dealer or in the sewing-machine department. Any other oil may be too heavy for the precision parts and would only give added trouble. After each oiling, you should stitch several times through scraps of fabric to absorb the excess oil. If you neglect to do this, you may get oil spots on your work, so keep stitching through the scraps until there is no sign of oil on the cloth.

It is a good idea to have your sewing machine tuned up and cleaned by a reliable person every now and then, especially if it does not operate to your entire satisfaction. He will either come to your home or you may take the head of your machine to his shop. Removing the head from the cabinet is not so difficult as you may think, and you will undoubtedly get quicker service this way. The repairman may even give you explicit instructions over the telephone as to how the machine head is removed from the cabinet, although any man in your family could do it easily.

TO BASTE OR NOT TO BASTE? It is a proven fact that overhandling a garment while sewing often is the reason for homemade-looking results. Speed and accuracy go hand in hand; working with confidence will create both. Basting darts and seams first, and then sewing them on the machine, is time-consuming and unnecessary. Simple pinning of seams and darts is preferable to basting, not only because it is faster, but also because pinning holds the work much more securely for stitching. All sewing machines will sew over pins when the pins are inserted properly for stitching. Some machines have a hinged foot that simply glides over the pins. If your presser foot is not of this type you need not hesitate to sew over pins anyway. Just insert the pins horizontally, at right angles to the line of stitching, pointing them from the right toward the left.

A word to women who have qualms about sewing over pins. Pin your work as recommended, and sew right up to the pin. Slow down a little, remove the pin, and then continue on your way to the next one. Do this until you complete each seam or dart, and so on to the end of the garment. This is still a modern method compared to tedious basting.

If you construct your garment in the order that makes for greater accuracy and cuts down your sewing time, your finished product will surely compare with any custom-made article. Any other way involves too much handling, and will cause your garment to look tired and worn out before you have finished.

Making darts and stitching seams

Whether darts are featured as part of the styling or designed to mold the cloth to the figure, the stitching should be done with equal precision. When darts are stitched haphazardly, they will distort the styling of the garment.

We will begin with the jacket fronts first and make the darts on the side front pieces. The point-to-point darts that have previously been marked with chalk will now be pinned and stitched. Place the garment section flat on the table, with the marked side of the fabric facing upward. Place the tips of your thumb and forefinger on the midsection of the point-to-point dart, where it is the widest, and pinch the cloth together between finger and thumb. The dart marks will come together accurately and willingly, especially if you moisten slightly the tips of your fingers. A sponge can be used for this purpose, but if you have no sponge, beware of getting lipstick stains on the cloth. Now insert a pin horizontally into the middle of the dart with your free hand. Pin again at each point of the dart. Then hold the fabric in both hands, stretch it between two pinned sections, and continue to insert additional pins about 1 inch apart. The reason for stretching the dart while pinning is to eliminate the possibility of the dart twisting.

Before placing the fabric on your sewing machine for stitching, turn the wheel of the machine by hand so that the threaded needle is inserted into the needle plate as far down as it will go. Pull the ends of the bobbin thread and the top thread toward the back of the machine, so that they do not become snarled when the stitching is begun. Slide one of the pointed ends of the point-to-point dart directly up against the needle, just as close as it will go, and lower the presser foot of the machine. The needle is not inserted into the cloth as yet, but it will insert itself into the point of the dart with the very first stitch.

The stitching should taper very gradually from a long, slender, sharp point to the wider midsection of the dart, and continue with a very gradual taper toward the other end of the dart, ending with another sharp point. These points must be very sharp and slender so that they blend right into the garment. (Fig. 4.)

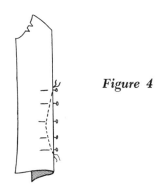

Figure 4

When darts end abruptly without gradual tapering and sharp points, the ends of the darts will budge and spoil the appearance of the garment. The fit of the garment will also be affected by poorly made darts. Allow the machine to continue to sew two or three extra stitches after the dart has passed beyond the needle. The bobbin and spool threads are automatically twisted tightly when this is done, reinforcing the ends of the darts without the need for tying thread ends. The top point of the dart was reinforced by starting the stitches with the needle inserted into the needle plate rather than the fabric. The threads at each end of the darts are then clipped off to 1-inch lengths. Do not cut them shorter, or they will not hold the firmness of the stitching.

65

Even if the machine sews backward as well as forward, you will have much sharper points on darts if you treat them in the manner just described, instead of sewing backward for reinforcement. You can never sew quite so sharply in reverse as when sewing forward.

When there are darts on the right side of the cloth for decoration, the ends of their threads are pulled through at the points and tied on the wrong side of the work. The same is done with tucks and with pleats when they are stitched on the right side of the garment: all thread ends are pulled through to the wrong side and tied securely.

When several darts are grouped together as a special detail, it is much better to pin and sew each dart individually before pinning another. Pinning all of them first and sewing them all at once is not satisfactory, since the fabric cannot be manipulated easily with too many pins in the way. If the darts are located in different areas, however, they can all be pinned at one time and then stitched, as for instance when some are located in the middle of the styling area and some in the side seams, under the arms.

The V-shaped darts are pinned at the widest end first and then at the points, with additional pins inserted in between, 1 inch apart, with the moistened tips of thumb and forefinger doing the pinching as in the first type of dart. Remember to hold the pinched cloth taut while pinning to prevent the dart from twisting. This type of dart is sewn from the wide end and tapered gradually to a sharp point, with the stitching continued off the fabric for reinforcement. Again, cut the threads to 1-inch lengths. (Fig. 5.) It is not necessary to start the stitching with

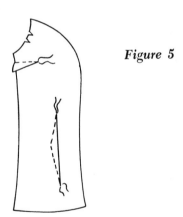

Figure 5

the needle inserted into the plate when making a dart of this type. That is done only when the dart has two points and you have no alternative.

PINNING THE SEAMS   The jacket front and side front sections are pinned together next, with the right sides of the material facing each other.

Start to pin at the top of the jacket to be sure not to distort the shape of the shoulders. Pinning is always done from the top downward, on every part of the garment, so that the tops of the units remain accurately matched. Occasionally two seam edges won't come out evenly at the ends, especially if lengths have been added or disposed of. It is wise, therefore, to start the pinning operation at the top of all sections and work downward to keep the important parts of the garment intact. Any slight discrepancy can easily be taken care of at the bottom.

Insert the pins horizontally into the seam edges, pointing them from right to left and pinning 2 or 3 inches apart. The notches which are along the seam edges for matching purposes will automatically come together, unless some extra fullness has been allowed on one of the edges for easing: easing is usually found around the bust area as well as at elbows of sleeves and at shoulders. In such places, match the notches accurately first and then fit the edges together between the notches. The correct way to ease a loose edge against a shorter one is to drape the two fabrics—the looser on top—over the fingers of one hand and pin them together at 1-inch intervals. Allow the top layer to roll freely on the underneath one as you pin so that a slight looseness forms between the pins. In the rolling process the fullness is distributed evenly and smoothly from one notch to the other.

If the fabric is not supple, it will often be necessary to stretch the under layer a little during the pinning, while you are rolling the top one—a manipulation which is not as difficult as it may sound. If you treat seams in this manner, you will avoid wrinkles in the seamline.

Work the back unit of the jacket in the same manner as the front. The darts in the side back section should be pinned and stitched first. Then the center back and side back pieces should be pinned, right sides facing each other. (Fig. 6.) Again, if there is any easing, roll over the finger and pin with the fullness on top for good results.

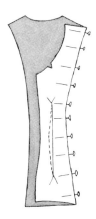

Figure 6

Sleeve sections can also be pinned together at this time. In a tailored garment such as a suit or coat, the sleeves generally consist of an upper section and an under one. Pin an upper section and an under section to each other, with the right sides together. Start pinning from the top of each seam and proceed downward, inserting pins horizontally from right to left, so that the top of the sleeve, which will be inserted in the armhole, remains undisturbed. (Fig. 7.) When one-piece sleeves are

Figure 7

featured in the design, the V darts at the elbows are chalked, pinned, stitched, and pressed before the seam is pinned together for sewing.

Frequently you will find markings that indicate a small dart at the back of the shoulder. This is sometimes marked as a V but at times it is just a straight line, indicating that it must be folded at the line, pinned, and then stitched into a very narrow, sharp, V-shaped dart. Darts of this type are also found at the back of necklines. They are pinned and sewn exactly the same as those described at the side seam of the jacket front, from the wider part to the point, with the stitching continued for reinforcement. When stitching a dart that is marked with just a single line, the stitching is started ¼ inch away from the fold and tapered to nothing at the point or end of the line.

UNDERLINING THE GARMENT FABRIC   There are many lovely but loosely woven and knitted fabrics that require a complete underlining to provide shape and opaqueness. Your pattern may suggest that an underlining be used, and it is wise to do so if your fabric lacks necessary body. Show your pattern to your salesperson and ask what weight and type of underlining to use.

The lightweight underlinings are cut like the outer fabric parts and are sewn into the seams along with the garment fabric. You can run a line of machine stitching around the outer edges of each piece first, or, if the fabric does not stretch, just hold the two layers of each part together and pin them. With either system, however, run a line of machine stitching right through the middle of the darts through the two fabrics before you sew the darts into their right shape. Otherwise, it will be impossible to sew perfect darts on the outside cloth, as the outer layer will slip away from the underlining fabric before the line of stitching reaches the pointed end of the dart. To avoid bulk, slash the dart through the middle to within ⅜ inch from its point and spread the raw edges apart.

Constructing the units of the garment

As noted, all pattern companies allow a ⅝-inch seam edge on all parts of their pattern pieces. This seam must be maintained throughout the complete construction of the garment if it is to fit well when completed. The only places where there is apt to be a variation in the width of the seams is in the "hidden areas" at the sides, where individual fittings are done. The personal contours of your figure can definitely change the seam edges here.

If the seams are taken in more than the allowed ⅝ inch in the styling areas of the garment, the garment will be too small, even though the difference between you and the pattern has been accurately added to the "hidden areas." On the other hand, if the seams are not sewn the full ⅝-inch width, the garment will be too large in the important areas and taking it in at the side seams would only spoil the effect of the design. This matter of consistently sewing the right kind of seam is one of the important "little things" that have great bearing on the appearance of the finished product.

One of the best ways to maintain a uniform width in your seam is to place a short strip of adhesive tape, about 2 or 3 inches long, on the needle plate of your machine, just ⅝ inch to the right of the hole in the plate. For real accuracy, do this: Take one of the pattern pieces that has a straight seam edge and place the pattern under the presser foot of the machine, as if you were going to sew through it. Turn the wheel by hand and insert the needle through the line that indicates the width of the seam. Lower the presser foot so that the pattern will be held firmly under it, and then press the adhesive tape onto the needle plate, directly up against the pattern edge. You now have a very accurate seam guide with ⅝-inch space between the needle hole and the tape edge. Just be sure that the tape is placed in a straight vertical position in front of you as you sit at the machine. This tape will not only keep your seam edges a uniform width throughout the construction of your garment, but will also make them come out perfectly straight every time. Keep the edge of the seam directly up against the edge of the tape, and that's all there is to it. Even the experienced person will benefit by this helpful little trick.

You can purchase commercial seam guides that screw on to the base of your machine, but the flatness of the tape enables you to sew around curves and points with greater ease. Some of the new sewing machines have grooves marked on the needle plate, to indicate different fractions of an inch, ¼ inch, ½ inch, ⅝ inch, and even ¾ inch and 1 inch. But it is much easier to see the edge of the tape than fine printing engraved on the plate lines.

There is no definite rule about the direction from which a seam must be sewn, although some sewing instructions stress a certain direction as a "must." Certainly, you should PIN from the top downward so that the units to be joined will match well, but the stitching may be done from either end. If possible, keep the bulk of the fabric to the left of the sewing machine when starting to sew. Occasionally, you will find yourself sewing with the bulk under the arm of the machine, even though you started on the left side of the needle. Some of the construction steps will bring this about, as you will see later.

When easing needs to be worked into one of the seam edges, as in the bust area or the elbows of two-piece sleeves, or when joining skirts and waistbands, the work should be placed under the presser foot with the smoother edge on top of the loose one. Hold the work slightly taut during the stitching process, with one hand behind the presser foot and the other in front of it, without pulling the work away from the needle in either direction.

Whenever seam edges differ in length, but must be made to conform to each other, join them together in this manner. Your results will always be smooth, with no sign of a pucker. On the other hand, if the looser edge of the seam were placed on top of the short, smooth one, the slackness would be pinched into little folds between each pin, and the appearance of the seam would be spoiled. Pressing will always produce a perfectly flat surface on an eased seam edge if the cloth has been properly handled in pinning and stitching. If the slackness has been caught into tiny folds in stitching, however, pressing will not flatten it down.

Stitch the front and side front sections of the jacket to each other, placing the edge with the easing underneath the smoother one. Whether you sew from the bottom of the jacket to the top, or the other way around, does not really matter, as long as the eased edge is sewn correctly and the seam width is an exact ⅝ inch.

The back of the jacket is the next unit to be stitched. With the darts

70

already done in the side back sections, the center panel is joined to the two side sections. (Fig. 8.)

Sew the sleeve sections together with the looser of the two seam edges on the bottom, so that the ease can be worked in smoothly at the elbow area. With sleeves, it is especially important to take the precaution of chalking large crosses or scrolls on the wrong side of the cloth, to avoid the possibility of ending up with two left or two right sleeves.

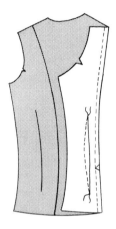

Figure 8

Press as you go

Pressing is another of those ultra-important "little things" that play such a big part in creating a handsome garment. Your talent for doing fine work will be to no avail if you underestimate the importance of pressing your work properly as you assemble the different parts. It is most essential to press each unit perfectly before it is joined to another unit. The importance of this cannot be stressed too much. How, when, and where you press will have a tremendous bearing on the appearance of your finished product, whether it is a high-fashion creation or one entailing simple, basic sewing ability.

When pressing is done haphazardly, even the finest work will look "home grown." But quite often the eye can be diverted from imperfect workmanship when a good pressing job is done in the process of construction.

Pressing is always done on the wrong side of the cloth, using a light touch, and gliding the iron on the seams slowly, with long back-and-forth movements rather than short, quick ones. There may be an occasional need to touch up the right side of the work, but the general blocking is done on the wrong side of the cloth as you go along. Don't bear down on the iron, as heavy pressure will flatten the surface nap of your material and produce a shine on any dark-colored fabric. Too much pressure may also produce ridges along the seams. For best results, use a light touch in pressing and give the job the proper amount of time.

Because of the resiliency of animal fibers, woolen materials must be pressed with dampness in addition to heat. A steam iron is wonderful for this purpose, with the dial set for "wool." Just separate the seam edges on the wrong side and press them out flat, starting from the bottom of the seam and gliding the iron toward the top, so that the edges do not fray. Remember, the slower and lighter this is done, the better. Seams fray much more readily when they are pressed from the top downward, as all the yarns on the seam edges are in a natural upright position. You will retain them in the correct position if you press the seams from the bottom up.

All fabrics, regardless of their basic fibers, may be safely pressed directly on the wrong side with a steam iron. In using a dry iron, however, the following method will prove excellent: Regulate the heat of the iron to suit the type of cloth you are using. In the case of wool, wipe the seam on the wrong side of the fabric with a dampened sponge or an old terry face cloth. Then glide the iron directly on the fabric, without using a pressing cloth, starting from the bottom of the seam and working toward the top, moving the iron lightly and quickly. This initial pressing, besides separating the seams and putting them into position for final pressing, will save wear and tear on your back, as it eliminates the necessity of peeking underneath the pressing cloth to see if the seams are behaving themselves properly. The pressing cloth is then placed over the seam and the seam is thoroughly pressed.

A crash dish towel makes an excellent pressing cloth, as it holds the moisture long enough to create steam for a really good pressing once the heat of the iron has been applied. If the pressing cloth is too thin, it dries before the steam sufficiently permeates the cloth. The pressing cloth should be thoroughly moistened, but not wet enough to spot your fabric.

No pressing cloth is needed in pressing silk, rayon, cotton, linen, or any of the synthetics. Just wipe the seam with either the sponge or the terry cloth, and slowly iron as you did in the initial pressing, working from the bottom of the seam toward the top to control the fraying of the seam edges.

The proper pressing of darts is another thing that adds the professional touch to a finished garment, since the direction into which the dart is pressed affects the draping of the cloth. Home sewers are often confused about this matter. Darts on the front of your garment should always be pressed with the fold directed toward the center front. Back darts are pressed with the folds directed toward the center back. No matter where the darts are located, at the shoulders, neckline, midsection, waistline, or skirt top, the rule of pressing is still the same. Underarm darts, located at the side seams, as well as elbow darts in sleeves, are pressed with the folds of the darts in a downward position.

The fabric alongside a dart is spread out with the fingers of the free hand while the pressing is done. This little manipulation blends the darted part of the material right into the garment and molds the right side of the cloth into a perfectly smooth shape. If you fail to keep the cloth spread out flat while pressing, you may press folds into the cloth next to the darts.

Use the small end of the ironing board to achieve good results when pressing darts. When pressing point-to-point darts, it simplifies matters if the pressing is done close to the edge of the ironing board. In this way you avoid pressing wrinkles into the fabric next to the darts.

When darts are featured on the right side of the garment as part of the styling, there may be occasional exceptions to the rule of the pressing direction. In such cases, they should be pressed as indicated in the design. It is usually necessary to do the pressing on the right side of the garment at such times, placing a dry cloth over the darts to keep the iron from marking the fabric. If your suit fabric has a resilient nature, give it a very light touch with a thoroughly squeezed-out sponge before placing the dry cloth on the darts. This will help you get a flat pressing job.

When working with heavy fabrics, such as coatings, it is often advisable to slash darts right through the folds after they have been stitched to about ½ inch from the point. Then press them open, separating the edges in opposite directions. This will greatly eliminate bulk in the seams into which the darts are sewn.

Sleeve seams are pressed open over a sleeve board. If you do not own a sleeve board, you can improvise a very satisfactory substitute by using a rolled-up magazine (not a small thick one, but rather a large one with fewer pages), wrapped up in a dish towel. Insert this into your sleeves and it will serve the purpose very well. Be sure, however, that you roll a towel around the magazine, or you may transfer the cover design onto your sleeves. (The moisture of the pressing cloth and the heat of the iron will loosen the inks on the cover and transplant them onto your garment.) When two-piece sleeves are being made, you can simplify pressing by sewing and pressing one of the seams before making the second. In this way you will have only one seam to press in the confined area of the sewn-up sleeve.

Pressing as you go is of utmost importance, it is very true. But don't feel that in order to do a good job you must knock yourself out by jumping for the ironing board as soon as any dart or seam has been sewn. Accumulate several individual seams and darts, and press them all at once. For example, you can press the seams and darts of each front, the seams and darts of the back, as well as the seams of the sleeves, all at the same time.

Before a good press job can be done on a curved seam on which one edge was eased and the other was not, as at the joinings of the front panels, you must clip inward through both edges at once: about ⅜ inch deep and ⅝ inch apart. Otherwise, the short edge will not spread flatly during the pressing and the full one will form into ripples. (Fig. 9.) The clippings allow the short edge to spread and the full edge to overlap smoothly.

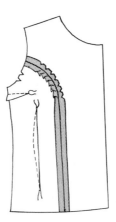

Figure 9

Every so often you will need to press a curved seam over a curved surface. This happens around the bust area more than anywhere else. A tailor's mitt can be used for this type of pressing, but if you don't have one, you can improvise a very handy curved surface. Do this: Make a fist of your free hand and wrap it up in a small terry-cloth towel, so that it resembles the head of a miniature mummy. Place the curved seam on top of this handy curved surface, with the cloth wrong side up, and go ahead and press. If you have several layers of the towel on your fist, you need not worry about burns.

Before venturing on to the next tailoring step be sure that you can answer "yes" to the following questions: Are the darts in each unit as sharp as they can possibly be at the ends? If they cause the cloth on the right side to ripple, either they have not been pressed well, or the ends of the darts aren't tapered enough. Are the darts pressed in the proper direction? Are the seams in each unit exactly ⅝ inch wide, and have they been pressed perfectly flat? If so, you have paved the way for the next step.

STEP THREE

Interfacing the units of the jacket

All tailored suits and coats have certain parts interfaced with materials that are made for this purpose and which give the garment a firm foundation, helping to keep it perpetually trim and shapely. Your suit would resemble a soft, tailored two-piece dress if the interfacing were omitted. Some dresses are also interfaced in parts in order to achieve some specially desired effect. Besides insuring a permanently trim appearance, interfacing also has a priceless disguising quality, for it conceals irregularities in the upper part of the figure.

The yardage is specified on the pattern envelope when interfacing is required, and generally special pattern pieces are provided by which to cut the interfacing. When there are no special patterns, you are instructed to use parts of the actual jacket pattern for this purpose. A glance at the layout chart on your pattern sheet will tell you which pieces should be used.

Even loosely knit or woven materials which you underline for extra body will need still another firm fabric in the places where permanent perkiness and trimness are necessary. Just treat the parts of such garments as if they were made of single layers of cloth when you attach the interfacing fabrics to them.

TYPES OF INTERFACING   Interfacing material comes in several types, and you will need to know when to use one kind and when another. Tailor's canvas, also referred to as haircloth, is an old stand-by for interfacing woolen suits and coats. It consists of part cotton fibers and part animal hairs, and has great resiliency and a good adhering quality.

The interfacing is placed between the outer fabric of the garment and the facing, which is also of garment material. The animal hairs in the canvas adhere to both the garment and the facing fabric, holding them together as one, once they have been properly tacked. The haircloth is a "natural" for interfacing woolen suits and coats, because both contain animal fibers. The resiliency of hair canvas will keep the collar and lapels of your garment rolled over becomingly without creasing or folding, even after many seasons of wear.

A special firmly woven linen is also made for interfacing. It is most satisfactory to use when a soft, semi-tailored effect is desired, or when your tailored garment is made of silk, rayon, linen, or cotton. Haircloth is not recommended for these fabrics, because the animal hairs in haircloth would work through the fabric weave and cause discomfort to the wearer.

A WARNING Sometimes the interfacing material shows through the garment cloth. To avoid this, make sure that the interfacing used is not any darker than the outside fabric: natural-colored interfacing shows through white and pastel colors even when the weave is close. It is therefore important to test the garment fabric with the interfacing underneath it to be certain that it is absolutely invisible. If a shadow shows through where the tailor's canvas is, get some other type of a material for the interfacing. Although it may not be made of the same fibers as the tailor's canvas, it will give support and do the job well. Look for about the same weight as the medium tailor's-canvas weight. There are many substitutes for haircloth on the market, and you should have no problem finding a satisfactory one.

The many lovely miracle fabrics must also be interfaced when tailored effects are desired. Remember that most of these fabrics require little if any pressing when laundered. Therefore, you will defeat your purpose in using them if you don't use fabrics of like quality throughout your entire garment. Unless your interfacing and your lining fabric are both of the miracle type, you will have to iron or press the parts of the garment which are made of something else.

Even though hair canvas and linen interfacing are not recommended for use with fabrics made of miracle yarns, the miracle interfacings can be used satisfactorily inside of garments made of natural fibers. This is especially true in items that can be washed at home, such as cotton and linen suits, and in lightweight silk, rayon, or cotton outfits where the linen interfacing may be too heavy. The nonwrinkling quality of the miracle interfacing would simplify the pressing also, as only the outer fabrics would need to be pressed. There are all types of interfacings made for the miracle fabrics, from those heavy enough to use in coats to sheers that resemble curtain marquisette. Do not make the mistake of using interfacing that is too heavy for the texture of your garment fabric. This goes for both the natural and the synthetic interfacings.

77

PREPARING THE INTERFACING   When hair canvas or linen is used for interfacing, it is a good idea to wipe it with a damp sponge and dry it with the iron before cutting. If there is any possibility of shrinkage, let it happen now, and not after the garment has been worn and sent to the cleaner. This can be done on your ironing board, as it is not necessary to dunk the canvas or linen into the water. They probably won't shrink at all, but it is always better to be sure.

The interfacing must occasionally be darted in certain areas to follow the design. Darts in the interfacing are stitched from the wide sections toward the points, and the fold of the dart is then slashed to about ½ inch from the ends, and pressed open.

PINNING INTERFACING IN PLACE   The two jacket fronts are the first units to work on after the interfacings have been cut and the darts sewn. The technique for applying the canvas to the jacket fronts will be the same for all other sections in which interfacing is used. Select a solid surface for your work. Be sure that it is not some choice piece of furniture, as it will surely get scratched during this operation. If you use your dining table, protect it with a leatherette pad. Otherwise, an old card table, or your kitchen table or counter top will do nicely. Your ironing board or a soft table pad should not be used, as softness would interfere with your work.

Place one of the jacket fronts on the flat surface, with the wrong side up, and place the interfacing on top of it. When darts are stitched in the canvas, the smoothest side should always be placed against the garment; otherwise the raw edges of the darts would make an impression which would show through the outside fabric.

Start pinning the canvas and wool to each other at the top of the front edge, right at the neckline, and continue toward the bottom, matching edge to edge and inserting the pins vertically about 2 inches apart. The canvas molds the garment into the proper shape, and the woolen cloth underneath the canvas must be made to conform accurately to it. If the garment cloth has a tendency to curve inward at the waistline of the jacket, where the fitting darts are sewn into it, you must gently force the wool into a straight line with the edge of the canvas, as this is one of the most important functions of the canvas. Keeping the front edges of the jacket perfectly straight would be impossible without the foundation of the canvas.

The neck and shoulder sections are matched and pinned next. Quite often in tailored items the interfacing is cut to reach directly across the upper chest and over to the armholes, so that greater smoothness can be acquired and retained in that area. When this is the case, the canvas and the cloth are matched at the armholes and pinned to each other. In other patterns, the interfacing is cut into a panel to fit down the front of the jacket, just the width of the woolen facing that eventually covers it.

When the outer edges of the canvas and garment have been completely pinned edge to edge, the inner edge of the canvas must also be pinned accurately to the inner sections of the front in the following manner: Place the palms of both hands on the canvas and flatten the canvas down against the jacket front to make sure that the woolen fabric is perfectly smooth underneath it. Keep your fingers spread out so that a large area of the jacket can be taken care of at one time. Keep one hand spread on the canvas while the other hand pins the inner edge smoothly to the jacket front. Start at the shoulder area and work downward for best results, smoothing constantly until the complete canvas has been pinned.

As you pin the canvas, much rippling and distortion of fabric take place directly alongside of the inner edge of the canvas. This is how the jacket gets into its proper shape. The canvas controls the parts that must remain straight, smooth, and firm. The rippling and bulging, on the other hand, will conform themselves to the contours of your figure in the most becoming way, as long as the interfaced sections are as smooth as they can possibly be.

If you have combined the pattern pieces of front and facing and cut them together, either trim away the ⅝-inch seam allowance of the interfacing front edge or just fold it under and press it flat: trim if the cloth is firmly woven and you wish to reduce bulk; fold to supply additional support to a garment made of loosely woven or lightweight fabric. Then place the canvas against the inside of the garment, matching the edge or fold of the interfacing to the crease in the garment. Stab stitch the canvas into place, making sure that the canvas is attached to the garment proper and not to the facing part.

STAB STITCHING THE INTERFACING   The canvas is now ready to be attached permanently and invisibly to the jacket front, using a fine needle and mercerized thread in the exact color of the garment fabric. Lay the garment flat on the table with the front edge nearest to you, canvas side facing upward. The stitching will be done vertically, parallel with the front edge. This is one of the reasons why the stitches will be invisible on the right side of the garment. Another is the unique way in which these stitches are executed.

Start the first row about ⅜ inch from the front edge. It does not matter whether you work from the top of the front to the bottom or vice versa, as long as you keep the stitches going in a vertical direction on the garment, even when the canvas takes on a curved or angular line. When the stitching is done with the rows running in the same direction as that in which the garment is to be worn, the stitches blend naturally into the weave of the cloth. Tie a tiny knot in your thread to anchor the first stitch, and stab the needle into the canvas so that it penetrates directly through to the right side of the cloth, and then with a quick twist of the wrist, pick up just a thread or two of the canvas on the needle, including an invisible amount of the garment cloth also. It is the quick stabbing, plus the twisting motion of the hand, which will enable you to pick up such a small amount of both materials on the needle that the stitch will not be visible on the right side.

Repeat the stitches every 1½ inches, working from the right toward the left. If you are left-handed, you may work from the opposite direction. The thread must be extremely loose between each stitch, so loose, as a matter of fact, that two fingers could fit comfortably into the thread loop without crowding. When the first row has been completed, just clip off the thread: no reinforcement is required. The second row should be started about 1¼ inches away from the first one. Each row is done in the same manner as the first, until the canvas is completely covered with stab stitching, the rows spaced about the same 1¼ inches apart. (Fig. 10.) It will amaze you to see how quickly you will get into the swing of doing this work.

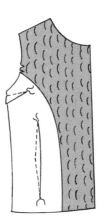

Figure 10

Every so often you should take a look on the right side of the garment, to see that the stitches are not visible. The looseness of the stitching will keep the surface of the wool perfectly smooth and flat. If the stitches were not loose enough, there will be a dent in the garment cloth wherever a stitch was taken, and although the stitches themselves won't show, the surface of the cloth will be dimpled and tacky in appearance. Furthermore, if the rows of stitching were done horizontally instead of in a vertical direction, the garment cloth may pull inward where the stitches are, even though the thread loop was loose enough between the stitches.

Do the second jacket front next, using the same method in pinning and stitching, and making sure that the garment and canvas are perfectly smooth against each other.

You are now ready for the next step in the construction of your jacket, so see if all the important little factors which go toward making beautiful clothes have been carried out to your entire satisfaction.

Did you keep the interfacing and the garment cloth perfectly lined up edge to edge when stab stitching them together? Are the canvas and the outer fabrics smooth against each other, so that neither of them is puckered or bubbled? The bubbles should be only alongside the canvas, where you will fill them out with your own curves. Do any of the stitches show through? Do you have dimples on the right side of the material, caused by too-tight stitches?

If you've passed this quiz with a good percentage of. *yes* answers, and corrected the ones which were answered *no*, proceed to have fun with the next step. You are off to a good start!

STEP FOUR

Bound buttonholes

The ability to make beautiful bound buttonholes, as well as set-in types of tailored pockets, used to be considered one of the great accomplishments in sewing, something that required lots of experience and practice. The wise beginner shied away from bound buttonholes. All that is changed now, by simplified methods.

With the very first sample or two you will be completely convinced that these lovely functional details can be made easily, even by the rawest beginner. There are several ways of making bound buttonholes, but none is quite so simple as the method set forth here for you to follow, consisting of the four easiest steps you have ever been instructed to take.

Even if you have been making buttonholes for a long time, and have been happy with your results, it would be to your advantage to try this newer way, just to see how easy it is to get all your buttonholes looking exactly alike in shape and size. Sometimes one buttonhole is very nice, but the one next to it may differ somewhat in appearance or size, or both. To line them up properly on the garment and then make them uniform in size and appearance is of utmost importance. It will be easy if you follow these simple instructions. Again you will find that the "little things" stressed in each step along the way will produce precision workmanship.

Before starting to make sample buttonholes, prepare the strip of binding which will be the finish of the buttonhole edges. Cut a length of fabric 1 inch wide, either on the length weave or cross weave of the cloth, whichever way will fray the lesser. The bindings can be made from short lengths of cloth or long ones, just so that the weave runs in the same direction on all the strips. A long strip will later be cut into shorter strips anyway. Fold the strip lengthwise through the center, right side out. Sew through the strip exactly ⅛ inch away from the fold, and then trim away the raw edge of the strip, leaving exactly ⅛ inch at the edge. The machine stitching should be in the direct center of the strip, with ⅛ inch on either side. These widths must be identical in order for your buttonhole to come out perfectly, because the raw edge of the strip acts as a spacing device for bringing the bindings together in the finished buttonhole. If the raw edges were wider than the fold, the finished buttonhole would have empty spaces between the bindings at each end. On the other hand, if the raw edges were not so wide as the folded side of the binding, the buttonhole space when cut would be too narrow for the folds to fit into properly, and they would overlap each other. You will learn to overcome any of these trifling errors in the sample making, and thereby avoid them in the buttonholes you make on the garment.

Follow the instructions for each step as set forth here, reading one sentence at a time as you proceed, and you will be delighted with your accomplishments. These will be sample buttonholes; therefore, make any size you want.

One: With your chalk sharpened to a pencil point, mark the length of the buttonhole desired on the *right* side of the cloth, in the form of a tiny "goal post," such as seen on football fields, or an oversized letter H, whichever you prefer to call it. (Fig. 11). The horizontal crossbar of the symbol represents the length of the buttonhole and should be drawn directly parallel with the cross weave of the cloth. The guideposts at the sides are parallel with the length weave of the cloth. That's all to that step.

Two: From the binding which you have prepared prior to starting, cut two strips 1 inch longer than the horizontal line of the symbol. Place one of the strips above the line, with the ends projecting evenly beyond the sides of the goal post and the raw edge of the strip resting on the line. Stitch through the strip from post to post, making sure that the stitching is done directly through the preliminary sewing. (Fig. 12.) Cut the thread ends at the start and end of this stitching to

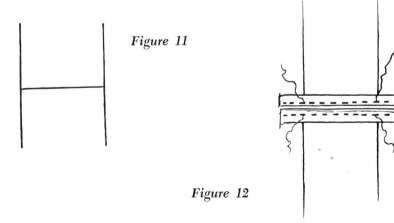

Figure 11

Figure 12

1-inch lengths and no shorter, for reinforcement. The second binding is now placed below the horizontal line of the goal post, with the raw edges butted right up against the ones on the first strip, and sewn in the same manner.

Three: This next step is done on the *wrong* side of the cloth. Mark the center area of the buttonhole between the two rows of stitching with a "bull's-eye," a dot, with your chalk. (Fig. 13a.) Pierce the dot with the point of the scissors. Then insert the point of the scissors into the hole at an angle, and cut directly to the end of one row of stitching, cutting only the uppermost fabric, and not the bindings on the other side. Reinsert the point of the scissors in the same manner to cut to all four ends of the stitchings, starting from the bull's-eye each time and not cutting any farther than the ends. The cuts will resemble an "X." (Fig. 13b.) You now have a fairly large triangular tab of cloth at each end of the buttonhole which will make it good and sturdy when finished. You are ready for the finishing step.

Four: First turn the wheel of your machine by hand until the needle is inserted into the needle plate, and bring the threads toward the back of the machine to keep them from getting snarled when stitching. Then gently pull the bindings through the cuts from the right side of the cloth to the wrong side, and finish the ends of the buttonhole as follows: Lay your work to the left of the sewing machine, with the fabric right side up. Fold back the cloth at the end of the buttonhole which is nearest to the needle, so that the triangular tab and the ends of the bindings underneath it are visible on the wrong side of your work. You now slide your work, holding it in that very same position, right up against the needle until you can't slide it any closer. Then lower the presser foot, and stitch down across the projecting triangular tab and the ends of the bindings, keeping just as close to the fold as you possibly can without catching it in the stitches. (Fig. 14.) Take care of

Figure 13a   *Figure 13b*

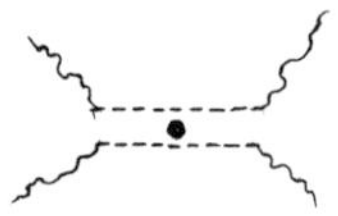

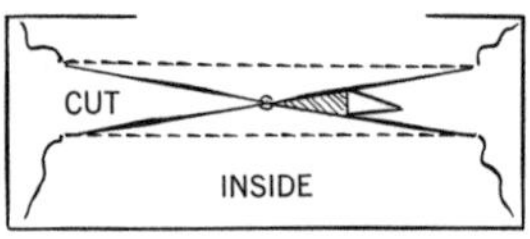

CUT

INSIDE

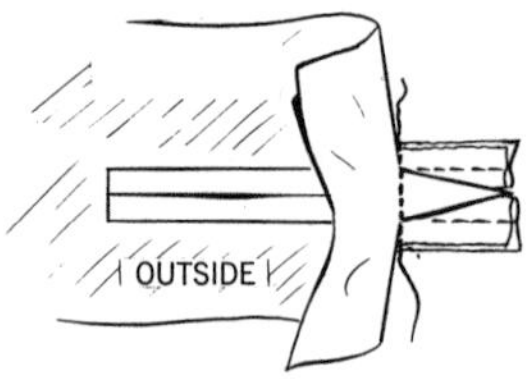

OUTSIDE

Figure 14

the opposite end of the buttonhole in the same manner. All the raw edges of the bindings will eventually be covered up with the facing of the jacket.

Here's a helpful hint: Use a bright contrasting thread in the bobbin when preparing the bindings for the buttonholes. This will simplify the steps and give visual aid in the construction where precision stitching and cutting are of prime importance. The preliminary stitching on the binding is used as a guide for producing perfectly formed buttonholes, so it is necessary that this stitching be visible. When working with loosely woven or tweedy cloth, the stitching often becomes buried out of sight in the weave so that it is difficult to see it on the bindings. The colored stitching will show up readily in all textures. The bindings are placed on the goal post with the bright stitching facing up and are sewn into place right through it. When the buttonholes are finished, the bright stitching will not show, as it will be covered with the facing of the garment.

Make a few sample buttonholes first before attempting the steps on your actual garment. Even though they are easy and fun to make, a certain amount of practice will give you added confidence. Beautifully tailored pockets of the set-in variety are made by using the basic buttonhole steps, so you will not only become a proficient buttonhole maker but also an expert on pockets.

Buttons and buttonholes are both functional and decorative, and their sizes are determined by the style and type of garment you are making. The sizes featured on your pattern have been determined after much consideration by the designer, so it would be advisable to make the buttonholes in the recommended size for good effect. When several buttons are featured on a garment, the size is usually kept rather small, but when only one or two are used, the buttons are much larger. Too many big buttons will detract from the style, but when only one or two are featured, they would look insignificant if they were too small.

It is not necessary to purchase the buttons before you make the buttonholes, as there are choice buttons available in every color and shape you may desire. If you are purchasing buttons to fit buttonholes that have already been made on your garment, take a sample buttonhole with you. This will be of great help not only in choosing the size, but also in determining the best color.

Now that you are familiar with the four steps of buttonhole making, you must learn how to transfer the markings for them from the pattern to the garments. After all, it is not enough to know how to make perfect buttonholes; it is also necessary—and very important—to know how to align them properly and make them match in size. You need to become familiar with the symbols the pattern companies use for marking buttonholes, for each is just different enough from another to be confusing unless you know them.

One pattern company uses a symbol resembling an ordinary nail lying on its side, a line projecting from the nailhead to show how long the buttonhole should be. For accuracy here, the buttonhole would be marked from the head to the end of the nail. Another manufacturer prints the symbol for the buttonhole as a common pin, the line emerging from the pinhead to show the length of the buttonhole, so it is marked from head to point.

Some patterns use large dark squares to indicate the size and placement of buttonholes; others use dots with stems heading out of their centers. Holes are punctured in the pattern pieces, and marks made through the holes to the cloth. But make the holes on the outer edges of the large squares or dots, *not* at their centers, to prevent the buttonholes from being shorter than intended and to make sure they are the right distance from the edge of the garment.

Occasionally two large dots or two large squares show the size of the buttonholes. Then the dots should be made at the two outer ends of the symbols, *not* at their middles.

Next, remember that on women's clothes, the buttonholes are on the right front and the buttons on the left, just the reverse of the way men wear them.

The pattern piece should be pinned edge to edge on the *inside* of the garment through the canvas and fabric. With the point of a pencil, puncture through the pattern and mark the buttonholes on the *canvas* at both ends of each buttonhole symbol, and then remove the pattern.

With the pencil, draw horizontal lines on the canvas from one dot to the other, and then with a yardstick draw parallel vertical lines through the dots from just above the top buttonhole to just below the bottom one. You have now produced a symbol very closely resembling a ladder, the rungs of which are the accurate length of each buttonhole.

Adjust your sewing machine for the largest stitches it can make, and thread it in bobbin and spool with colors that contrast vividly to both the color of the garment material and the color of the canvas. Then sew through the ladder-like pencil lines so that the symbol will be seen without any trouble on the outside fabric as well as on the canvas: this symbol will be your foolproof guide for getting the buttonholes alike and in perfect line.

A warning: Do use a light touch with the pencil marking, especially when working with light-colored fabrics, for if you bear down too strongly you will send powdered pencil material right out to the surface of the garment—no fun to remove. The machine stitching will do the job for you: you need only see the pencil lines enough to sew through them properly on the canvas side.

Put your two hands on the canvas with your fingers spread out and press down with them a little as you sew through the ladder symbol to prevent the presser foot from separating the cloth and canvas from each other, as well as to prevent the stab stitches from getting caught in the presser foot.

If you are making bound buttonholes on a delicate fabric, do not machine stitch the ladder symbol, because you may be left with needle marks. Stitch the symbol by hand instead in a bright color—after penciling the interfacing lightly. Just be sure that the hand stitches are close enough together to give you a clear line to follow for a straight arrangement of buttonholes.

Functional buttonholes are rarely made without an interfacing of some sort to give them strength, but even those used only for decoration look better if they are interfaced. In suits and coats the buttonholes are made right through the canvas. If you have prepared the binding ahead of time, now cut two strips for each buttonhole, 1 inch longer than the actual length of the ladder rungs. Make sure that the raw-edge sides of the binding equal exactly the width of the folded sides before you start to sew them to the garment. As stated before, these edges are spacing devices that make the folded edges come together properly in the finished buttonhole. They even up the cutting space.

Sew a pair of bindings on each rung with the raw edges together, making sure that you start sewing exactly on one side line of the ladder and stop directly on the other. Stitch right through the preliminary stitching line of the binding, and leave the threads 1 inch long at each end, so that they will be caught into the next operation. Sew the binding to each rung in the same manner. (Fig. 15.) When they have all been

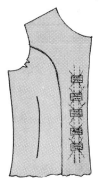

Figure 15

sewn, inspect the canvas side of your work to make sure that each of the horizontally stitched lines is exactly the same length, the same distance from the front edge, and that the space between each pair of bindings is the same. (Fig. 16.) The large machine stitching that guided you on the right side of the garment will also guide you on the wrong side. You can see at a glance if the pair of stitching lines that hold the binding securely to the ladder are even. If they are not, they can be corrected easily before you cut the buttonhole. When these stitching lines are not exactly even with each other, one being a stitch or two longer than the other, the buttonholes will slant at the ends and lose their rectangular shape.

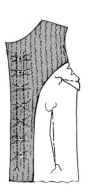

Figure 16

After you have checked each parallel line of stitching on the canvas side for accuracy and corrected as necessary, remove the ladder symbol very carefully, as it has performed its important purpose. Clip the threads here and there on both sides of the garment—canvas and outside too—and remove the threads gently first from one side of the front and then from the other, so that there is no strain on the material.

Then mark the buttonholes with "bull's eyes" on the canvas side. You will cut and finish one buttonhole at a time so that the materials don't fray from handling. Before you do any cutting, however, take hold of the thread ends with both hands and give them a gentle pull to tighten the stitches in case they have loosened up a bit. Pull on the canvas side as well as the fabric side to avoid having stitching threads visible at the ends of the buttonholes. After you have cut through the buttonholes and finished them at the ends, baste the bindings together to close them up. Then press them closed, using a moist cloth to block them. Leave the basting in place until the garment is completed, but trim the bindings at the ends to no longer than ¼ inch to avoid interfering with the front seam edges.

If you are making bound buttonholes on a very loose basket weave or tweedy texture, you will need to provide more support than just canvas to keep the buttonholes from fraying. Ideal for such reinforcement are the adhesive types of lightweight fabrics which are pressed on with a warm iron. Attach either a strip or a patch to the wrong side of the material at the buttonhole location before you stab stitch the canvas into position. The extra layer will not show through to the outside of the cloth once the buttonholes are built into the garment. Back the bindings of the buttonholes with the same cloth to make sure that they don't fray either.

If the suit features pockets, they should be inserted at this stage of the tailoring progress. Some pockets are built in along with the construction seams and styling lines of the design, while others are separate units, such as patch pockets, and are superimposed on the garment. There is also the set-in variety that is made much in the manner of a bound buttonhole. Slight variations in the buttonhole steps will produce several different types of set-in pockets. Information on this subject is completely covered in the section on "Pockets."

The fronts and back of the jacket are now joined together across the shoulders, and the seams are pressed open. The edge of the canvas interfacing is not sewn into the shoulder seam. Lap it over the seam, and later on you will catch it in with the collar and sleeves.

STEP FIVE

Making the collar

When fronts of garments are interfaced with canvas it is customary to interface the collar as well, so that a uniform appearance will be maintained in that area. The collars of tailored suits and coats usually consist of an upper section, cut in one piece on the straight of the goods, just like the rest of the garment, and an under collar, cut in two pieces on the bias weave of the material. The under-collar pattern is used for cutting the canvas, unless a special pattern piece has been provided. The canvas is cut on the bias, like the under collar. This gives the finished collar a flexible quality that makes it conform nicely to the individual's neck, even though the upper collar has been cut on the straight of the goods.

The two under-collar sections that were cut from the garment cloth are sewn with the right sides facing each other, and the seam is pressed open. The canvas is then pinned against the wrong side of the under collar and stab stitched into place. If the canvas has been cut in two pieces, the center edges are not joined, but are just overlapped and caught together with the stab stitching, because some of the flexible quality of the bias weave would be lost if the edges were sewn together. The stab stitching does not have to follow any particular direction, as it did on the fronts, since this part of the collar is not visible anyway. The stab stitching should be just a little closer together than on the garment fronts, and the threads pulled flat against the canvas.

The collar is now ready to be completed as a unit. The upper- and under-collar sections are pinned with the right sides placed against each other. The pinning is done 1 inch apart. The neck edge is left open. Usually the upper collar is slightly larger than the under collar, so that a bit of easing is necessary to make the edges fit each other. This is to allow for take-up, or rolling, when the collar is finished. If the upper-collar piece is held on top of the under section and the unit is rolled over the fingers while being pinned around the outer edges, the slight difference will ease in with no trouble.

To sew the collar, place the work under the presser foot of the machine with the canvas facing up. The presser foot often causes supple materials to slide a little as they are being sewn, especially when there are more than two layers to sew through, even though the edges have been securely pinned. Because the canvas is much firmer than the garment material, if the canvas side is placed up for stitching, the edges of the article will remain smooth and even, and sliding will be avoided.

When collars are interfaced, the seams are trimmed off in a special way before the work is turned right side out, so that the outer edges are tapered gradually to blend in with the rest of the collar. Only when the seam is trimmed off in the "customary tapered manner" will the edges behave and look well. Here's how it is done:

Trim the seam edge of the canvas completely off, right up to the stitching. Do not worry if the canvas separates from the stitches here and there, as the stab stitching will hold it in place. The middle layer, the under collar, is cut off to ¼ inch. The third layer, the upper collar edge, is not cut at all, but is left to act as padding and to hold the outer edge of the collar in shape after it has been pressed correctly.

Many a home sewer, anxious to do a good job and thinking that she is eliminating bulk, trims the whole seam evenly around the outer edge of a unit, only to find that the sudden change in thickness has produced a ridge that spoils the appearance of the article. Only with the staggered manner of trimming will you achieve a gradual tapering that prevents ridges.

Square and pointed ends must be trimmed off before the collars are turned to the right side, so that an even smoothness can be attained around the complete outer edge. Seams on square corners are cut off diagonally, quite close to the stitching at the turning point, so that the remaining seam edges will dovetail when the collar is turned. (Fig. 17.) Thus bulky corners are eliminated.

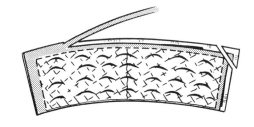

Figure 17

When collars are shaped with sharp points, more angular than the one just described, the trimming is a little more drastic. First, the point is cut off diagonally and then the seam edges on both sides of the point are "whittled" down gradually, starting about one inch below the point and trimming up toward the point. Do this as if you were sharpening a pencil with a knife, except, of course, that you are using scissors. (Fig. 18.) If too much seam edge is left inside corners and points it is most difficult, and sometimes impossible, to get perfectly shaped corners on the finished collar.

Collars with rounded ends, such as the Peter Pan type, must be treated in a different manner after the seams are trimmed off in the customary manner. The remaining seam edge will ripple and wrinkle around the outer edge of the collar if precautions are not taken before turning the collar to the right side. Do this for permanent smoothness: From the outer edge clip inward in the direction of the stitching line, every ⅜ inch apart, clipping right up to the stitching. (Fig. 19.) Do not

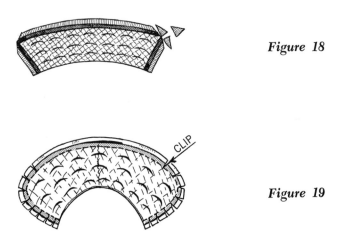

Figure 18

Figure 19

cut away any of the edge of the collar when you clip, as that would cause little "valleys" to form on the edge of the finished collar. The clipping will keep the edges from becoming ruffled inside the collar, as all the little wedges of the seam will overlap one another when turned, and they will lie flat inside the collar.

The collar is now turned right side out, and the outer edge basted flat so that a good pressing job can be done. Hold the right side of the collar toward you while basting, and roll the edge of the upper collar slightly away from you with the thumb and forefinger, so that the under-collar edge is not visible. Roll and baste an inch or two at a time, repeating the operation until the complete outer edge of the collar has been done. The rolling is important, but it should be done only enough to bring the seam slightly away from the outer edge of the upper collar, so that the under-collar edge does not show when the jacket is worn. Too much rolling may distort the neck edge of the upper collar. The pattern piece of the upper collar is purposely cut slightly deeper than the under one, to allow for this manipulation. Nevertheless, it is advisable to baste several rows as you continue to roll, just to be sure that the under collar will not show. This happens much too often on home-sewn clothes, and it is a sign of tackiness which can be avoided if the collar is handled correctly.

Press the under-collar section, so that the right side, the part that will show, will not have iron markings on it: even when a pressing cloth is used, some fabrics become shiny when pressed on the right side. Remember to press slowly and lightly for best results.

If trim stitching is going to be featured, either by machine or by hand, it should be done now, before the collar is attached to the neckline. Whether or not you stitch the outer edge of certain parts of the garment is a matter of personal preference. Some styles and some fabrics may look better one way than the other. Try a row of stitching around your collar, and judge for yourself. The stitching can be ripped out easily if you decide that the collar would look better when left plain. See how hand sewing with silk twist would look, instead of machine stitching, especially if your fabric is soft cashmere, camel's hair, or any cloth with a surface pile. These look exceptionally elegant when hand picked, as hand sewing is often called. You will find out how to do this under the heading of "Trimming Tricks."

The collar unit is now ready to be attached to the jacket. If you have decided to feature stitching on the edge, be sure to press again when the stitching has been done. No matter how well pressed the article was before the trim stitching was applied, it must also be pressed after the stitching.

Attaching the collar and facings to the jacket

The neck edges of the collar unit should be lined up evenly before they are pinned to the neck of the jacket. If the under-collar and canvas edges protrude below the neck edge of the upper collar, they must be trimmed off. Otherwise, the outer edge of the finished collar will curl up when worn. On the other hand, if the upper collar hangs over the edges of the under sections, this edge is not cut off. Push it upward to line up with the other edges, and pin them evenly together. The extra width in the upper collar will eventually be taken up when the collar

93

is rolled into place on the finished garment. This condition is not a general one, but you may be faced with it from time to time.

Markings on the pattern will indicate the place to which the ends of the finished collar must extend on the neckline of the jacket. The symbols are in the form of either dots, lines, or printed instructions on the pattern. These should be marked with chalk or pins on the outside of the left and right fronts of the jacket before attaching the collar.

Some ways of stitching collars to garments are easier than others. The method used here is a very simple one, and may be quite different from the instructions given on the pattern instruction sheet. Therefore, to avoid confusion, just disregard the notches at the neck edges of the pattern pieces. Follow these instructions instead, for if you attach the collar in the way suggested, the notches on the pattern will no longer have a purpose.

Pin the center of the collar, all three thicknesses, to the center back of the jacket neckline, with the under collar against the outside of the jacket. Then pin the collar ends to the right and left fronts of the neck at the symbols. These important pins will make it easy to fit the collar and neck edges to each other accurately. Hold the pinned seams at the center back with one hand, and hold one of the pinned collar ends with the other hand. Now stretch the neckline slightly by pulling in opposite directions, and the jacket neckline will conform to the collar edge with ease. Then pin all the edges together 1 inch apart, and repeat the same operation on the opposite side of the neckline. (Fig. 20.) After pinning, check to see that the extended fronts of the neckline are equal in width on both sides. Since these extensions will eventually be your jacket lapels, they must be exactly alike. Although they were marked accurately, they may have slipped a little in pinning. No stitching should be done until the facings are also pinned into place on the fronts.

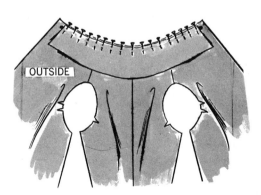

Figure 20

94

Now pin the facings, cut from the garment fabric, against the fronts of the jacket, with the right sides of the materials together. Work from the top of the front toward the bottom, and insert the pins horizontally to simplify the stitching. (Fig. 21.) Pin about 2 or 3 inches

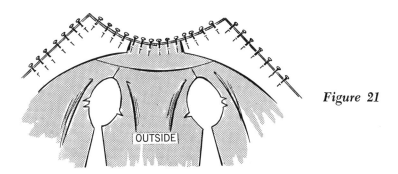

OUTSIDE

Figure 21

apart. Then match the neck edges of the facings to the neckline of the collar. Withdraw the pins that hold the collar in place, and reinsert them with the facing included. Don't allow the collar to slip out of place while doing this.

When pinning the neck edges of the facings, it is of great importance to see that the shoulder edges of the facings are lined up perfectly with the shoulder seams of the jacket. Unless they are accurately matched, both in pinning and stitching, the finished lapels will twist and ripple, and the neckline also will be greatly affected. It is very easy to distort a neckline, because of its round and flexible shape, but it is just as easy to keep it right by seeing that everything stays in its proper place at every step of the preparation.

The stitching of the collar and facings to the jacket is done in one operation, with the canvas side of the jacket facing up when placed under the presser foot of the machine. Just as when sewing the collar, this position will avoid "crawling," and the fabric edges will remain flat and smooth. Start stitching at the bottom of the right-hand front, continue upward toward the neck, pivoting at the point for a sharp turn, and then continue around the neck edge. Pivot again at the point of the left lapel, and continue to sew downward on the remaining front edge.

Trim off the two front edges of the jacket in the customary staggered manner, the canvas completely cut off, the middle layer trimmed to a

95

¼-inch width, and the third layer left untouched. Clip the corners diagonally, as usual. To make the collar hug the neck becomingly, trim the seams around the neck in this way: From the shoulders to the points of each front, trim the seams of the neck down to an even ¼-inch width. This includes the edge of the facing, the collar, and the jacket, but the canvas is trimmed completely down to the stitching. The part of the neckline that is not covered with facing is left uncut, to support the collar. (Fig. 22.) When working with heavy textures, such as coat-

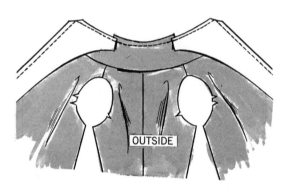

Figure 22

ing fabrics, some of the center layers of this seam should be cut out. These center layers, the under collar, and the canvas edges should be trimmed off to ¼-inch widths, but the jacket and upper collar seams should be left intact. The lining will eventually cover them.

Pattern instructions often recommend that a facing of the garment material be used continuously across the back of the neck, to cover up the seam between the shoulders. When this facing is used, the piece is attached between the shoulder edges of the front facings and sewn in with the collar. The facing provides the support. The complete neck is then trimmed off to an even ¼-inch width, from one front to the other, including the back of the neck.

Now turn the work over to the right side for a thorough pressing. Do you remember how the upper-collar edge was rolled over a certain way so that it slightly overlapped the under-collar part? That is the way the jacket fronts must be treated after they have been turned over to the right side. Here is what you do: From the top buttonhole down, toward the bottom of the jacket, roll the jacket edge over slightly so that it overlaps the facing edge. Baste it that way, close to the edge, so that it will stay put. Then, from the top buttonhole up, toward the neckline, roll the facing edges over slightly to overlap the jacket edges. Then baste the neck of the jacket so that the edge can be pressed properly.

Do the pressing in this manner: From the top buttonhole down, press on the facing side. From the top buttonhole up to the neckline, press on the jacket side. On the neckline, press on the under-collar side, using the small end of the ironing board so that you can press without wrinkling the collar. The reason for pressing in this piecemeal fashion is to avoid shine on the part of the cloth that will show when worn. It is advisable to use a cloth when pressing these parts, even when a steam iron is being used, to prevent shine on the surface.

For a jacket that is meant to be buttoned right up to the neck, roll the whole length of each front edge inward so that the seam joining the facing and fronts is just slightly inside the garment. But if the jacket is to be worn partially open, start the rolling process at the second buttonhole from the top; in that way, though the lower part of the front will have a seam inside the garment, the upper part—from the second buttonhole to the top—will have the seam on the edge where it will be as unobtrusive as possible. You start at the second buttonhole because that is where the fronts usually turn into lapels when the top button is left open.

The jacket is now ready for a fitting. If you used the right pattern size and followed the instruction steps in the order and manner set forth here, any problem you may have in fitting will be of minor consequence. Major problems in fitting are the results of starting wrong.

STEP SIX

Fitting the jacket

One of the most common faults of women who sew for themselves is that of trying on the articles they are making much too often and too soon. In their anxiety to see how a thing will look and fit, they often attempt to "fix" some part of the garment that would automatically adjust itself to a good fit if only it were left alone until a further stage in the construction. Trying on too early can be quite misleading. It takes an experienced eye and a keen imagination to be able to visualize how a garment is going to look in the finished state when there are still seams to be taken in here and shaped edges to be clipped there.

Many a beautiful neckline has been botched by being trimmed off too soon. The individual, trying on the garment prematurely and finding it a little snug around the neck, trims the edges, not realizing that by the time a ⅝-inch seam is sewn and the edge is trimmed, the size of the neckline takes care of itself and fits perfectly. "Fixing" makes it too large. Armholes, too, should not be touched. Do you know that armholes can be enlarged considerably without cutting away any of the material? Just refrain from trying on too soon and too often, and you will never get into trouble with scissors.

It is a known fact that even the most beautifully formed human body is slightly irregular in shape, one side just a little different from the other. One eyebrow may be more arched than the other, the left shoulder may be higher than the right, the hips may not be in an even line. Countless irregularities are taken for granted as being natural and average. Needless to say, no one purposely accentuates an irregularity of any kind, but rather tries to conceal it in the best possible way.

In some people, these differences may be more pronounced than in others. But whether your figure is obviously out of kilter or the difference is so subtle that it isn't noticeable, it is still important to fit your clothes with the right side of the material facing out, just as the finished garment will be worn.

Many home sewers fit their clothes wrong side out, not realizing that they are fitting the left side of the garment to the right side of the body, and vice versa. The irregularities of the figure are only accentuated when garments are tried on in this way. Make it a rule, then: Always fit the garment right side out.

Pin together the underarm sections of the back and front of the jacket, with the wrong sides of the fabric together and the seam edges projecting out. Insert the pins vertically, ⅜ inch away from the edges and about 1½ inches or 2 inches apart. When both sides have been pinned together, try on the jacket and pin the fronts together, just as if it were buttoned up, lapping the right side over the left about 2 inches, if the garment is single-breasted (Fig. 23) or more than that

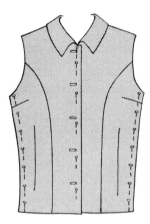

Figure 23

if it is double-breasted or if the front closing is of an unusual design. In such cases, it is advisable to mark the center front line of each front section from the pattern piece, so that the centers can be matched accurately, one over the other, when fitting. This is not necessary on the usual single-breasted style of jacket or coat.

Now inspect yourself in the mirror and note the fit of the garment. A fitted design should follow the contours of the figure closely without being too tight. It should not be loose either, just easy and smooth. If the necessary additions have been made in the hidden area of the design when cutting the garment, a good fit will be achieved without any difficulty. It may just be a matter of moving a pin here and there.

Of course, some women will have more fitting problems than others.

Regardless of the fact that you may be somewhat different in figure from what is considered average, you should treat yourself as average until you reach this stage of your work. Now you do something just a little different.

If you are either shorter waisted or longer waisted than the average person and are making a suit jacket in which the waistline is clearly defined by the shape of the point-to-point darts, you will have to change their shape so that the widest part of each dart will come to your own waist. This is how that is done: After you have pinned the sides of the jacket and overlapped the fronts properly, tie a good strong string around your waist rather tightly, right over the jacket. Don't look in the mirror to do this; just do it by instinct. It is important that the string be a round one, rather than the flat tape kind, so that it will roll right to your natural waistline when tied. The string should be located where a belt looks best on you. Now be sure that the jacket above the string lies perfectly smooth. Then, with chalk, draw a line directly below the string, first across each of the fronts and then directly across the back, from side to side, keeping your shoulders in as normal a position as you can while you are chalking, so that the line is accurately drawn. Someone else may do this for you, but it is easy enough to do by yourself.

Remove the jacket and insert pins through the chalk line, or run a line of hand basting through the line, so that the waistline may be seen on the inside of the jacket. Now check to see how the darts correspond with the chalked and pinned waistline. Darts are shaped to control the fit of the garment, nipping in the waist area. The widest part of the dart is meant to be located at your waistline.

If you are longer waisted than the average person, the widest part of the dart will be higher than your chalk line. If you are shorter waisted than the average, the wide part of the dart will be lower than your chalk line. All you need to do to make the darts right for you in either case is to reshape them slightly, bringing the nipped-in or broader part of the dart to the location of the chalk line that represents your individual waistline without changing the location of the dart itself or its length. Only the shape of the dart is changed, inside of the jacket, but the outside appearance of the garment doesn't alter in the least.

Changing the shape of the darts is very simple. You need only to open up the stitching in the center section of the darts and restitch them, seeing to it that the widest part of the dart corresponds with the accurate waistline that you established with the string.

How about establishing the waistline at the side edges of the jacket? Nothing to it! Remember that the waistline was by-passed in chalking the adjustments and cutting the cloth. At that time it was advised that, even though your waist measurement was the same as the pattern measurement, the addition of the fabric should be carried along the complete hidden area of the garment, by-passing the waistline. That was done to provide enough cloth in case your waistline had to be re-located during this first fitting. You can now relocate the waistline properly and easily merely by shifting the pins to fit.

Do not approach your fitting with doubts in your mind. These are foolproof methods of sewing and fitting, and they have been a boon to women who have to depend on themselves for such things. There is not always someone at hand to help you do a good fitting job. You should be the authority on how your clothes should look on you, so if you please yourself, you most definitely will be pleasing to look at.

When the fitting of the jacket meets with your entire satisfaction, take it off and turn it wrong side out. Wherever there is a pin holding the back and front underarm sections together, mark with chalk, rub-bing the chalk on both seam edges at the same time so that both front and back are marked identically. This marking is done on the inside of the jacket to serve as a stitching guide. When both sides have been chalked, remove the pins from the right side of the materials and pin the jacket in preparation for stitching. The seam edges of the back and front of the jacket are placed with the right sides facing each other this time, and the pins are inserted horizontally, starting from the armhole and working toward the bottom, pinning 2 or 3 inches apart, making sure to keep the seam edges even.

Stitch both sides of the jacket at the underarm sections and press the seams flat. If the darts were altered to lengthen or shorten the waistline, these, too, should be thoroughly pressed again before going any further.

Inserting the sleeves

The sleeves were sewn at an earlier step, and are waiting to be inserted into the armholes. The manner in which this is done has important bearing on the general effect of the finished jacket and also on its fit. Only when the sleeves are inserted into their respective armholes fault-lessly will the garment have a custom-made appearance and fit com-fortably without binding or bulging.

Before starting, be sure that the sleeve seams have been pressed open. Some garments have sleeves that are cut in one piece, while the more tailored types of apparel, such as suits and coats, usually have two-piece sleeves, consisting of an upper and under section. Whatever type of sleeve yours happens to be, inserting it will entail the same technique.

Upon inspecting your sleeves, you will note that they bear notches corresponding to those in the armholes. These will have to be matched accurately when the sleeves are set into the garment. You will also note that there is much more seam edge on the sleeve than there is in the armhole. These edges must be made to fit each other by easing, so that none of the sleeve fullness is forfeited. This extra fullness will make the garment fit comfortably in the upper chest and across the back of the shoulders. If the sleeves were minus this extra material, the garment would draw across these parts and be uncomfortable to wear. Its appearance, too, would be greatly affected.

Many women with vast experience in sewing have never stopped struggling when setting in a pair of sleeves. There are others who won't use a pattern with set-in sleeves because they have never been satisfied with their results. But no matter what your experience, you will be delighted with your sleeves every time if you follow the instructions just as they are set forth here.

On the right side of the fabric, exactly ⅝ inch away from the seam edge, run a large machine-stitched line around the upper part of the sleeve, from one notched section to the other. (Fig. 24.) Leave the threads about 2 or 3 inches long at each end of the stitching. Be sure to have the right side of the cloth facing up when this stitching is done, and be sure that the seam edge is not less than ⅝ inch in width.

Figure 24

There is a definite reason for all this exactness, as you will soon see. This large machine stitching is referred to as a "magic stitch" for the very good reason that it contributes magically toward the ease and accuracy with which a beautiful effect is achieved in the upper area of the garment. Without this magic stitch, the work involved would be greater, and the results nowhere so gratifying and effective.

The sleeves are now ready to be inserted into the armholes. Match the notches at the peak of the sleeves to the shoulder seams of the jacket, and pin them with the right sides of the materials facing each other. If the notches at the top of the sleeves have not been made beforehand, it would be advisable to re-lay the pattern piece on the upper section of the sleeves and make them now. They are important guides for placing the fullness of the sleeves in the area of the armhole where it will do the most good. Make a habit of always clipping these notches before the pattern pieces are removed from the cloth, as it is much easier to clip accurately at that time than when the sleeves have been assembled.

The importance of the way you hold the garment when pinning the sleeves into the armholes cannot be overemphasized. Not only can you simplify the work greatly, but you can guarantee perfect results every time. After the top of the sleeve has been pinned to the shoulder seam, turn the garment so that its wrong side faces you, and take hold of each side of the armhole just as if you were taking hold of the steering wheel of an automobile. The inside of the sleeve is visible through the arm- hole, and it resembles a tunnel that is looming ahead. This position should be held throughout the complete process of pinning the sleeve. "Steer" or turn the armhole to the left, and match the notches of the sleeve to those of the armhole, and pin them to each other. Then steer to the right and do the same thing with the notches that are located there. Note all the slackness that is present in the sleeve edges between the shoulder and the notches at each side. All this fullness is now going to be eased in with the magic stitch. When this stitching was done around the upper part of the sleeve, it was stressed that the right side of the material should face up. The reason for this was so that the bobbin thread, which is the easiest to pull, would be facing toward you when it was needed. And that time is now. Take hold of the bobbin thread at one end of the magic stitch and draw up the fullness until the sleeve edge equals the length of the armhole section between the notch at one side and the shoulder seam. (Fig. 25.) Distribute the fullness evenly between these two points with your fingers, so that a uniform

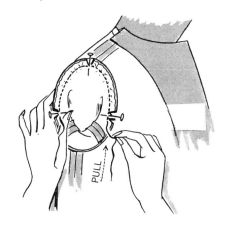

Figure 25

smoothness is achieved, and pin the seam edge of the sleeve and arm-hole together 1 inch apart, keeping the edges flush with each other at all times. The same easing operation is done on the opposite end of the magic stitch, and the edges of sleeve and armhole are pinned evenly together 1 inch apart.

On some patterns there may be more fullness to ease in on one side of the sleeve peak than on the other. When this happens, do not be tempted to even up the fullness, as it is meant to be eased in that way because of the nature of the design.

When the upper section has been eased and pinned, the underside of the armhole and sleeves is steered, hand over hand, just as if a U-turn were reached, and the bottom of the tunnel is now held just as the shoulder part of the jacket was held before, and pinned in the same manner. At times it is necessary to stretch this underarm section slightly so that the edges of the armhole and sleeve conform to each other easily as they are pinned together. It is quite probable that there will be a slight difference between the armhole edge and the sleeve edge, if an addition was made in the hidden area of the design when the garment was being cut. The curved edges of the armholes and sleeves are quite flexible, so there will be no trouble in getting them to fit each other easily. (Fig. 26.)

The sleeves are sewn into the armholes with an exact ⅝-inch seam edge. If the seams were narrower, the garment would end up being too broad across the shoulders, and if the seam were wider than the customary ⅝ inch, the shoulders would be too narrow. Exact sewing is the only way to achieve a perfect fit every time. The stitching is done inside the tunnel (Fig. 27), starting on the under-sleeve section and

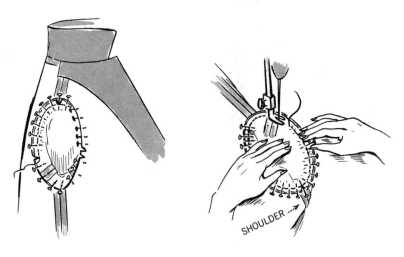

Figure 26   Figure 27

continuing right over the magic stitch when that part of the sleeve is sewn. The fullness at the top of the sleeves, between the notches and the shoulders, will always ease in smoothly without a sign of gathers or puckers if you place the fingers of both hands on each side of the magic stitch and hold them that way while sewing through the fullness. The magic stitch, besides controlling the fullness, acts as a wonderful guide for keeping the seam edges the right width around the armhole.

The edges of armholes and sleeves are flexible because of their curved shapes. Therefore the sewing around them must also be made flexible. If there is any tension whatever in the stitching, the threads will break and the seam would have to be restitched. To avoid having this trouble after the garment has been completed, stretch the armhole slightly after the sleeves are sewn in: hold the shoulder edge with one hand and the underarm section with the other. If there is any tension at all in the stitching, the threads will break now and the damage can easily be repaired by running another row of stitching directly through the one already there. Do this even if the stitches do not break, as it will make the armhole edges that much stronger.

A permanent smoothness is produced around the upper section of the shoulders and sleeves when the seams of ONLY THE SLEEVES are trimmed away to ¼ inch along the magic stitch, where the sleeve edges are rippled because of the eased fullness. (Fig. 28.) If these edges are

Figure 28

not disposed of, they will eventually cause the upper section of the sleeve to become fluted and uneven. The under section of the sleeve is not trimmed away, nor is any part of the armhole edge. These are needed for support to the armhole area.

Here is a pleasant surprise! Never press the seams around armholes at this stage of progress. You may not have to press them at all, even when the garment is finished. In the past, much stress was placed on the need to shrink, steam, and press sleeves in order to fit them properly into the armhole. Many a well-fitting shoulder line has been fouled up by unnecessary torture with the iron on this very important part of the garment. Remember, these edges are very flexible, and they can be stretched out of shape permanently with pressing done at the wrong time. The sleeves and armholes are made for each other, and will fit well and look well when properly handled. Leave them alone after they have been sewn to each other, and everything will be fine. When the garment is completed, a light touch-up can be administered with the iron if necessary. The shape cannot be spoiled then.

STEP SEVEN

Streamlining the shoulders

The woman who needs a bit of camouflage on some parts of her figure need not be too unhappy. The fact of the matter is, even the lucky girls with gorgeous figures occasionally need to resort to camouflage because of some new trend in fashion. Fashion is fickle. One never knows when the perfection of some part of the figure will be deemed outmoded, and changes here or there will be necessary to conceal the true figure and bring forth a new look. Perfection of form has often been sacrificed on the altar of fashion, sometimes for rather ludicrous effects, to say the least.

Be that as it may be, it is natural to want to be modern, especially in fashions. We follow the prevailing trends, adapting them to our own personal needs. The style of a dress or suit does not have to feature the very latest thing in cut or detail to be considered smart and fashionable, nor must it be in the color which is the current rage. You can wear a classic style in a color that is seen every season, but you will look up-to-date as long as the silhouette of the shoulder line is modern. No other part of the garment can affect the general appearance as much as the shape of the shoulders.

The shoulders of a garment will conform to whatever kind of foundation is used underneath the outer fabric. A suit jacket or coat foundation is especially important if a trim, tailored look is to be achieved. Only when these foundations are the right shape and compare to those used in good ready-mades will the shoulders of your garment be up-to-date.

In the past thick shoulder pads were used for creating unusual fashion effects which obliterated the natural shoulder contours. Padding has become less and less from year to year, and at the present time garments conform pretty closely to the natural shoulders; there is just enough firmness built into the contours of the armholes and sleeves at the shoulder areas to support the joining seam which might otherwise collapse and lose its shape. Support is needed especially for loosely woven fabrics, but even some of the firmer ones benefit by the use of a modern shoulder shaper.

Even women who have objected to wearing shoulder padding in the past will agree that the modern shoulder shaper is comfortable and serves to streamline, rather than emphasize. Certainly a trim shoulder shape does a lot for the rest of the figure. And these shapers will make your own shoulders equal in size in case there is a difference between them.

It is not necessary to pin them into the jacket at this stage, as they are not large enough to affect the fitting. So just fit without them. Don't bother to make your own shaper's even if pattern pieces are provided for them, unless your design is so unusual that ready-made foundations are not available for it. For the most part, though, you will find the shaper you need in fabric stores or at the notion counters of important department stores. Look for the kind used currently in ready-mades, and you will produce the modern effect you want.

SHOULDER SHAPERS FOR SET-IN SLEEVES   The shapers for designs with set-in sleeves come in pairs meant for the left and right: they are not interchangeable. They are made like a saddle and are covered with tailor's canvas and layers of cotton flannel which give just the right amount of "rise" to absorb whatever ease there may be in the tops of the sleeves. Large loose stitching holds the layers together. The front of the shaper is square, while the back is cut on an angle. The square fronts make it possible for the garment itself to drape becomingly even on the thinnest person who might otherwise have trouble with shoulder fit. (Fig. 29.)

Shoulder shapers should be inserted with the utmost care, as only then will they serve their true purpose. If they are put in haphazardly, they will detract from your good work. Follow the instructions here, and you won't go wrong. All shapers are inserted in this manner in garments with set-in sleeves. Shoulder shapers for kimono sleeves are handled a little differently, and will be explained in the next section.

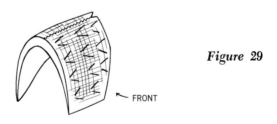

FRONT

Figure 29

108

Drape the shoulder seam of the jacket directly over the shoulder line of the shaper, matching the two accurately, holding the garment with the right side facing out. The whole operation of inserting the shaper is done from the right side of the cloth so that the effect can be seen. It is also the only way to attain smoothness in the garment. Project the end of the shaper ½ inch into the sleeve tunnel, the area which is in a direct line with the shoulder seam, and pin the garment to the shaper at this point, first making sure that the armhole edge inside the jacket is in its normal position, aiming toward the tunnel, just like the shaper edge. The direction in which an armhole edge is placed is an important matter, because it has great effect on the behavior of the sleeve fullness at the top of the shoulder area. The right way produces perfect smoothness, while the wrong way results in unexpected puckers and dents around the upper part of the sleeve, even though the fullness has been correctly manipulated when being installed.

When the first pin has been inserted at this junction, where the peak of the sleeve and the end of the shoulder line come together, continue to pin downward in the groove of the armhole seam, 1 inch apart, smoothing the garment as you pin. (Fig. 30.) First one side of the shoulder is stroked and pinned, and then the other. It doesn't make any difference whether the front or the back part of the garment is pinned first, or whether you start with the right sleeve or the left one. Although the seams of the garment and the shapers have been accurately matched on the shoulder line, directly from the neckline to the outer shoulder, they should not be pinned through this seam. Matching them is only a means of correctly lining up the curved edge of the armhole and the projecting edge of the shaper. Only in kimono sleeves is the shoulder seam pinned.

Do not be surprised, upon inspecting the inside of the garment after pinning, to find that the shaper and armhole edges have shifted slightly away from each other during the pinning process. This is quite natural and it happens frequently, depending on the cut of the design. Even though the shoulder part of the shaper was extended ½ inch into the tunnel, by the time the pinning of the garment reaches the bottom of the saddle, both on the back and the front, the projecting part of the shaper will diminish. At times it may be reduced to nothing even before the bottom of the saddle edges has been pinned.

Here is another surprise. Shapers are always sewn by hand from the outside of the garment, in order to retain the smoothness that has just been achieved. If the sewing were attempted from the inside of the jacket, the smoothness would be disrupted. A tiny backstitch is used, made directly through the groove of the armhole seam. Make the stitches 1 inch apart, starting at one end of the saddle and ending on the other. (Fig. 31.) The tiny stitch is laid flat on the surface without any

109

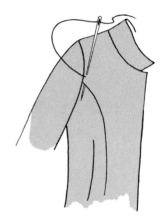

Figure 30   Figure 31

tension, to avoid dents. Only a small amount of padding is taken up on the needle in this tacking, and stitching never shows when properly done.

SHAPERS FOR KIMONO AND RAGLAN SLEEVES   The shoulder shapers used in kimono sleeves are quite different from those used in the set-in type. They are cup-shaped and fit over the bone structure of the shoulders, producing the soft and natural line that the kimono-sleeve design requires. They are interchangeable, as there is no difference in shape between the front and the back. (Fig. 32.)

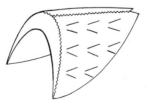

Figure 32

The cup-shaped foundation is used for a raglan or dolman type of sleeve, too. But in the kimono-sleeve garment a seam extends from the neckline across the shoulder, and right down to the bottom of the sleeve. In raglan sleeves, diagonal seams run upward from the armholes toward the neckline on both the front and the back, and a dart between these seams forms the actual shape of the shoulder. For any of these sleeves, the foundation is inserted as follows:

Drape the shoulder of the garment over the shoulder seam of the shaper, with the point of the shaper 1 inch away from the neckline of the garment. In this position the cup fits properly over the bone structure of the shoulders. If the point of the pad is too close to the neckline, the garment may look too narrow across the shoulders. On the other hand, if the point is too far away from the neckline, the shoulders will droop and give the garment a bedraggled appearance.

The garment is pinned to the shaper through the shoulder seam, and sewn with the same backstitch that is used in the set-in sleeve. Stitch 1 inch apart from the point of the pad to the end of the shoulder seam. Do not continue down on the extending bit of felt that gives the foundation its cup shaping. Stitching down on this piece would cause the sleeve to pull into a dent. The lining of the jacket will help to keep the shaper in its proper place.

Tacking the bottom and facings into place

The bottom of the jacket is now ready to be turned up. The amount usually recommended for a hem by the pattern instructions is about 1¼ inches. Although this is flexible, depending upon the length you desire, you might turn up that amount first and try on the garment. You will decide on your preference much more easily if you see the garment first in its original length.

The hem's seam lines are matched and turned first, with pins inserted vertically. When all the seams are pinned, the hem between the seams is eased in and pinned also. Usually there is some slackness of cloth between these seams, especially in fitted garments. The slackness must be manipulated a certain way to avoid making folds in the hem, as this would cause the hem line to become irregular.

To distribute the slackness of the hem between the pinned seams, place the fingers of both hands on the unpinned sections of the hem, just as if you were putting them on the keyboard of a piano. This position will break up the slackness, and spread it evenly and naturally from seam to seam. Then insert the pins vertically into the hem, 1 inch apart. (Fig. 33.) The shape of the hem is preserved in this way, and the little ripples at the top edge of the hem will be taken care of in the sewing.

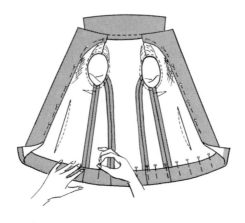

Figure 33

When the hem has been pinned, the facings are arranged in their proper positions. Start to pin at the top of the facings and work downward, inserting the pins up and down. Keep the garment perfectly smooth with the palms of your hands, and work on a flat surface for best results.

Now try on the jacket to see how it looks. Check the length to see if it is even all around, and make changes if adjustment is needed in the hem line. Take in or let out a bit on the "hidden area" if you are not quite satisfied: these are minor alterations. You can even shorten it if you wish, for you will now know just how much shorter you would like it. If you would like the jacket to be longer, drop the hem and face the bottom with a strip of the garment fabric cut 1½ inches wide on the cross weave of the material and sewn to the bottom of the jacket with ¼ inch seam allowance. The strip will act as a facing. Lots of garments are made with separate facings at the bottoms, so you won't be original.

For loosely woven or lightweight fabrics, it is recommended that a strip of interfacing 1½ inches wide, cut on either the straight or cross weave of the canvas, be attached to the inside of the jacket. Place the lower edge of the canvas where the jacket bottom turns up and sew the canvas into place with two or three rows of stab stitching. Attach the top of the jacket hem to the canvas with loose running stitches made ¼ inch away from the raw edge. The canvas makes the jacket stand out from the body and at the same time helps to keep the bottom of the jacket in shape.

When the jacket meets with your approval, hand sew the edges of the woolen facing to the interfacing, with a plain in-and-out running stitch, ¼ inch away from the edges. Just take care not to sew through to the outside of the garment. If the canvas interfacing fails to come out to the very edge of the garment facing, tack the edges of the facing to the outside cloth, using stab stitching: make the stitches 1½ inches apart and leave them loose, so that they will not dimple the outside. The stabbing too is done ¼ inch away from the raw edges of the woolen facing.

You can hand sew the hem into place at this time also, attaching the top edge to the strip of canvas, or stab stitching it invisibly into position if no canvas has been used. The outer edges of the jacket should now receive a slight touch-up with an iron to get it ready for the lining. (Fig. 34.)

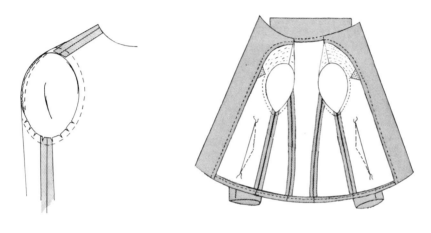

Figure 34   Figure 35

HERE IS A VERY SPECIAL FITTING HINT When you pin yourself into the jacket to observe the effect, you may feel that you would like more room in the armholes—as much freedom as you can get—but still want the jacket to fit smoothly. Here's what you do: At the lower part of the armholes, between the notches on front and back, clip inward through both the armhole and sleeve raw edges about ¼ inch deep at ⅜-inch intervals. (Fig. 35.) Since each clipping releases the inner circle of the armhole ¼ inch, four of them will give you an added inch. You can keep clipping until you've used up all the space under there. So help yourself to more comfort if you wish it, for there will be no visible change on the outside.

STEP EIGHT

Cutting and assembling the lining

Any lightweight fabric can be used for lining the jacket. The material should be of a pliable nature so that it will not affect the outer lines of the jacket. When lining is too stiff or heavy, it tends to distort the line and fit of the garment. The outer material should always be the firmer of the two.

Rayon, silk crepe, and satin are suitable materials for lining dressier suits, while rayon twills do nicely for more casual apparel. Taffeta may also be used, as long as the texture is not of the paper-stiff kind. It is not unusual to use cotton for lining casual jackets or coats, especially when the model is semi-fitted or boxy. When using cotton for lining purposes, remember that the fibers will adhere slightly to woolen sweaters and cotton blouses. This can be quite uncomfortable, unless the jacket is a roomy one.

For a practical lining job, it is advisable to match the color of the lining to the garment fabric, although it can be slightly darker in tone if a choice must be made. For the all-purpose suit, self-colored lining will allow greater freedom in choosing accessories; contrasting lining or lining matched to a blouse has its limitations. When blouse and lining are the same, the texture of the material used should be equally suitable for both items.

The yardage requirement for the lining is specified on the back of the pattern envelope, and the layout chart shows how to lay the pattern pieces on the cloth. Frequently, the lining is cut from the same pattern pieces as those used for the jacket. Specific information on the pattern will show what parts to use for this purpose. If the garment is highly stylized, involving intricate workmanship, a special pattern piece is provided, minus the jacket detailing, to show the basic lines or darts needed to give the lining the same shape as the jacket.

It is necessary to make the same additions in the hidden area of the

114

lining as were made in the jacket. Chalk these increases before cutting. A 1-inch pleat is required in the center back of the lining, so that there will be no chance of the lining disrupting the fit of the jacket, in case of shrinkage during cleaning. If the same pattern piece is used for cutting the lining as was used for the jacket, the pleat is allowed for as extra fabric in the center. This will be illustrated in your pattern layout chart. On the other hand, if a special pattern piece is provided for the back lining, this extra material will be included in the pattern piece itself.

Too often when the same pattern pieces are used for the lining as for the jacket, there is a printed line near the bottom to indicate the end of the lining. It is better to disregard this line and cut the lining the full length of the jacket, for if you cut the lining shorter than the jacket, it frequently comes out too short and as a result the jacket material buckles when worn. It is, after all, easy enough to cut off any excess lining later if necessary.

When the pieces have been properly arranged on the wrong side of the material, cut the lining and mark the darts. Stitch the darts in the same manner as they were on the jacket. Sew the sides together with the same seam width as on the hidden area of the garment using the jacket seams as guides. Do not try on the lining. Treat it as if it were another jacket, using the same techniques for seams, darts, and sleeves, magic stitch and all. Do nothing about the center back pleat at this time as that will take care of itself later on. If there is a seam in the center back, sew it together, but if there is a fold, leave it unpleated.

Press the seams open as you assemble the lining. The upper seams of the sleeves, along the magic stitch, do not have to be trimmed away as they were in the jacket.

Inserting the lining into the jacket

Slip the sleeves of the lining into those of the jacket, match the tops, and pin the top of the lining to the shoulder shaper, inserting the pins on the outside of the lining. Now reach under the lining and hand sew the shoulder edge of it to the underlayer of the shoulder shaper right at the pinning: use a double thread and go back and forth from shaper to lining several times to form a durable thread shank about ¾ inch long. The shank will hold the jacket and lining together but will allow for enough independent action between them to prevent strain on either.

Next, match and pin together the underarm seams of the lining and jacket, and secure them with the shank stitching. These are the only places where it is necessary to attach the lining to the seams of the jacket. Your garment and lining are well anchored to each other.

Now pin the side seams of the lining to those of the jacket, starting at the armhole and working downward, inserting the pins horizontally on the outside of the lining, about 2 or 3 inches apart. This is only temporary pinning, to keep the lining divided into sections for easier handling.

Starting at the shoulder area of the fronts, turn under ⅝ inch edge of lining, and place the fold on the facing ⅝ inch away from the edge. Insert the pins vertically from the top to the bottom, first on one front and then on the other. Then bring the back of the lining across the shoulders and continue pinning around the back of the neck, working from the shoulders toward the center, covering the stitching on the base of the collar. Any excess lining should be folded into a one-way pleat at the center of the back. The pleat is continued down to a point 3 or 4 inches from the neckline, and pinned into place. It is also pinned at the waistline. (Fig. 36.)

When the complete neckline, including the back, is faced, pin the lining in the same manner; clip the edge of the lining inward about ¼ inch here and there so that you can curve it as you are pinning around the edge of the back facing. Some materials, especially those that are firmly woven, would pucker if not clipped in this manner.

In pinning the bottom of the lining to the jacket hem, sufficient length must be allowed for easing, to avoid horizontal wrinkling in the finished garment. On the other hand, if the lining is too long it will hang below the hem of the jacket. Here's how to arrive at just the right amount of slackness in the lining length.

At the side seams, measure the lining exactly the same length as the jacket, and turn the extra length under, inserting a pin through the fold of the lining but not attaching it to the jacket as yet. Do the same at the center back, holding the lining straight from the neckline down to the bottom, and adjusting it there by folding the extra length under and pinning through the fold. Now measure the two fronts of the lining ¾ inch shorter than the jacket length, and pin these through the folds also, still apart from the jacket. These five pins will be the means by which the right amount of slackness will be reached, so that the jacket will be faultlessly smooth when finished and worn.

With one hand hold the lining at the bottom of a front at the point where it is pinned under. With the other hand, take hold of the lining at the side seam where another pin is keeping it folded. Now stretch the lining between your hands to make a continuous fold between the held pins. Insert additional pins horizontally 2 inches apart through the fold. Then treat the other lining front in the same way. The back of the lining, too, is stretched between your hands from sides to center and pinned through the fold. This is how you make the lining the right

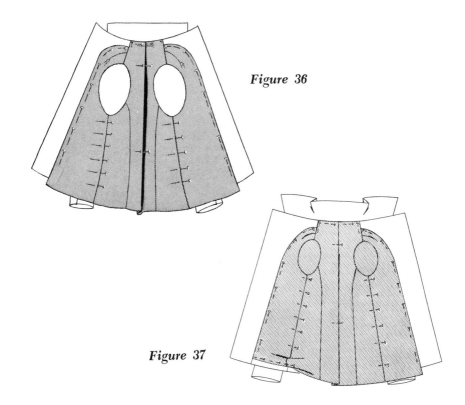

Figure 36

Figure 37

length while keeping it loose enough so that the jacket will not pucker and yet not so loose that the lining hangs below the jacket.

Once the fold has been pinned, trim away the turned-under material so that it is no wider than 1½ inches to be sure that excess lining does not form wrinkles when the garment is finished.

To pin the lining to the bottom of the jacket, start at the side seams. Slide the fold upward and pin it over the hand stitching at the top of the jacket hem. Continue pinning toward the fronts. The lining naturally works out right at the facing edges. Insert the pins horizontally, about 1½ inches apart. With both fronts taken care of, the back is pinned in the same manner, starting at the side seams and working toward the center back. A one-way pleat is made there, folded in the same direction as the pleat at the neckline. There is just enough slackness in the length of the lining to avoid puckering or sagging below the bottom of the jacket hem. (Fig. 37.)

The lining is now ready to be hand sewn into the jacket. Try on the jacket to make sure that everything is in order before starting the hand sewing. If the pins have to be adjusted here or there for some small reason, now is the time to do it.

STEP NINE

Sewing the lining into the jacket

The stitch used for inserting the lining into the jacket is useful for many things. It is simple, invisible, and fast. Because the stitches do not show at all when properly done, a double thread is used in the needle for extra strength. Follow the instructions, word for word, for the first few stitches, until you get into the full swing of it. All you do is this:

Hold the lining side of the jacket facing you, and if you are right-handed, prepare to sew from the top of the right front. If you are left-handed, start the stitching from the top of the left front. With a knot tied at the end of the thread, begin by bringing the thread through the fold of the lining and concealing the knot inside the jacket. Now insert the needle into the facing, directly alongside of the thread which has just come through the lining, and take a ¼-inch stitch into the facing, going downward on the front. Then take a ¼-inch stitch back into the lining fold, starting it exactly in line with the thread from the facing stitch, again descending downward. (Fig. 38.) When the stitches are

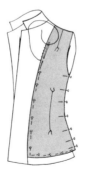

Figure 38

done properly, a straight horizontal thread "bridge" forms between the lining and the facing, a bridge which is visible only when the stitches are loose or when the facing and lining are pulled apart. The thread should disappear completely when the stitches are drawn up to their proper tension. But if each new stitch was not started exactly in line with the end of the last one, the bridge will be tilted, and the thread will show. Do the bridge stitch around the entire outer edge of the lining, the last stitch bringing you back to the starting point.

At the bottom of the fronts, where the facings are turned up against the garment fabric, there is an open space that should now be sewn together by hand with the bridge stitch done loosely. If the style of the garment has rounded or cutaway fronts, this part of the jacket would have been sewn by machine, as a continuation of the stitching that attached the facings to the jacket. When the garment front is even with the rest of the hem line, the facings are sewn to the front by hand so that they do not pucker at the bottom.

Another bit of sewing that still needs attention is on the inner edges of the facings, just below the lining fronts. These raw edges are tucked under neatly with the point of the needle, and hand sewn with the same bridge stitch used on the lining.

The pleat in the center back of the lining is caught together with cross-stitches. Make sure not to sew through to the jacket. Copy this stitching from a garment in your closet, imitating as closely as you can. Inspect something of a similar nature whenever in doubt as to what to do in your particular case, and you'll find an answer every time.

Adjusting the sleeve lengths

The sleeve lengths should be determined next, if they are to be full length. They could have been done earlier, but will be measured much more accurately now that everything has been sewn into its proper place. Sometimes sleeve lengths become affected when they are measured too soon, because they work themselves up with the additional sewing needed for the completion of the garment.

Try on the jacket and turn up the sleeves to the proper length, which is at the break of the wrist, just where the arm ends and the hand begins. Insert a pin only at the front of the wrist, in line with the thumb. Measure each sleeve separately, since there may be a slight difference in the length of your arms.

Remove the jacket, turn the sleeves inside out, and turn up the sleeve length evenly, using the first pin to indicate the amount. Sleeve bottoms are shaped so that the length is right whether the arm is in its normal downward position or bent at the elbow for action. By using the first pin as a guide, the original shape of the sleeve will be maintained. If the fabric turnèd up exceeds 1½ inches in width, trim off the excess. Less than this width can be used if necessary.

If the jacket features a less than full-length sleeve, just turn up the amount recommended on the pattern piece, so that both sleeves look the same when your arms are in a downward position. You will not have to measure each sleeve individually.

Pin the hem vertically, with pins 1 inch apart. If the raw edges of the hem seem tight and do not fit smoothly, clip in about ¼ inch every here and there on the turned-up edge, until the results are flat. Tack the hem to the sleeve with stab stitching ¼ inch away from the edge and 1 inch apart. The lining must then be brought over the hem and turned under to be sewn with the bridge stitch. (Fig. 39.) Make sure

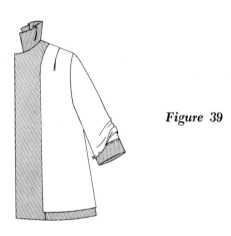

Figure 39

that the lining is not too short, as that would cause the sleeves to buckle.

Cutting and finishing the buttonholes on the facing

Cut and finish the buttonholes on the facing side of the jacket in the following manner: Insert pins at each end of a buttonhole on the right side of the garment so that they penetrate through to the facing side of the front, and then cut the facing from one pin to the other in one clean slash. Finish the raw edges of the facing by tucking under a minimum amount of facing edge with the tip of the needle. Sew the fold to the binding of the buttonholes, making sure not to sew through to the right side. The bridge stitch is used for this work, with stitches done quite close together. There will be nothing to turn under at the ends of the slash, so an extra stitch or two should be taken there for reinforcement purposes, keeping the stiches as invisible as possible.

Cut and finish one buttonhole at a time, to keep the facing edges from fraying. When all the buttonholes have been finished in this way, press them on the facing side of the garment. Then remove the bastings that have held the buttonholes closed up to now.

A light touch-up with the iron on the outside of the lining is just about the only pressing the jacket will need, if the iron has not been spared too much during the assembling.

STEP TEN

Joining the skirt units

The experience you gained in the construction of the suit jacket will greatly simplify the making of any other item of wearing apparel, because so many fundamental principles of sewing were applied and special stress was placed on the steps responsible for professional-looking results. Making a suit skirt, or any other average skirt for that matter, is surprisingly easy. It takes less time to make a perfectly fitting skirt from start to finish than it does to alter a badly fitting one.

A skirt with a three-panel back was chosen to re-emphasize that it is at the "hidden areas" of a garment that any necessary adjustments are made. Remember that each of the skirt pieces within the "styling area" were cut just like the pattern.

Mark the darts on the wrong side of the cloth and sew, starting the stitching at the wide ends at the top of the skirt and continuing to the points, ending very sharply. Pin the back panels together from top to bottom with the pins placed horizontally. Stitch from either direction. Press the seams open and press the darts toward the middle of the units.

If the jacket has been underlined with another fabric to give the outer cloth more body, underline the skirt too, and then treat the skirt parts the way the jacket was handled. (The way to use a finishing lining to cover up the raw edges inside of the skirt will be explained later.)

Pin the front and back units of the skirt together at the side seams, with the wrong sides of the cloth together and the seam edges projecting on the right side of the skirt. Insert the pins vertically on the right side of the cloth, about 2 inches apart, leaving a short opening on the left-hand side so that the skirt can be tried on. (Fig. 40.)

Slip into the skirt, and pin the left-hand seam. Allow the skirt to rest easily on the waistline, just on top of the hipbone, not so loose so that it will slide off, but not too tight either. If the skirt is too snug at the

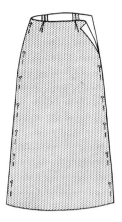

Figure 40

waist and across the stomach, there will be horizontal wrinkling just below the waistband when the skirt is worn.

Look yourself over in the mirror from all angles, for now is the time to make whatever kind of adjustment is needed to correct the draping of the skirt for your figure. Figure irregularities and personal posture can cause skirts to drape peculiarly, but slight alterations at the waistline will correct the problem and at the same time camouflage the figure fault.

IF SIDE SEAMS OF SKIRT JUT FORWARD   A flat backside or a prominent tummy can cause such jutting. To correct it, all you do is tie a string tightly around your waistline on tope of the skirt. Then, starting at the middle of the back, pull up the skirt gradually to bring it further above the string until you see that seams are vertical on both the left and right sides. Pulling up on the back of the skirt throws the fullness more equally around the front and back. (Fig. 41.) Then draw a chalk line around the back from side to side directly underneath the string. Remove the garment and trim away material above the chalk line, leaving only ⅝ inch for seam allowance.

WHEN THE SEAMS SWING BACKWARD   The cause for this problem is a pronounced derriere. The solution lies in tying the string around the top of the skirt and pulling up on the front of the skirt, starting at the middle of the front and continuing until the sides straighten out.

The sides of the skirt will barely be affected by adjustment of either the front or the back units since the raising at either place is gradual and the amount of cloth removed is more or less like a crescent, deeper at the middle and very shallow at the sides. (Fig. 42.)

123

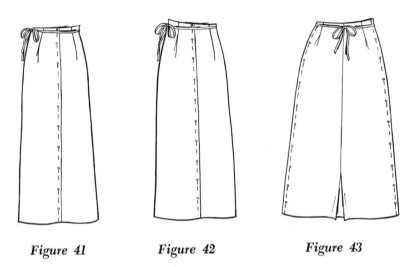

Figure 41   Figure 42   Figure 43

WHEN THE HIPS ARE DIFFERENT IN SHAPE   It is very common for hips to be different in shape or in height. As a result, the fullness of the skirt is thrown to one side, causing the garment to drape closer to the body on the flatter or lower hip and further away on the other side—and making the hemline tilt noticeably. The string trick will not only correct the draping and the hem but will also conceal this figure fault. Tie the string around the waist over the top of the skirt. Pull the skirt up on your flat side and keep pulling until you see the garment on the opposite side of your body becoming less full while the material you are pulling becomes fuller. When the fullness is exactly alike on both sides, you are ready to chalk underneath the string, for by this alteration you will have made the bottom of the skirt hang properly also. (Fig. 43.) Be sure that the chalk line is a continuous one across the side being raised, so that you will remove an even amount from front and back units. Then cut the extra material away, leaving ⅝ inch for seams.

You are now ready to continue with the rest of the construction steps quite confident that you will have a skirt that will not only look good but will conceal your figure fault and be comfortable to wear.

While unpinning the skirt to take it off, reinsert the pins at the left side through either the front or back skirt unit, so that they can be used as stitching guides later. Chalk the inside of the fabric before removing the pins from the right side.

Pin the left-hand seam first, right sides of the fabrics together, and then stitch it completely—without leaving an opening for the zipper. Press it flat. To make it easy to put the zipper into the left side of the skirt and to achieve a streamlined effect which will compare with the smoothness of the right side, leave the right seam open until the zipper job is done. In this way, you will be inserting the zipper when the material is still flat, rather than tubular.

How to "peg" slim skirts

Only slim styles can be pegged or tapered to conform to a fashion trend. But no matter how fashion-conscious you are, it will not be wise for you to peg a skirt (or slacks, for that matter) if your hips are larger than average or if your legs are heavy, as this type of reshaping will only draw attention to your problems.

If pegging is in order, pin the sides of the skirt gradually closer to the figure from the hip area, instead of allowing the fabric to fall in a straight line: the taper should be quite gradual or else the hips will appear heavy even if they are not. Continue to taper to the very bottom of the skirt, but allow yourself enough room for walking and getting into a car or bus! The very slim skirt can be left split at the hemline a couple of inches to make walking easier, if there is not already a walking pleat either in front or back.

Inserting the zipper

After the shape of the left hip has been pressed into the seam of the skirt, rip the seam down 7 inches from the top, the length of the zipper to be used. The stitching does not have to be reinforced at the end of the opening, as it will not rip any farther. The pressing folds make wonderful guides for keeping the zipper side of the skirt as streamlined and flat as the side without a zipper.

There is always excess tape at the top of zippers. Before starting to pin the zipper into the skirt, cut off this tape to an exact ⅝-inch length, otherwise there will be an open space between the waistband and the top of the zipper in the finished skirt, causing a gap.

Place the front fold of the skirt over the zipper teeth, overlapping just a trifle more than enough to cover the zipper teeth. Insert the pins diagonally, pointing them up, and pin about 1 inch apart until the bottom of the opening has been reached. Then place the back of the fold right up against the zipper teeth, and pin from the bottom of the opening toward the top, inserting the pins diagonally, still pointing up and 1 inch apart. (Fig. 44.)

Here's a pleasant surprise! It's easier to sew a zipper into any part of a garment with the regular presser foot than it is with the regular zipper foot. The little zipper foot is a good gadget to have around for many other uses, but the regular presser foot can't be beat for controlling the behavior of the cloth as well as the zipper when they are being sewn to each other.

Keep the zipper closed while sewing it into the skirt, except at the very beginning: it will be impossible to sew a straight line unless the zipper is left open about 1½ inches from the top, because of the bulk of the zipper tab. Start sewing at the top of the skirt front, ½ inch away from the fold, and withdraw the pins when you get to them. The cloth crawls a little as it is being sewn, and puckers would form between the stitches if the pins were not withdrawn.

When you have stitched down about 1¼ or 1½ inches from the top of the opening, leave the needle in the work while you raise the presser foot and push the zipper tab up to the top of the opening so that it will be out of the way. Then lower the presser foot again and continue sewing to the bottom of the opening. Place your hands flat on each side of the work as you sew to prevent the presser foot from pushing the cloth. (Fig. 45.)

At the bottom of the opening, leave the needle plunged into the work and raise the presser foot to allow the work to be swung into position for stitching across the bottom of the opening. Then lower the presser foot and sew across the bottom of the opening, directing the line of stitching slightly downward instead of straight across: Turn the wheel by hand for this short length of stitching to prevent breaking the machine needle in case some part of the zipper is underneath. If a part of the zipper does happen to be underneath the line of stitching, work the wheel to see whether it can go into the work with a little help: sometimes it can go between the zipper teeth without trouble and with no ill effects to machine, zipper, or the skirt. But if the needle does not go in, lift the presser foot, withdraw the needle, and shift the work a little—just enough to make it possible to get the needle to penetrate— and then continue to the opposite side of the closing. The one or two stitches that may be disturbed or thrown out of line by this little shifting will not be noticeable, especially since the stitching was done in a slightly diagonal direction.

Once the needle is on the opposite side of the zipper teeth, leave it inserted in the work, lift the presser foot, and pivot the work again to place it in position to sew upward on the closing. Hold the top fold out of the way and stitch on the extreme edge of the back fold, directly against the zipper teeth. When you near the top of the opening, you will have to move the zipper tab again in order to continue a straight line of stitching. This time, however, you must not only lift the presser foot but also withdraw the needle and pull the work away from the foot a little in order to be able to get the zipper tab down and out of the way. Then you can continue stitching in a straight line to the top of the skirt opening. (Fig. 46.)

Note: In many of the lovely custom skirts zippers are sewn in by hand with tiny back stitches about ¼ inch apart. The back stitch is done

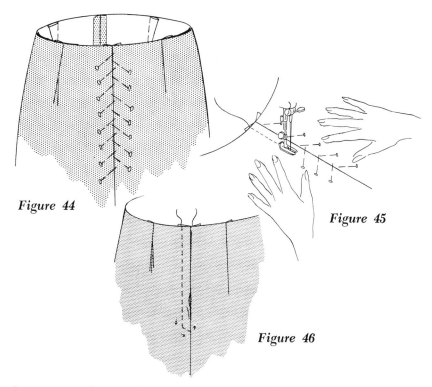

Figure 44

Figure 45

Figure 46

by inserting the needle just a tiny bit behind the thread from the last stitch.

When you have finished with the zipper, pin the right-hand seam of the skirt and stitch it. Press the seam thoroughly and you will be ready for the waistband.

Attaching the waistband

The combination of a smoothly fitting skirt, not too snug, and a firmly fitting waistband, just the way you like it, is most desirable. It is achieved when the work is properly held in the hands in the pinning as well as in the stitching process. Do just as the instructions say, and the results will be gratifying.

Cut a waistband 3½ inches wide and 3 inches longer than your waist measurement. The band can be cut either on the length weave or the cross weave of the fabric, but never on the bias, since that would cause the band to stretch and wrinkle. It is true that some fabrics are more stretchy and supple in one direction of the weave than the other, but this fact won't affect the waistband too seriously so long as the straight of the goods is heeded. When the garment is made of striped material, or a fabric with a striped effect such as corduroy, piqué, or ottoman, the lines should run horizontally around the waist for a more pleasing and slimming effect. Short, vertical lines, confined in the limited area of a waistband, create a broadening illusion.

Unzip the skirt and make sure that the fabric is turned right side out, the way it will be worn. Now hold the skirt with the front facing you. Place the RIGHT side of the waistband against the WRONG side of the top of the skirt front, allowing ⅝ inch of the band to project to the right of the skirt opening. Pin the two together, inserting the first pin so that it points in an upward direction. Roll the band over the fingers of the left hand with the skirt on top of it and pin again, in an upward direction. By holding the work in this position, the skirt will be eased into the waistband evenly. Repeat the rolling over the fingers and pinning every inch apart around the top of the skirt. (Fig. 47.) Little ripples will form between the pins but they will completely disappear when the band and the skirt are sewn to each other, if the work is placed under the presser foot in the right position.

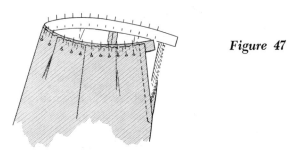

Figure 47

Nine times out of ten, if the skirt was cut with just the right amount of additions made in the hidden areas, the seams sewn with the right amount of edge, and the skirt fitted neither too loosely nor too tightly, the waistband will fit perfectly the first time. But don't stitch until you have tried the skirt on, to see that the band fits just the way you like your waistbands to fit.

If the band is found to be a little too snug for comfort, unpin the back section of the band from the zipper to the right-hand seam and repin it. Hold it in the same position as before, but do not roll it quite so much. This will flatten some of the ripples between the pins and release a bit of extra length in the band without affecting the fit of the rest of the skirt.

On the other hand, if the band is not quite tight enough, unpin the whole band and start from scratch, rolling the work over the fingers in the manner described, but pushing a tiny bit of additional skirt to be eased between the pins. Be sure to push only a little bit or you'll get it too snug.

Woolen fabrics are quite expandable, so remember that the waistband will stretch somewhat in wearing. Because of this, it is a good idea to have the band a bit snug when new.

Place the work under the presser foot of the machine with the BAND FACING UP. Always sew on the shorter edge when one piece of fabric is to be eased into another at a seam. Start stitching on the front section with a seam allowance of ½ inch instead of the usual ⅝ inch.

Hold the work taut with both hands while sewing, one hand ahead of the needle and the other behind it. This keeps the little ripples from turning into folds underneath the waistband. At the same time, the important ease is retained in the skirt top without puckering. This is how straight-of-the-goods fullness is controlled. The "magic stitch" would not work on this type of easing, being practical only on bias or curved edges. Don't trim the seam at the top of the skirt.

Both ends of the band are now folded edge to edge, wrong sides out, and sewn. The skirt is then placed in an upside-down position in front of you for ease and accuracy in the final pinning before stitching. Working from the front toward the back, from left to right, turn the band over to the right side of the skirt and fold under a ½-inch seam. Place the fold directly on top of the stitching, overlapping just enough to cover the stitches. The left hand holds the skirt and keeps it smooth while the right one inserts the pins. (Fig. 48.) Pin 1 inch apart, stretching the work slightly as you pin, to eliminate twisting of the waistband. If the work were held in any other position, good results would be harder to achieve. If you are left-handed, follow the instructions above, but work from right to left, holding the skirt with your right hand and pinning with the left.

When you reach the little extended piece of waistband at the back part of the skirt, fold the edges generously inward so that the width is narrower at this end than the rest of the waistband. This extended

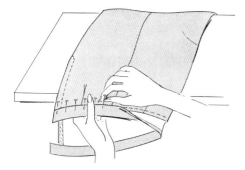

Figure 48

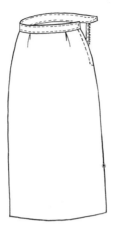

Figure 49

piece is a "reserve," in case the skirt needs to be altered. It is also a means of achieving a neat, flat closing. All well-made skirts are finished in this manner. When the waistband is finished off evenly with the front fold, the left side is as streamlined as the right. A button and buttonhole with a triangular-shaped waistband end would show through a fitted jacket. That's why it is not used here.

For a nice professional look, stitch the waistband on the very edge of the pinned fold on the right side of the skirt, starting on the front end and continuing to the back, stretching the work as you sew. Although it is not necessary, the stitching can be carried completely around the band, including the top and ends. (Fig. 49.) This gives the band firmness and keeps it from folding over and wrinkling, especially with soft fabric. If additional firmness is desired, a narrow piece of grosgrain ribbon can be invisibly hand sewn to the back of the finished skirt band. It is much better to secure additional firmness in this manner than to use an interlining in the band, since interlining may cause extra bulk as well as twisting.

Now press the top of the skirt. Turn it wrong side out and slide it over the ironing board. It should be zipped and hooked at the top. Place a pressing cloth over the top, even when using a steam iron, and press horizontally across the waistband area with a slight curved motion. If you put a hand into the part of the skirt that hangs under the ironing board, and pull on that part of the waistband, the easing dimples will flatten completely with pressing, for paper-smooth results.

Use small hooks and eyes for closing the waistband, two on the front lap and one at the end of the underlapping end.

Just in case you don't know the right way to sew hooks and eyes on skirt bands, here's how to do it: First always use small hooks and long

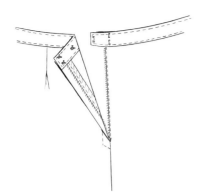

Figure 50

eyes that look like little dumbbells rather than the rounded ones that look like tiny horseshoes. (Fig. 50.) The long ones will hold the band flat against your waist. The hooks should be sewn ½ inch in from the front edge of the band. Stitch through the holes, one at a time, and then bring the needle invisibly to the hook end and secure that with a few stitches. Otherwise, the hook will allow the end of the waistband to stand away from the under section. The little long eyes are sewn through each hole individually, with the thread transferred from one to the other.

Another popular way of attaching a band to a skirt top is to pin it to the outside of the garment and machine-stitch it into place, easing the skirt top in the same way as for the first method. Then turn in a narrow edge of the band against the inside of the skirt so that no raw edges will show, and hand finish it by catching the stitches to those that have been done by machine. If you are using a heavy material, finish the raw edge of the band with seam tape instead of turning it, so that you do not create bulk around the waist. No machine stitching will show when the band is handled in this manner, and it is a very nice way to finish silks as well as heavy materials.

If you are working with a bulky fabric, you might try eliminating the waistband completely and using instead a strip of firmly textured grosgrain ribbon 1 inch wide. Match the ribbon to the color of the fabric if you can; otherwise, use a neutral color. Look for the firm grosgrain among the less expensive varieties: the costlier ribbon is usually too soft. Work with the skirt turned inside out. First, drape the ribbon over your hand and then drape the skirt top over the ribbon, lapping the top over half the width of the ribbon. Pin together at 1-inch intervals, inserting the pins vertically. Allow the ribbon to extend about an inch or so at the ends of the zipper closing. Ease the skirt onto the ribbon, as you would when using a waistband; ripples should form between the pins so that the slackness can be taken up in the skirt top. Try on the skirt before stitching the ribbon into position to make sure that the waist fits well. Then turn the skirt right side out, and stitch through the edge of the ribbon. Next, turn the ends of the ribbon inward and the ribbon itself to the inside of the skirt. Hand sew the ribbon invisibly to the darts and seams of the skirt. You can make a line of machine stitching on the top of the skirt to give it more flatness if you wish, or you may leave it just as it is. Use a round hook and eye to close the ribbon.

Hemming the skirt

The skirt should now be tried on and the length determined. You needn't be too strict in following the current fashion dictum on skirt lengths. In fact, it's smart to adapt the prevailing trends to suit your own personal looks and requirements. The hem line can be dropped or raised a trifle without throwing you out of focus in the fashion picture, provided you do not go overboard in either direction.

How much liberty can be taken, and in what direction, depends on you. Are you tall or short, slender or otherwise? Are your legs good, bad, or indifferent? Is your skirt slim or full? All these factors must be considered when deciding the proper length for the individual.

For a person of average height or taller, the current fashionable length is generally most becoming, especially if your legs, too, are of average size. On the other hand, if your legs are heavy, plan to wear the skirt a trifle longer than the popular length so that the calves can be slightly concealed without forfeiting a stylish appearance. If your legs are too thin, reveal some curve of the calves to create a more feminine effect.

The fullness of a skirt also makes a difference in the length. A narrow skirt is apt to look skimpy when worn too short, while a full skirt will be ungraceful if not short enough.

You can mark your own hems with one of the self-operating types of marking gadgets. If another person is willing to help you, all the better. It is important, no matter who does the marking, that the marker and you keep an even distance apart consistently around the complete skirt. In other words, you pivot around on your heel and toe, and the marker remains in one spot. Only when this is done will the hem line be even all around. In marking a very full skirt, where some of the ripples fold out and some in toward the body, bring forth the ingoing ripples to be marked, rather than inserting the marking gadget between the folds. If the marker moves in and out of the ripples, the hem line will be wavy, short in one place and long in another. Keep your distance and mark every 5 or 6 inches apart. (Fig. 51.)

With the hem line evenly marked, you next consider the width of the

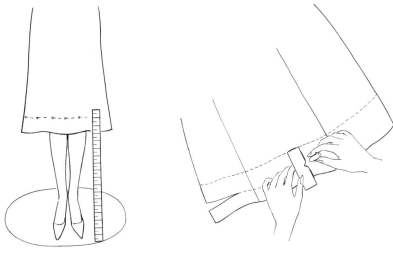

Figure 51   *Figure 52*

hem. If the skirt is a slim one, 54 inches or less, the amount of hem to be turned up should not exceed 3 inches, although it could be narrower if necessary. If the skirt is medium full, a 2-inch hem is satisfactory. If the style has considerable flared fullness (not pleated or gathered), the hem should not exceed 1 inch in width, although it would not matter if it were even narrower. The more flared the skirt, the narrower the hem must be in order to look well. Too much hem weighs heavily on the bias drape of the skirt and causes the hem line to become uneven. (Fig. 52.)

Trim the hem allowance evenly, and for best results sew the rayon seam binding to the hem edge without pinning or basting. Just place the binding on the right side of the hem, half of the width on the hem and the other half off it. Sew close to the edge of the binding with the machine, easing the skirt under the needle, but pulling the binding just a trifle as you sew. Without this combination of skirt easing and binding stretching, the binding is apt to end ruffled, giving you trouble later on. Arrange only 3 or 4 inches of work at a time and sew that much; then arrange 3 or 4 more inches and sew that until the very end. Each time you stop to arrange the hem and binding for further stitching, be sure to leave the needle inserted in the work; otherwise, when strain is put upon the binding, the work will shift out of place from underneath the presser foot.

Place the skirt on a flat surface with the bottom of the hem nearest to you. Turn up the hem, matching seam upon seam first. Then place your fingers, piano fashion, on the unpinned sections of the hem, to distribute evenly whatever fullness may be between the seams. Insert

133

additional pins vertically into the hem 1 inch apart. If there is rippling between the pins, don't worry about it: it will all work out in the sewing. The more flare there is in the hem line, the more rippling there is apt to be. That is the reason for limiting the width of a hem in a flared skirt.

Here is a warning: Never press a hem into the bottom of a skirt before hand sewing is done. Women often do this, thinking to make the hemming easier. But when hems are pressed prematurely, the top edge of the hem becomes stubborn and hard to handle. The pressing of all hems should be left until last.

The stitch used for hand sewing hems is a speedy one that is durable and almost invisible. The visible threads, when sewing is properly done, will resemble the front teeth of a tiny animal, or if you are the literary type, you may want to compare them to ditto (") marks. A professional-looking hemming job is not one with fine stitches closely spaced, but rather one that is sparsely sewn with stitches meant only to hold the hem in place until you decide that it's time to change it. After all, skirt lengths do change from time to time.

The hemming stitch is similar to the "bridge stitch" used to insert the lining into the jacket. The same alternating procedure is used, except that in the bridge stitch the stitches were even in both lining and jacket facing, while in the skirt hem they are irregular. Only a thread or two is taken in the skirt material, but a stitch ⅜-inch long is taken in the binding. You may need to "sew a word at a time" for the first few stitches, but you'll soon get into the swing of this hemming stitch.

Hold the bottom of the hem nearest to you and prepare to sew from right to left, starting at a side seam. Conceal the knot inside the hem and bring the thread to the outside of the binding at the top edge. Right above the binding, and in a direct line with the thread coming from it, take a tiny stitch in the skirt, just a thread or two. (Fig. 53a.) Now take a stitch into the binding, ⅜ inch long, starting it directly below the thread in the skirt. (Fig. 53b.) Repeat every ⅜ inch apart until the hem is done. The stitches will look like "mice teeth."

This is an excellent stitch for hemming because so little thread is exposed on the surface of the hem. This reduces the chances of catching your heels in the hem, and of wearing out the thread from constant friction against your hosiery. Most important, this hem won't show on the right side of the skirt.

Turn the skirt inside out, slide it over the ironing board, and press the hem in this manner: Place the pressing cloth over the lower half of the hem only. Even when a steam iron is used, the cloth is necessary to control the behavior of the hem line, especially if there is some easing in it. Press parallel with the bottom of the hem, but only on the lower half of its width. When the bottom of the hem is knife-edge flat,

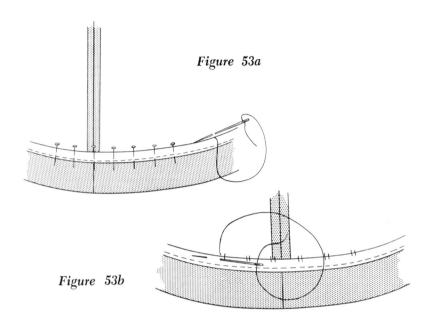

Figure 53a

Figure 53b

touch up the upper half lightly, just to even up the pressing job. If the whole width of the hem were to be thoroughly pressed, the impression of the whole hem would come through on the right side of the garment.

The most popular way to line skirts

The ultimate reason for lining skirts is to take the strain of wear off the outside fabric so it will stay in shape. The lining material often wears out before the skirt does and so should be inserted so that it can be removed easily. Make the lining completely separate of the skirt, seam for seam and dart for dart.

Skirts with slim lines often have a walking pleat in the front or back. When cutting a lining for such a skirt eliminate the pleat and leave only a seam allowance to be stitched from the top to the place where the skirt pleat hangs free. Leave the rest of the lining seam open for freedom of walking. Reinforce the end of the stitching line for about an inch. Finish the slit edges of the lining neatly either by hand or machine.

Now put the lining into the skirt with the raw edges facing you or facing the wrong side of the skirt, according to your preference. However, if the skirt fabric is the clinging type in which raw edges and folds of darts may show through, put them on the inside of the completed garment so they will be completely invisible.

Turn the top of the lining ⅝ inch in toward the inside of the skirt, pin it to the bottom edge of the waistband, and hand stitch it into

135

place. Turn under the raw edges around the zipper opening too, and hand sew to the zipper tapes. The hem is also sewn by hand; make it 1 inch shorter than the skirt. As you can see, it will be no job at all to replace the lining at any time, as no part of the skirt has to be pulled apart in the process.

Often, the lining is caught in at the waistline with the top of the skirt and sewn along with the waistband, but this presents a problem if

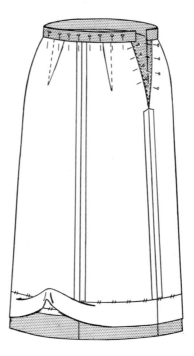

Figure 54

the lining does not ease sufficiently to be worked smoothly with the skirt into the taut waistband. (Fig. 54.)

THE BACK STAY   A stay is a partial lining cut to fit over the inside of the skirt back. It usually extends three quarters of the skirt length from the waistline. Darts are sewn, but any pleat featured in the skirt is omitted in the stay. The stay may be incorporated into the seams and darts, but it is preferable to attach it by hand when the skirt is fin-

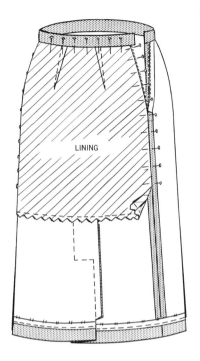

LINING

Figure 55

ished, because then there will not be a dent where the stay ends at the side seams. Furthermore, when the stay is completely separate and hand attached, it can be changed easily if it wears out or if it shrinks during cleaning.

Finish the lower edge of the stay with a row of stitching through the single layer of cloth about ½ inch in from the raw edge; then pink close to the stitching. The stitching keeps the bottom of the stay in shape, and the pinking prevents fraying. This makes a nice flat finish and does not cause ridges to form on the outer cloth as a hem might. Turn under the raw edges at the two sides and the top, and hem them invisibly to the inside of the skirt. (Fig. 55.)

If the skirt has been finished with grosgrain ribbon on the inside top instead of with a waistband, either turn the stay over the lower edge of the ribbon or slip the stay underneath the ribbon edge. Both methods work well. Sew the ribbon by hand to the stay.

HOW TO MAKE A COAT

Making a coat involves practically the same construction steps used in the jacket. Each unit is assembled and constructed as completely as possible before it is joined to one another. Only the bottom of the coat is sometimes treated differently from the jacket.

A full-length coat should be about 1 inch longer than anything that is going to be worn underneath it. Measure the length carefully and mark it with chalk or pins. After establishing the correct length, cut a strip of the tailor's canvas about 3 inches wide on the straight or cross weave of the grain, and arrange it across the bottom of the coat with the lower edge of the canvas on the line where the hem will be turned up. You may piece the canvas if necessary, but if you do, overlap the edges instead of machine stitching them into a seam. Stab stitch the canvas into place on the inside of the coat, just as for the fronts of jackets. The stab stitching will not show if it is done loosely.

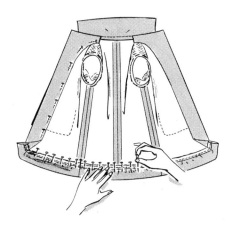

Figure 56

138

Leave the hem of the coat about 2 or 3 inches wide. If you plan to allow the coat and lining to hang free of each other at the bottom, finish the top edge of the coat hem with seam tape and then stitch the tape edge by hand against the canvas, making sure that the stitches do not go through to the outside. (Fig. 56.)

If you plan to attach the lining to the bottom of the coat, do not use seam tape to edge the hem. Just turn the hem up and attach it to the canvas with a running stitch ¼ inch from the raw edge. Both ways of treating the lining of a coat are equally popular, and the results are about the same.

Now it is time to start the coat lining.

All about coat linings

Assemble the lining completely. Then insert it into the coat, tacking it with the shank stitch at the shoulders and underarms just as for a jacket. Pin the lining's side seams temporarily to those of the coat for easier handling. Then pin the two front sections of the lining against the facing edges and continue pinning across the shoulders and around the back of the neck. Fold a one-way pleat at the center back if you have extra lining to dispose of there.

Now measure the lining bottom 1 inch shorter than the coat if it is to hang separately from the coat. Leave a 1½-inch hem to be turned up and sewn by hand, turning the raw edges under for clean finishing. Shank stitch the lining and the coat to each other at the hem line of the side seams. The shank should be about ¾ inch long. This helps the lining and the coat to hang together properly. More tacking may cause the garment to pucker. (Fig. 57.)

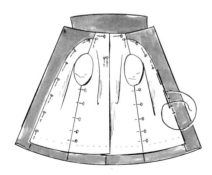

Figure 57

If the lining is going to be attached to the top edge of the coat hem, follow the directions given for handling the bottom of a jacket lining.

What you should know about interlinings

Interlining is used in coats and jackets in addition to the outer lining material for extra warmth. The interlining fabric is cut exactly to the shape and size of the lining and then incorporated into the construction seams as one cloth. The lining fabric is laid on top of the interlining and evenly pinned around the outer edges. After the lining is completely assembled, the edges of the interlining are trimmed off on the inside of the work to achieve greater smoothness if interlining is bulky. The seams are pressed open. The front edges of the two materials are basted together so that they will not slip away from each other when the lining is attached to the front facings.

When there is a pleat in the center back, the interlining should not be pleated with the outer fabric, but slashed down about 6 inches instead and the edges overlapped and made to fit the outer lining material. Pleating the interlining would produce bulk.

Lightweight interlining is preferable to the bulky type. The loosely woven types will generate more warmth than those that are heavy and closely woven, because of the "breathing space" between the yarn. There are many choice interlining materials on the market, some of natural woolen and cotton fibers as well as synthetics. Your garment style should determine your choice.

Some interlinings are woven all in one with the outer lining fabric, the fleecy wool on one side and the decorative fabric on the other. This combination eliminates the work of cutting two separate fabrics and pinning and stitching them together.

Insulated lining may be used without an interlining. It is specially processed to be nonporous and windproof. If you generate heat with no difficulty even in the middle of winter, use this lining alone. Otherwise, use a lightweight cotton or woolen interlining in conjunction with it: you will be lots more comfortable.

HOW TO MAKE A BASIC DRESS

How to select the style

There are many more style variations in dress designs than there are in coats and suits, for fashions in dresses change more frequently, and generally more drastically, than in coats and suits.

The more familiar you are with the fundamental principles of sewing, garment construction, and simplified techniques, the easier it will be to make a variety of dresses like an expert. Making the suit laid the groundwork toward your becoming an expert, and the dress will add even more to your self-confidence.

Naturally, you should choose a style that suits your figure type. And if you have limited sewing experience it is advisable to select a design without too much intricate detail. Only experience and basic knowledge will teach you to handle the unusual features. That doesn't mean, though, that because a style is simple it should lack attractive and interesting features. Some simple designs are extremely smart and flattering, frequently more so than those involving intricate workmanship. Study the design of your choice and analyze its construction and details from the viewpoint of your skill. The person who realizes the limitations of her capabilities is the one who enjoys her work.

Let us assume that you are making a dress that is fairly basic in design, such as the one shown here. (Fig. 58.) Follow the instructions step by step, deviating only when and where the details differ on your dress. Complete each unit as fully as possible before joining it to another, unless its completion involves another unit.

The fabric used for this dress is lightweight wool crepe. This fabric should be shrunk before you work on it, if there is any doubt as to whether it was shrunk before leaving the mill. True, few fabrics reach the market without being preshrunk, but don't take chances.

Along with the correct pattern size, essential for good-fitting shoulders and neckline, a very important factor in the appearance of the

141

Figure 58   *Figure 59*

dress is the location of the waistline. This is especially true when a
waistline seam joins the bodice and the skirt. Unless this seam is accurately placed, the fit of the garment won't be right.

When there is no waistline seam, as in princess designs, or when the
waistline is established with fitting darts, as in the suit jacket, the waist
of the garment can be fixed by changing the shape of the darts or
reshaping the vertical seams.

But a waistline seam is another story, especially for the long-waisted
person. If you are long-waisted, allow extra cloth at the bottom of the
bodice front and back when laying the pattern on the fabric. Be generous, because you can easily dispose of excess fabric after you find
your true waistline.

If you are short-waisted, do not fold or tamper with the pattern
pieces before laying them on the cloth. Just cut them to their original
style and shape. Folding the pattern may alter the style of the design
at the cost of its smartness. You can take care of the waist length in
the fitting later on.

Laying the pattern and cutting the dress

Lay the pattern pieces on the wrong side of the cloth, with the straight-
of-the-goods symbols parallel with the selvages: consult the layout
sheet when in doubt. Add the necessary amount to the hidden area of
the garment wherever needed, as explained in the directions for mak-

142

ing a suit. Note on the diagram (Fig. 59.) that additional length has been added to bodice pieces for long-waisted people. Be meticulous about your "hidden-area" additions, because dress patterns generally have less extra cloth allowance for bust, waist, and hip areas than do suits and coats. Even if you later had to dispose of some of what you added to the suit jacket, be sure to make your "hidden-area" additions here.

Cut the garment pieces as you did when making a suit, following the chalk lines wherever additions have been made, and marking the notches where needed, especially on the armholes, sleeves, and the peak of the sleeves. If your fabric has no definite wrong side, identify a wrong side by chalk scribbles, to avoid confusion when the pattern pieces are removed.

If you intend to underline the whole dress with another fabric and to sew the seams of both layers of cloth together, cut the underlining cloth now too and put the fabrics together. If you wish to line only the skirt; make the dress first and the lining later, just as you did with the suit skirt. Even if you wish the whole dress lined, you can put the lining in as a last step: you will probably find that the garment is easier to construct and to fit if lined separately. You should underline only if the outer fabric is sheer or delicate.

Constructing the dress units

Start by sewing the darts in front and back bodice units, and join the units at the shoulders. Press the seams open, and press the darts toward the centers.

THE LONG BACK ZIPPER   This closing requires special attention, for if the dress's waistline is too long, the zipper will cause the bodice to hump, and if the waistline is too short, the skirt will not hang right. As we noted, it is always important to have the waistline right, but for a style featuring a long zipper, it is essential.

When installing a back zipper, sew the center back of the bodice together with large machine stitching, press the seam edges apart, and then rip the large stitches. The large stitches serve as guides for a good press job and prevent the seamline from stretching during the pressing.

If the tapes at the top of the zipper are too long, trim them down to ⅜ inch before starting to insert the zipper into the back opening. Then lap the left back of the bodice over the zipper teeth and sew it into its permanent position right over the zipper, ½ inch away from the folded edge, just as on the skirt opening. Continue to stitch from the neck down until you are about 1½ inches above the bottom of the bodice. Then sew the right back to the opposite side of the zipper with

143

Figure 60

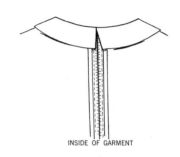

INSIDE OF GARMENT

Figure 61

the fold of the bodice directly against the zipper teeth, again stopping 1½ inches above the bottom of the bodice. Leave the rest of the zipper dangle until the bodice is fitted. (Fig. 60.)

Face the neckline next. The facing cut from the garment fabric should be interfaced with light cotton, the weight of sheeting, to give support to the neckline. Join the facings through the shoulder seams. Then finish the outer edges of the facing by running a line of stitching ½ inch away from the raw edges through both fabrics at once. Trim very close to the stitching with pinking shears: the stitching holds the edge of the facing in shape, and the pinking prevents fraying. This is about the flattest type of finish for necklines.

Now stitch the facing to the neckline, placing the interfaced side on top to prevent the neck of the dress from stretching. Catch the tapes of the top of the zipper into the line of stitching.

Trim the neckline seam in the staggered manner: the interfacing cut off to the stitching line, the middle layer ¼ inch wide, and the third layer left in its entire width. Clip inward to almost the stitching line at ⅜-inch intervals through all remaining layers, so that when the facing is turned over to the inside of the garment it will lie flat.

Finish the two ends of the facing by turning in the raw edges and arranging them against the zipper teeth: make an angle in the fold of the facing on the overlapped side of the bodice (where the zipper is furthest from the edge); on the opposite side, just fold straight down from the top. Hand sew these ends into position. Roll the neck edge to bring the seamline a shade inside of the garment, so that it is completely out of sight. Baste the edge, and give the neckline a good pressing. (Fig. 61.)

Don't do too much hand sewing when tacking neck or front facings

144

into place. This is a common fault with home sewers. In fact, the word "tacky" when applied to home-sewn clothes refers to this very fact. The facing around the neckline of a dress needs to be hand tacked only to the shoulder seams. If there is a seam or dart to which extra tacking can be done, well and good. Otherwise, tack only at the shoulders. Press very carefully around the neck edge to avoid stretching, and press lightly to make sure that the outer edge of the facing doesn't make an impression on the right side of the dress.

How to fit yourself

You have now reached the stage at which you can accurately locate your waistline on the bodice of the dress. The importance of establishing the correct waistline on a dress cannot be emphasized too much, as it has an effect on the general fitting as well as on the appearance of the dress. The more complete the details within the units, the more accurately the waistline can be marked. If you tried when some of the units were only partially finished, the chances of the finished garment fitting well would be *poor*.

FINDING YOUR WAISTLINE Pin the bodice with the wrong sides of the fabric together and ⅝-inch seams extending outward. Put on the bodice and zip it closed in the back. Tie a firmly twisted string around your waistline rather tightly, tighter than a belt would be worn, so that the string will roll to your natural waistline. (Fig. 62.) A tape or ribbon is not satisfactory, because it will stay where originally placed instead

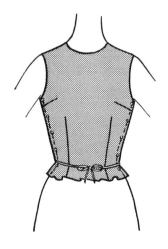

Figure 62

of rolling. Now see that the bodice looks well on your figure above the string. If it is form-fitting, make sure that both front and back are smooth and even above the string. Any fullness that disrupts this effect should be moved over to the side, away from the styling area.

After approving your appearance in the mirror, chalk the waistline by drawing a *broken* line across the back and front, just below the string, keeping your shoulders in natural position during the chalking. Do not move your shoulders too much, as this will affect the line on the bodice and you may have to make it over again. Draw a *continuous* line on the underarm sections of the bodice pieces, from the front to the back, so that the skirt sections will line up evenly at the waistline in the hidden area when the sides are joined together. Otherwise, one section may be higher or lower than the other.

When the chalking is completed, remove the bodice. Don't be too much concerned about the fit of the bodice anywhere but in the waistline section. Unpin the sides and, placing the work on a flat surface for accurate marking, make a continuous line out of the broken one that was drawn for the fitting. Occasionally it is necessary to make slight changes in this line, but this is a small matter and needn't upset you.

Irregularity in the waistline is sometimes justified, because a figure fault may cause the line to wave. If there is a real reason for an uneven line, that's your shape and you must fit it as it is. But if the irregularity is caused by inaccurate marking or an improperly placed string, correct it before proceeding.

To fit a bloused bodice in which the fullness is controlled by gathers at the waist, do not put in the gathers before you establish your correct waistline. After you have tied the string around your waist, pull down the center front and center back of the bodice underneath the string, and then pull down on the side seams so that they too will be where they belong. The fullness of the bodice will now be draped between the centers and the sides. Tug again at these four sections until the fullness is concentrated in line with the bust and the shoulder blades. Next, hold the string at your waist with both hands and shrug one shoulder, without letting the string shift. Shrug the other shoulder, and then shrug both of them together. The shrugging will cause the material underneath the string to pull up just enough to make the blousing becoming to your figure and height. The taller you are, the more length will be released in the bodice by the shrugging.

Now chalk around the waistline just below the string. After removing the bodice, check the chalk line to make sure it is continuous. Then make the gathers where the chalk indicates your waistline to be. Run two rows of "magic stitches," ¼ inch apart, and draw them up to the right size so the bodice units will match the top of the skirt units.

Joining skirt and bodice

Before joining the skirt units to the bodice, draw a chalk line on the right side of each skirt unit ⅝ inch away from the top waistline edge. Rip down the center back seam of the skirt about 4 inches—so that each side of the skirt can be joined to its respective side of the bodice pieces—and unfold the pressed edges on skirt and bodice. Then start in the center of either back or front to pin the chalk lines of the skirt directly on top of the line that represents the accurate bodice waistline, inserting the pins about 1 inch apart, at right angles to the waist seam. (Fig. 63.) Pin from the center toward each side, keeping the units smooth against each other. Always work with the skirt on top, so that you can gauge the stitching by the seam allowance on the skirt. Sew the two parts together with large machine stitching so that you can make changes if necessary. Let the zipper dangle.

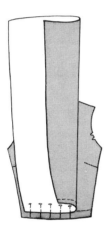

Figure 63

Fitting and stitching the side seams

Pin the side seams with the wrong sides of the cloth together and the seam edges projecting on the right side of the dress. Insert the pins vertically on the right side of the dress, about 2 inches apart, starting from the waistline seams of front and back, to the bottom of the skirt. Return to the waistline and pin the edges of the bodice. If there is a slight difference in length at the side edges of the bodice, match the armhole area with pins first and then hold the edges taut between

147

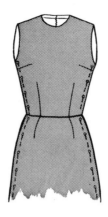

Figure 64

the waistline and the bottom of the armhole to make the edges conform: the shorter edge will stretch to meet the longer one, and the longer one will ease a bit. (Fig. 64.)

Now put on the dress to check the fit of the waistline and to make whatever adjustments are needed. Zip it closed in the back.

Inspect yourself critically in the mirror. Is the waistline long enough and in its most flattering location? You can imitate a longer waistline than yours if you wish by dropping the waistline of the dress just a fraction of an inch below the natural waist. Don't go too far, though, or the garment will look like a misfit.

Put a narrow belt around the waist during this fitting, and make sure that it covers the waistline. If the seam shows either above or below the belt, the seam will have to be adjusted so that it is completely covered by the belt when the belt is worn.

If your pattern is the right size, if you made the additions accurately, and if the waistline is placed where it belongs, there is no reason why the dress should be anything but a total success both in fit and becomingness.

Do not hesitate to take off the dress to move the pins at the sides either closer to your body or farther away. The waistline should fit snugly enough so that its seam will stay firmly placed. With a bloused bodice, it is particularly important that the waistline be fitted well, or the extra length of the bodice will cause the waistline to droop and thereby throw the dress out of shape. Put the dress back on again after you have shifted pins and check the results before continuing. It pays to be particular.

When you are satisfied, remove the dress, chalk the side seams on the inside of the garment, and take out the pins. Pin a piece of seam binding, or some other lightweight tape, across each waistline seam, on the skirt side, and sew through the first row of large stitches. This will

148

make the waistline firm and keep it from stretching. Then press the waist seam in a downward position. This is the natural direction for waistline seams, except when the skirt is fully pleated or gathered. For such skirts, a downward seam would be too bulky, so it is directed upwards. The waistline seam should be trimmed down to ⅝ inch wherever necessary.

The dangling end of the zipper is now inserted into the rest of the opening. Rip up more of the center back seam in the skirt to accommodate the full length of the zipper. Resume sewing by overlapping a couple of the end stitches on the bodice for reinforcement. If you wish to insert the dress zipper by hand, follow the same procedure as for machine.

Now pin the dress together on the inside, matching the waistline seams first and then proceeding toward the bottom or toward the armholes, making sure that the horizontal seams at the waistline match well. Insert the pins at right angles to the seam edges, about 2 or 3 inches apart. Then sew through the chalk marks you made after fitting the dress.

If the garment has a zipper at the left side instead of the center back, work on the left seam first. Sew up the left seam, press it, and then rip it open where the zipper goes in, doing all this before you start pinning and sewing the right seam.

Sleeves, final fitting, and finishing

When sleeves are full length, they are inserted at this stage of progress. But because the sleeves featured in the dress here are short they should be completely finished around the bottom before being inserted. This can be done because there is no specific spot that the short length must hit. Remember that when the length must be exact, the sleeves must be inserted before the bottoms are finished.

In this case, the sleeves are given a 1-inch hem, turned up, and finished with seam binding. The hem is then hand sewn with the same stitch used to hem the suit skirt—the ditto or mouse stitch.

Make the magic stitch between the notches on the upper sections of the sleeves, and insert them into the armholes in the same way as for the suit jacket.

Try the dress on again for the last time before completion. Mark the hem to the correct length. The same principles govern the width of dress hems as those of suit skirts. If the skirt is full, the hem must be just so wide and no wider, or it will sag. Since this dress is slim in design, the hem can be as wide as 3 inches. Sew the seam binding to the top edge of the hem, and finish by hand with the usual stitch.

For a firm crease, press the hem of the dress, concentrating the

149

pressing on the lower edge of the bottom, using only a light touch on the upper half to avoid the hem width showing on the right side of the dress.

Edges of dress hems are often finished with a narrow strip of cotton or nylon lace instead of the usual seam tape, just to make them look nice. Garments made of the luxurious fabrics—silks, matelasse, blistered and raised surfaced materials—are especially suitable for lace hems. Sew the lace to the top edge of the hem by machine; turn the bottom of the garment up, holding the hem flat with the fingers of one hand and pinning with the other. (Fig. 65.) Use the same stitches for hemming with lace as when working with a taped hem edge. To press the hems of these special dresses, stand the iron up on its heel and glide the hems over the flat surface, so that the texture of the fabric is not affected.

If you desire, you can make your belt at home, either by following the directions under "Collars, Cuffs, and Belts," or by buying a belt-making kit from the notion counter of a good department store. Otherwise, you can send out a strip of the garment fabric to a shop that makes belts and self-covered buttons commercially. Just be sure that the belt is not too wide, especially if your waistline should be kept inconspicuous.

The completed dress should receive a light touch-up with the iron before it is considered finished or ready to be lined.

Figure 65

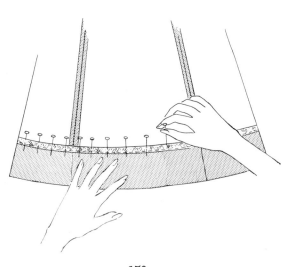

HOW TO LINE A DRESS Use a fairly lightweight material for the lining so that it does not overpower the texture of the dress fabric. Medium weight tafetta, china silk, sheath lining, flat crepes of rayon or other synthetic yarns are all suitable for this purpose and are available in almost all colors to match the outer cloth. Use the same pattern pieces as for the dress, but omit any sleeves: sleeves of dresses made from opaque fabric remain unlined, and those made of sheers, laces, or loosely knit fabrics are underlined along with the rest of the garment.

Put together the lining as you did the dress: press the seams apart after you pink them; fold and press the darts in the same direction as on the dress. Machine stitch a line completely around the armholes, ⅝ inch away from the raw edges, and then pink close to the line of stitching. The stitching will keep the armholes in shape, and the pinking will prevent fraying and ridges.

When you insert the lining into the garment, it usually does not matter whether the raw edges of the seams face toward your body or against the dress. Either way, the lining will protect the shape of the outer cloth. But if the dress cloth is very soft and clingy, place the lining so that the edges are toward you in order to make sure that the seam edges and dart folds do not show through.

Slip the lining into the dress and pin it at the shoulders from the sleeves toward the neckline. You will note that the lining comes not only right up to the neck but even beyond it. Trim off ⅝ inch all around the neck edge of the lining, and then at every ⅝-inch interval clip inward ⅝ inch so that when you turn the raw edge under to attach the lining to the garment, there will be no strain on the edge. Whichever way the lining is to be inserted, the edge of the neckline must still be tucked under out of sight and pinned against the outer edge of the garment facing. Once again, match the shoulders of the lining to those of the dress; then match the centers of the fronts and backs, and pin the lining between the matched parts. If the raw edges are to be worn against the body, clip the lining seams at the bottom end of the zipper right up to the line of stitching, and then tuck the raw edges out of sight against the zipper tapes.

Bridge stitch the lining around the neck and at the zipper closing. Measure the lining so that it is 1 inch shorter than the dress and hem it with "mice teeth" stitches. Secure the dress and lining to each other at the waistline by hand with double-thread running stitches. That is all that is needed to hold the two layers of fabric together for a nice smooth fit.

When you are lining a sleeveless dress, use facings of the same shape as the armholes, but you need no interfacing. For facing, use either the garment fabric, or if it is too bulky or would be uncomfortable to wear against the skin, pick another material in the color of the fabric.

151

Velveteen, for example, would be better faced with a fabric of the texture of taffeta for less bulk. No matter what facing fabric you pick, treat it as you did the neckline: trim off ⅛ inch of the lining around the armholes first and then clip inward at ⅜-inch intervals, the clippings ⅜ inch deep. The armhole edges of the lining will then tuck underneath neatly and without any puckers.

GLAMOUR BY THE YARD

The desire to be as lovely as possible is in the heart of every woman. A woman seldom feels more attractive than when she is wearing a beautiful dress on a special occasion, especially if the dress seems to have been created just for her in a favorite color and in a style which does full justice to her figure.

The cost of buying an exclusive design or of having it made for you is frequently prohibitive. But elegance is not hard to achieve if you know how to put your sewing machine to work effectively. For a very small fraction of the cost of ready-mades, you may have exclusiveness of your own. Glamour fabrics are available in every type, the choice is tremendous, and prices range widely. You can look like a million dollars at a very small investment if you so desire. It is the effect that the cloth will create for you that matters in garments of this type, not the 100 per cent pure gold threads that the cloth is woven from. After all, gold is not becoming to everybody.

With a creation of your own, you will never have the sad experience of meeting its double when you wear it: some very costly "original creations" have come face to face with each other at functions, much to the horror or amusement of the people wearing them.

Unless you are planning to make a wedding gown that will become an heirloom for future generations, you need not consider the wearing quality of the cloth, only its good looks. Even the most delicate materials will stand the amount of wear that a formal grown or dress receives. So you can forget about being practical in choosing fabrics and designs for these garments and indulge yourself by choosing exciting high-fashion designs and outstanding-looking materials if you like. Remember, though, that the more unusual the cloth, the more readily it will be recognized if worn again, so that if you want to make a formal you can wear repeatedly, you might wish to choose a less dramatic fabric.

Glamorous clothes are the "frosting on the cake" in your wardrobe.

You will be happy just to see them hanging in wait for the next time you can wear them: they may even spur you into going to places you would not go otherwise.

Fabrics featuring large scattered motifs

Choose styles with a minimum number of seams so that the design will not be cut up too much. It is often necessary to buy extra yardage to make it possible to cut the fabric as you want to. Arrange the design for your figure so that it will look right and flattering. Some mighty ludicrous effects are created when this type of printed fabric is cut hit-and-miss with no regard to where the motifs land. Picture a large cabbage rose decorating the middle of your tummy or a pair of giant-sized blooms growing smack on your derrière. Such things do happen unless the placement of the pattern is studied before the material is cut. It is a good idea to reproduce the pattern units from plain tissue paper, cutting full-sized bodice and skirt pieces, as if you were cutting cloth, and then shift the patterns around a little on the actual cloth to see where the designs will be most attractive in the garment: the transparency of the tissue will allow the motifs to show through.

Don't start to cut until you are certain you have enough cloth for proper use of the design. If a pattern cannot be managed well out of a piece of cloth you already have on hand, choose another style for it —one that will be cut to better advantage.

It is, though, very often possible to take liberties with patterns when a seam comes on a part of the garment that is cut on the straight weave of the cloth. Such a seam can be eliminated: fold the edge out of the way and place the pattern piece on the fold of the cloth instead.

Matelasse and other blistered fabrics

Glamour fabrics are often made from metallic yarns combined with silk and synthetic yarns. These outstandingly handsome fabrics deserve top billing in the choice of pattern selection. They come in allover designs as well as in large scattered motifs. Again it must be stressed that when the surface of the fabric is highly decorative, it is wise to choose a pattern design that is not too detailed so that the beauty of the cloth can be shown to best advantage. Some of the very interesting brocade and quilted effects are produced by blending several different yarns together. Unnecessary seams should be eliminated from such fabrics: they need only the seams and darts that have bearing on the fitting.

If the woven design of the blistered or metallic fabric has a one-way direction—as do some elegant paisleys—be sure you indicate the direction with arrows on the wrong side of the fabric—draw them in light-colored chalk or pencil them on pieces of paper—as a reminder for when you cut the garment parts.

Any of these fabrics deserve to be underlined to keep the garment in shape and also to make them confortable to wear: the metal yarns sometimes cause irritation to the skin. Sometimes a finishing lining is added for extra elegance, but this is optional.

The underlining material should be light in weight, like china silk or organza, if the style of the garment is meant to drape softly. Firmer crisper fabric like taffeta is used for a bouffant design. Cut both fabrics alike. Place the underlining against the wrong side of the glamour cloth; sew the pieces together on the underlining sides ¼ inch away from the raw edges. The marking of darts is done on the underlining cloth. Make a line of stitching through the middle of the darts to hold the two fabrics together before you sew the dart shape.

Assemble the garment now as if you were working with a single layer of cloth. The only difference comes when you are pressing the seams and darts: Instead of laying the iron flat on the cloth, stand it on its heel; hold the seams and darts in both hands and move them back and forth across the flat part of the iron to keep them separated. Treat the hems similarly: just move the fold of the hem back and forth across the iron a few times. A sharp crease is not desirable in such fabrics anyway. Note that steaming is not recommended for the yarns that produce the blistered effects, since they usually shrink when they come in contact with moisture.

Working with lace

Laces come in many different weights and types and start at a very modest cost. The rule for using lace is the same as for using other materials with interesting surfaces in print and weave: pick a simple pattern design so that none of the beauty of the fabric is lost.

Today there are laces available that are already underlined, the underlining having been bonded to the wrong side of the cloth by a special manufacturing process. However, there are many more laces which need to be underlined. Laces are underlined with other fabrics, either completely or only in certain areas: sometimes the lace alone is used for sleeves or for the upper back and the top of the bodice. Your pattern usually comes with pieces for the parts that must definitely be underlined and instructions as to how these parts of the garment are best handled.

Again, the weight and texture of the underlining material depends upon the silhouette of the pattern design. If absolute transparency is desired, as in some evening blouses or jackets, net is sometimes used as lining so that the mesh in the lace does not get blocked. In such a

155

case, the lace seams and darts must be trimmed very close to the line of stitching so that they are barely visible on the outside.

The best method of pressing is to place the lace face down on a turkish towel so that the design is not flattened by the weight of the iron. When pressing heavy lace, wipe it with a slightly moistened household sponge.

Beautiful effects can be produced with motifs cut from lace when the designs are outstanding enough to hold up around necklines and bottoms of sleeves. The designs are cut out of the lace, arranged into the desired shape, and hand sewn invisibly into place. Give vent to your artistic talents when working with lace! You'll never know what talents you may have until you have given them free reign.

Chiffon

Chiffon looks best when used over an opaque fabric. The upper part of the garment is mounted onto supporting underlining. You can create a richer effect by using two layers of chiffon for a bodice, and then adding an underlining either for the complete bodice or as a slip top (the top edge of the underlining slip caught by hand invisibly to the inner layer of chiffon to keep it in place).

Quite frequently the flared or gathered skirt is not underlined. Instead a sylphlike under skirt of opaque fabric is made and attached to the full chiffon one at the bodice waistline. The under skirt is made 1 inch shorter than the chiffon skirt. You may use a fuller underslip instead of the slim one, but a form-fitting slip underneath a flowing sheer skirt produces a sophisticated diaphanous effect.

The hems of chiffon skirts are usually hand rolled. Run a line of machine stitching ⅛ inch below the marks that show where the hem should be cut. Trim off the extra cloth right against the machine stitching. Do the rolling by holding the machine stitching between the thumb and forefinger of one hand while the other hand stitches through the

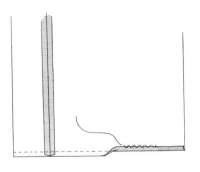

Figure 66

roll, using the usual ditto marks or mice teeth hemming stitches. (Fig. 66.)

Working with net

Net is a very popular material for evening clothes, especially for the young. Usually two or more layers of net are used over the opaque underlining material in the bodice, and the net seams and darts are caught in along with those of the foundation cloth. But the skirts are all done separately and then put together at the waistline after the net ones have been gathered. The opaque skirt can be bouffant or slim, but the net should be very full to be attractive. Net comes in widths of two yards and more, so it is possible to make an attractive net skirt with very few seams in it.

Try a fine net for the outer part of a gown and less expensive netting for the under layers; it is frequently done. And interesting effects— even iridescence—can be produced by using layers of different shades or colors of net. Place tones and colors on top of each other when you are shopping for the net, and you'll come up with some interesting ideas of your own.

Do not make a hem for a net skirt. Cut off the material to the correct length and leave it that way. When the bottom becomes slightly shaggy from wear or cleaning, just trim the extreme edges off, and the net will look like new again. Press with a warm iron on the wrong side.

Silk velvet

Silk velvets as well as those made of synthetic fibers are often manufactured with an erect surface pile. But it is still important to cut the garment parts with all the bottoms going in the same direction, for it does happen occasionally that a slight difference in color tone shows up only after the fabric is sewn. Draw arrows with chalk on the wrong side of the cloth to remind yourself that the pattern must be pinned a special way.

Velvet is not the easiest fabric to handle, and for this reason it should not be underlined. It would be impossible to produce straight seamlines if you included an added layer of cloth in the stitching. If you use a lining in the skirt, make it completely separate and catch it into the garment by hand at the waistline seam—either during construction or after the skirt is finished. Similarly, if a full lining is desired, make it separate and attach it to the facing edge of the neckline.

To produce straight machine stitching, turn the presser foot adjusting screw (on top of the machine at the left) counterclockwise a couple of times to lift the weight of the presser foot off the feeding dogs on the machine. The lightly treading presser foot will make the velvet less troublesome, and sewing the edges will be easier. Withdraw the pins that hold the edges together as you get to them: they may mark the outside of the velvet if they are stitched over.

Stand your iron on its heel, and press seams and darts against the flat side. You may drape a moist cloth over the iron to produce steam but be very careful not to spot the velvet. Darts are slashed through their folds and separated for more smoothness. Seams may be finished with pinking shears.

Neckline facings are made of other than the velvet in order to avoid bulk and to allow flatter steaming.

Hem tops are finished with tape and hand sewn into place; glide the extreme bottom of the hem line back and forth over the bottom of the iron to produce a slight fold rather than a crease.

Satin, peau de soie, and brocade

These formal fabrics come in silk, rayon, and other synthetic yarns— all ideal for glamour clothes. They all handle about the same. Use a slightly moist household sponge to wipe the seams when pressing, but don't bear down hard as the seams are apt to show through on the other side. It is not, however, necessary to use a press cloth.

Pink the edges or hand overcast them if you wish; some brocades fray more than others. The seams may also be finished with tape if you desire; just be sure to use the flat type, as the bias-folded kind will make the edges too thick. Press hems very lightly so that a crease is avoided; a soft fold looks richer in the hems of garments made of these stiff fabrics.

Although they do not have to be underlined, a finishing lining will make the insides of these garments handsomer. Use lightweight taffeta or sheath lining for this purpose.

PLAIDS ARE FOR MATCHING

As already noted, plaid materials will look their best when used for simple styles which require only the seams necessary for shaping. Too many seams will interfere with the fabric design and cause conflict between the plaid itself and the styling lines. Even if each line is perfectly matched in the joining seams, an overly detailed style will take away from the attractiveness of the finished garment. Remember, the beauty of a plaid is in its material.

Plaids can be used in many interesting ways. Bias and straight cutting can be combined in a garment for contrast. For example, a straight-weave dress can have necklines, armholes, or sleeves bound with bias stripping. Bias-cut pocket flaps and welts will add attraction to straight-cut garments. Put your own imagination to work. But just be sure that wherever there is a seam, the lines of the plaid design are matched with precision. Unmatched plaids are an eyesore.

Matching even plaids

Unfold the plaid material at both ends and trim the ends straight across through one of the horizontal lines; then refold it, and pin the ends evenly together. Next, to make sure that the two layers of material will be cut alike, pin the selvage edges, matching the horizontal lines perfectly the whole length of the cloth with pins 1½ or 2 inches apart. If you find you must reblock the plaid fabric because the long- and cross-weave yarns are not at right angles to each other, follow the instructions given on page 40.

Use the notches on the edges of the pattern pieces as matching guides: once you have pinned the first piece of pattern to the cloth, pin the second one so that its notch is on the same combination of plaid lines as those of the first notch. Shift the second pattern piece around until you have it correct before pinning it. You may not be able to follow the arrangement shown on the layout sheet: the size of the

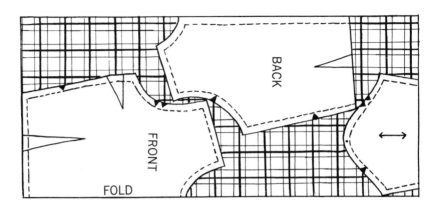

Figure 67a

plaid designs makes it impossible for the pattern company to illustrate the directions exactly. Use the notch procedure for matching each seam in the garment. (Fig. 67a.)

There will be times when you will find that after cutting, the notches on the top pieces of cloth are slightly different from those underneath: layers are apt to slip a little no matter how carefully you pin the ends and edges of the cloth. So, match the line of the plaid, and disregard the notches; after all, what the eye sees is most important, and besides, a slight slipping will not distort the garment.

When pinning, though, weave the pins into the seamlines with several in and out motions instead of the usual one: the whole length of the pin should be covered with cloth. After you have inserted the pins 2 inches apart, look at the right sides of the material to see whether the horizontal lines are matched all the way to the point. If they have slipped, correct them before you put the seam underneath the presser foot.

So that the lines remain perfectly matched, keep the seamline slightly taut while stitching—one hand holding the fabric ahead of the needle and the other the fabric behind it—but do not pull the fabric away from the needle itself. The tautness will prevent the presser foot from pushing the top layer ahead. It does not matter whether you stitch from the top toward the hemline or vice versa, just so long as the pinning is correct and the seamline held right.

Matching uneven plaids

Many plaids have a one-way direction of design. They cannot be matched unless every piece of pattern is placed on the fabric with the bottoms aiming toward one end of the yardage and the tops toward the

160

opposite end, just as if the material had a surface nap. The pattern pieces cannot be staggered or turned upside down. The notches that indicate places where fabric should be matched must be located on an identical kind of horizontal line in the plaid design. (Fig. 67b.)

If either the center front or the center back is placed on the fabric first, you will have no difficulty in matching the rest of the pieces properly.

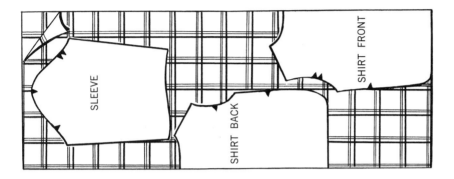

Figure 67b

HOW TO MAKE A PLEATED SKIRT
WITHOUT A PATTERN

It is easy to make a pleated skirt without using a pattern if the principles of pleating are understood. A good-looking pleated skirt is one that is not less than 3 yards around the bottom. Each pleat then lies smoothly in place on the figure and does not barrel out unattractively. A skirt with sufficient material in the pleats falls gracefully and flatters the figure, while one that is skimpy bulges around the hips and derrière.

Two lengths of 54-inch fabric can be used, or, if you wish, any of the other widths can be made to measure 3 yards by sewing the widths together and pressing the seams open. The fabric drapes much more gracefully and softly when the selvage edges run up and down rather than crosswise. On the other hand, materials are sometimes used on the cross grain to achieve different effects, as in stripes and border prints. In these, make sure to include sufficient length for a hem.

Sew the fabric widths together to make a gigantic rectangle. Leave it open until the pleating is done and the skirt is ready for a zipper. There are many different types of pleated skirts, but the knife-pleated style with 1-inch pleats looks well on most figure types and is always a favorite. Three widths of cloth are needed to make one width of pleating. In other words, if the hips measure 36 inches at their widest, 108 inches of flat material will produce enough pleating for a skirt that lies flat and even over the hips.

Permanent pleating can be accomplished with a pressing cloth and a steam or regular iron. Use a light touch when the pressing is done on the right side, but a heavier hand when the pressing is done on the wrong side.

How to mark the pleats

Work with the fabric facing right side up, as the marking must be done on the right side. The right-hand end of the cloth is folded under 1½ inches, from the top to the bottom, to form the first pleat. This may be pinned close to the fold, or pressed. This will guide the marking of all the other pleats. The pleats will all go in one direction, toward the left, when worn, and here's how to mark them.

Mark from the right toward the left side, working from the first folded pleat. Place a yardstick ½ inch from the top edge of the skirt, parallel with the top, and use chalk for marking. Put a chalk mark on the top of the skirt 1 inch away from the fold, and then skip 2 inches and make another mark. One inch from this last mark make another, and then skip 2 inches. Do this across the complete skirt top. The 1-inch space will be the width of the pleat showing on the right side of the garment and the 2-inch space will be the underfold of the pleat. After the top edge has been marked in this manner, do the same across the bottom of the skirt, making sure that the markings are in line with each other and that the weave of the cloth is parallel with the way the pleat will fall.

When the marking is finished, pick up the 2-inch space and fold it over the 1-inch space, pinning the top first, then the bottom, and last the center. (Fig. 68.) It is not necessary to mark the fold lines of the pleats. The vertical lines on the diagram are only for the purpose of illustrating which lines should be picked up and brought over to the matching markings.

After pinning, place the skirt right side out on the ironing board and press lightly with a damp cloth, concentrating on only a few pleats at a time. Do not worry about the pins making depressions in the cloth, since they will be removed as the work progresses. The pleated fabric should measure the same or a tiny bit larger than your hip measurement. If the pleats are not quite the size of your hip measurement, release a pleat or two here and there to make up the difference. This adjusting need not show on the outside of the skirt, as it can all be done from the under-pleat sections. Play around with it awhile and see how you can manage to squeeze out one or two more pleats if you need them, cheating a little in the depths of a few pleats.

With the pleats all in place and measured correctly, take care of

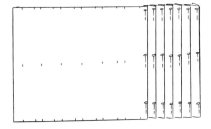

Figure 68

the waistline next. Pin down the pleats with another horizontal row of pins about 8 inches from the top. Then all around the top proceed to overlap the outside fold of the pleats a fraction of an inch, gradually tapering down to the pins, so that the hips will not be disturbed. The amount of overlapping depends upon the amount of difference between your hip and waist measurements and on how many pleats there are in the skirt. You do not have to be a mathematician to figure it out, however. Just remember, there are lots of pleats; therefore, only a tiny bit of overlapping is necessary on each pleat. It can be overdone very easily, so don't do any sewing on the pleats until the pinning has been measured.

If a really slimming effect is desired, you can stitch the pleats down on the extreme edge of each fold for about 8 or 9 inches. The pleats can also be left unpressed, especially if a too-slim figure requires softness and emphasis. When stitching the pleats, take care not to stitch through all the layers of the pleated material, as that will cause hardness and twisting. If the stitching is started with the extreme left pleat and worked toward the right-hand side, you'll have no trouble. Be sure to move the folds of the under pleats away from the path of the needle as each pleat is sewn down. Transfer the ends of the threads to the wrong side of the garment and tie them when all the pleats have been done. The skirt is still open on the left side.

How to insert a zipper into a pleated skirt

The zipper is inserted into the back edge of the skirt first, about 1 inch away from the last fold. (Fig. 69.) The material is then clipped and turned under at the bottom of the zipper and stitched into place. The front of the skirt is then placed over the back edge, with the front fold fitting directly over the zipper. Do the stitching ½ inch away from the fold, boxing it at the bottom. Only after the zipper has been completely inserted does the left-hand side of the skirt get stitched, the seam acting as an underlay fold of a pleat.

Before attaching the waist band, press the upper section of the skirt, where the pleats were overlapped for fitting. Press on the wrong side with a damp cloth. You'll note that new creases form in place of the original ones because of the fitting. If the fabric is thick and bulky, and the pleats are too cumbersome, some of the folds can be trimmed away so that they don't overlap into too many layers.

Attach the waistband in exactly the same manner as on the suit skirt. Belt slides can be inserted into the waistband operation, if desired. These are explained in the section on Bermuda shorts. The hem is measured and marked next. Trim it to an even width and finish either with seam binding or with a pinked edge in the following manner.

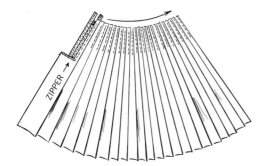

Figure 69

Run machine stitching through the single fabric, and then pink the edge of the hem close to the machine stitching. The stitching helps to hold the shape of the hem while the pinking prevents fraying. Pin the hem in the usual way, with pins inserted vertically every 2 or 3 inches. Hem by hand from right to left, holding the bottom of the hem toward you. Fold the top edge of the hem with the wrong side showing just enough so that the machine stitching is visible inside the hem. Start the hand sewing on the inside of the hem right in the machine sewing. Then alternate to the skirt, where a tiny stitch is taken on the level with the machine stitching at the top of the hem line, ⅛ inch to the left of the starting point. Every ⅛ inch, alternate back and forth from skirt to hem and back again until the hem is completed. (Fig. 70a.)

Thoroughly press the hem of the skirt, just as if it weren't pleated. Concentrate the pressure of the iron on the lower half of the hem, so that the impression of the top doesn't show through. Then place the skirt on the ironing board right side out, and rearrange the pleats at the bottom of the skirt. Doing a few pleats at a time, repleat the entire hem line. Then turn the skirt to the wrong side and give the whole skirt a pressing. Your skirt is now completed. (Fig. 70b.)

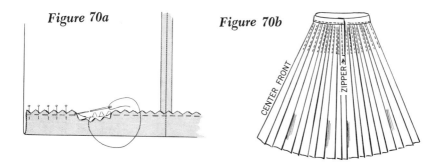

Figure 70a

Figure 70b

Pleated skirts of plaid material

Observe the handsome arrangements of the plaids in a Scotch kilt. Each pleat is folded through a similar vertical line of the plaid design at the hip area, and each pleat is tapered uniformly to the waistline. The gradual tapering produces a lovely fan shape: the pleats fall gracefully to the hem line without one fold out of line. There must, of course, be sufficient fullness in the pleats.

For a pleated skirt worthy of as much praise as the kilt, make the same precise pleat arrangement. Instead of using a yardstick for marking off the pleats, as you would for a plain fabric, let the line of the plaid design be your guide. Start by folding the pleats to your hip size—adding an inch for good measure—and then pleat the fabric the way you would like it best. Pin the fabric one way and then another to see what parts of the plaid designs you wish to have show most.

It is easier to make plaid skirts without patterns—unless you are making a swinging style or cutting one into bias units. But if the cloth is being used in the general way, pleat it as the design seems to indicate. For example, if the plaid repeats itself in both directions from the center as well as up and down, you can make it into a style that pleats from right to left. Or try a box pleat, using the center of the plaid design—or the center of a space between the plaids—as the center of the box pleat. A plaid which is uneven in design, repeating itself in one direction only, looks best when the pleating is done in only one direction.

Plaid dresses with pleated skirts

When using plaid fabric for a dress featuring a pleated skirt, cut only the bodice units and sleeves from the pattern; pleat the skirt yourself the way you think the plaid would look best. Then join the pleated skirt to the bodice to complete the job. Even if the skirt has pleats clustered only in some areas of the front and back, you should still pin the pleats as you think they should be, rather than folding and cutting them according to the pattern.

After you have pleated the cloth, fold the pleats of the pattern and pin them down flatly, so that the pattern is reduced to the shape it would be if there were no pleats at all. Then place the pattern over the pleated cloth and use it to guide your cutting. In this manner, you will preserve the original silhouette of the skirt design while using the pleats to the best advantage.

MAKE YOUR EXTRA SPECIAL
SPORTS SHIRTS!

With time so valuable in our lives, it is wise to be analytical in the matter of which items of wearing apparel are practical to make at home and which should be purchased ready-made. Even though sewing time is cut down considerably by using short-cut techniques, the fact remains that some things are just not worth making at home. One of these items is the sports shirt, for man, woman, or child. (Fig. 71.) Sports shirts are available in fine fabrics, with excellent workmanship at attractive prices, so unless your reason for making a sports shirt is a good one, you're wasting your time.

Does your shirt have to match a special sports ensemble, and can't be purchased ready-made because of the color or fabric? Do you have an unusual idea for your own sports shirt design? Did you pick up a unique piece of cloth in some foreign land? Or do you have a figure problem that makes it necessary for you to make your own? If your reason is logical, by all means make the sports shirt.

Figure 71

167

The workmanship on sports shirts is somewhat different from that on other types of wearing apparel. The inside of the garment must be clean finished so that no raw edges show. A few other items of wearing apparel are also finished in this manner, such as pajamas, lounging robes, and nurses' uniforms. The pattern will suggest this type of finish whenever required. Even the construction and the order of procedure are somewhat different from articles already covered.

Gather the lower back of the shirt on each side, just below the yoke, as indicated on the pattern. (Fig. 72.) Gathering is done with two rows of magic stitching, ¼ inch apart. Sew on the right side of the cloth, starting at the outer end and boxing at the inner end by taking two or three stitches vertically and pivoting before stitching the second row parallel with the first. Then pull the bobbin threads to gather the edge of the shirt to fit into the specified amount of space indicated on the yoke by notches or other symbols. Darts are also sewn and pressed toward the center back.

The yoke is usually double, although the under yoke does not have to be cut of the same cloth as the rest of the garment, unless the cloth is lightweight and non-transparent. It is often desirable to face the yoke with plain-colored fabric when the garment is made of figured material, so that the design doesn't show through the right side to distort the effect. Corduroy or flannel shirts should also be faced with lighter-weight fabrics in the yoke section. To join the yoke pieces to the lower section of the back, place the right side of the yoke against the right side of the shirt back, and the right side of the facing against the wrong side of the shirt. Pin them all together and stitch through the three layers. (Fig. 73.) Trim the seam to about ¼ inch and turn the work right side out. The bottom of the yoke is top stitched on the very edge, after the yoke pieces have been pressed into their upright position.

The facings on sports shirts are usually cut all in one with the fronts, thereby eliminating a seam on the front edges. These facings should now be pressed over to the inside of the garment, making sure to follow the vertical weave of the cloth. The outside edge of the facing should be turned over once and finished with a narrow hem.

Sew the two fronts to the yoke facing, with the insides of the front sections and yoke facings placed against each other, thus bringing the raw edges of the seams to the right side of the garment. Then bring the top yoke over and place it on top of the exposed seam edges. Sew it into place on the fold, matching the back stitching. (Fig. 74.)

Now make the collar. This is usually interfaced, even when the fronts of the shirt have not been, to help keep the collar permanently in shape. The procedure for making the collar is somewhat like that for the suit jacket. The under collar, however, is usually cut the same shape

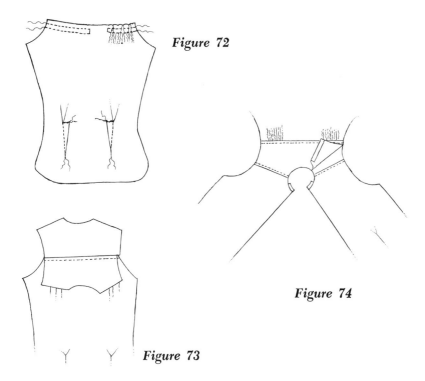

Figure 72

Figure 74

Figure 73

as the upper one, and on the same weave as well. You needn't stab stitch the interfacing to the collar. Just lay it against the wrong side of one of the pieces, and stitch around the three outer edges, leaving the neck edge open. Trim the edges in the customary staggered manner. Cut off the corners, turn the collar over to its right side, baste all around the edge, and press thoroughly. If you want feature stitching around the outer collar, do it now. The distance of the stitching from the edge and the number of rows of stitching are a matter of personal choice.

How to attach a sports shirt collar

Pin the collar to the neck edge, starting at the center back and working toward the fronts, matching the ends of the collar to the indicating marks on the fronts. Then bring the facings around to the right side of the garment and place them over the collar. When this has been done, the neck edge where the facings end on both front sections is clipped through all the layers of cloth, that is, the garment, the under collar, interfacing, and upper collar. Then stitch in this way: Sew through all the thicknesses from the front to the end of the facing, where you have clipped. Here lift up the upper collar piece and leave it free while you stitch all the layers of cloth underneath it. At the opposite end

169

of the neckline, where the facing is folded over the collar, the stitching is done through all the layers, as at the starting point. The neck edges between the clippings are directed upward, into the collar, and the upper collar edge is carefully pinned over the raw edges and blind stitched by hand. (Fig. 75.)

How to insert sleeves into a sports shirt

The sleeves are inserted into a sports shirt before the side seams are sewn. Put the magic stitch on the upper edge of the sleeves between the notches. With the WRONG SIDE of the armholes and the WRONG SIDE of the sleeves together, match the notches and the tops of each item to each other. Pin 1 inch apart, and stitch with the sleeve held on top during the stitching so that the easing can be manipulated with the tips of the fingers.

The flat felled seam

Note that the raw edges of the seam are on the right side of the garment. The regular ⅝-inch seam allowance has been taken. The armhole edge is left untrimmed, but the sleeve edge is trimmed away to ¼ inch. Now turn under the armhole edge ¼ inch, and place it flat on top of the sleeve, then sew on the edge of the fold. (Fig. 76.) Use the tip of your small scissors to tuck in the seam edge as you sew. It is much easier to make flat felled seams without pinning. It will surprise you to see how easily and evenly the raw edges turn under and take their place on top of the trimmed edge. Don't press these edges before stitching, as pressing tends to stretch them.

Pin the shirt together at the sides, and try it on for sleeve length. As long as the pattern is the right size, and additions were made in the

Figure 75 *Figure 76*

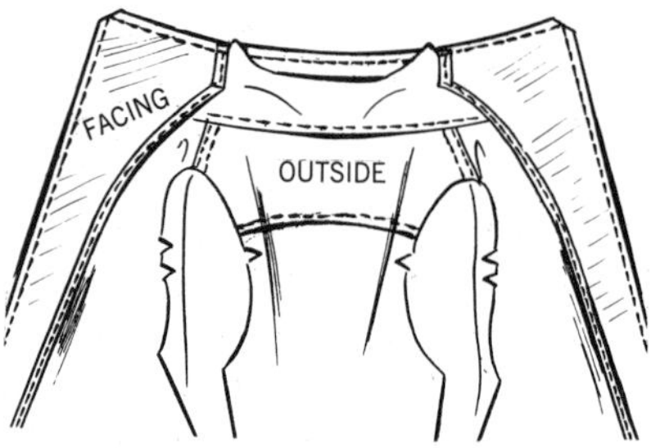

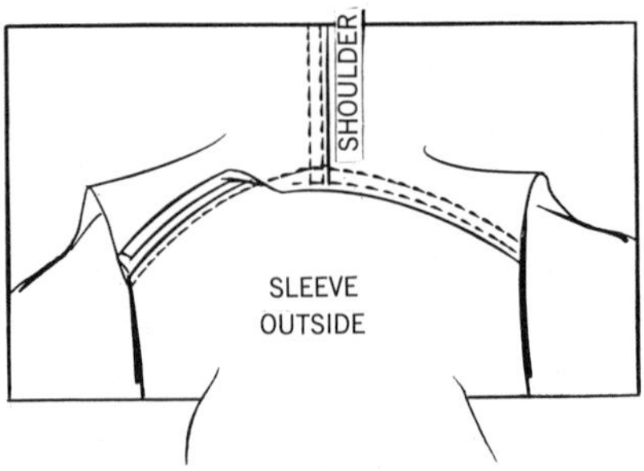

170

| Figure 77 | Figure 78 | Figure 79 |

hidden area, there is not much need to fit sports shirts through the body, since they are usually quite roomy. The slash at the bottom of the sleeve is finished with a continuous lap, a facing, or a tailored placket.

A continuous lap

The strip for a continuous lap is cut about 1¼ inches wide on the straight or cross weave of the fabric. It is placed against the wrong side of the sleeve opening and sewn with a seam slightly narrower than ¼ inch wide. (Fig. 77.) If the slash is completely flattened out and treated as a straight seam, so that it does a "split," there will be no problem in stitching the end of the slash without puckering. Now bring the strip over to the right side of the sleeve. Turn under a narrow edge of the strip and place this folded edge directly over the stitching. Sew down on the edge of the fold, making the opening do the split again for neater and easier sewing. (Fig. 78.) These are extended parts of the opening. The extension on the front part of the sleeve will be turned to the inside, while the one on the back section of the sleeve will remain extended without being turned.

Plackets on little girls' dresses with gathered skirts are also finished in this manner when there is no seam in the part that must have an opening. Usually this is located on the lower section of the back of the dress, right in the middle of a gathered panel.

A faced slash at the bottom of sleeves

A faced slash is treated in the same manner as the facing in the front of the dress. Cut the facing wide and deep enough to take care of the sleeve opening. The outer edges are turned over about ¼ inch and machine stitched. The facing is then placed against the right side of the sleeve opening and stitched with a seam slightly less than ¼ inch away from the edge. Make sure to have the stitching at the point of the slash shaped like a pointed U or a rounded V, so that the seam can be clipped right to the stitching without fraying. The facing is then turned over to the inside of the sleeve, and pressed. (Fig. 79.) Hand tacking will be necessary to hold the facing in place at the end of the slash.

171

The shaped placket sleeve opening

When the slash has been made at the bottom of the sleeve, clip ¼ inch at an upward angle on each side of the end of the slash. To the wrong side of the back sleeve opening attach a strip of fabric about 1¼ inches wide and about ¾ inch longer than the slash. Sew it with a ¼-inch seam, so that the raw edges are showing on the right side of the sleeve. (Fig. 80.) The strip is then brought through to the right side, and a ¼-inch edge is turned under. The folded underlap is placed over the raw edges and sewn down close to the edge of the fold.

Now cut the tailored overlap 3 inches wide and about 2 inches longer than the opening. Sew the right side to the wrong side of the front edge of the slash, with a ¼-inch seam, starting evenly at the bottom. It is then brought through to the right side of the sleeve. The top edge of the overlap is trimmed off at an upward angle, starting at the seamed edge and aiming toward the opposite edge. It is much easier to achieve a lovely triangular trim at the top of the overlap in this manner than it would be if it were originally cut into a triangle. If a pattern for this piece has been provided for you, use it, but if you are improvising your own placket piece, follow these instructions.

The loose edge of the overlap is now pinned over the raw edges and neatly arranged over the underlap. (Fig. 81.) The fabric is folded into a triangular shape at the top of the opening. Cut off the excess fabric on the underside of this trim after the shaping has been done and before it is sewn. Stitch on the edge of the pinned fold, carrying over on the opposite side of the placket to the level of the ending of the slash. (Fig. 82.) The little triangular tab that was cut at the beginning is now tucked in and caught with the stitching that is continued across the top of the opening.

Figure 80

Figure 81

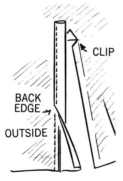

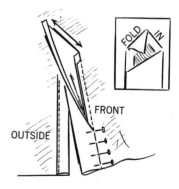

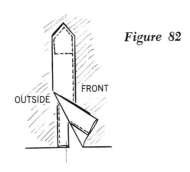

Figure 82

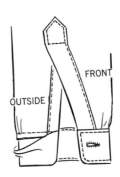

Figure 83

Side seams, hems, cuffs, and buttonholes

Now pin the side seams and sew them with the WRONG SIDES together. These are to be long, continuous seams, from the bottom of the sleeves to the bottom of the shirt, where the shirttails start to curve away from the side seams. The back edges of the seams are trimmed down to ¼ inch and the front edges are then lapped over, turned ¼ inch under, laid flat on the back sections, and sewn on the edges of the fold in the flat felled seam.

Roll and machine stitch a narrow hem on the bottom of the shirt.

The bottoms of the sleeves are drawn up to fit the cuffs, either by gathering or laying the fullness into pleats. The gathers will give a fuller appearance to the bottom of the sleeves, while the pleats will give the fullness a more confined and slimmer look.

Construct the cuffs the same as the collar, interfacing if the fabric requires extra body. Place the interfacing against the part that will be on the inside of the sleeve. If French cuffs are going to be used, cut the cuffs twice the necessary depth so that they can be turned back. Usually the French cuff is turned back through the center of the depth so that there is smoothness under the turned-up part. Whether the cuffs are to be turned back or remain plain, the workmanship in attaching them to the sleeves is exactly the same.

The underpart of the cuff, including the interfacing, is placed against the wrong side of the sleeve and sewn from end to end. Turn under a seam allowance on the outside layer of the cuff material, and place the fold over the raw edges. Pin the fold into place and top stitch on the fold edge. (Fig. 83.) You may continue the stitching all around the cuff edges if you wish.

Make the buttonholes last, after the cuffs have been thoroughly pressed. These can be done by hand or by machine, or can be combined: the base made by machine or with the buttonhole attachment, and then gone over by hand with the buttonhole stitch. The same can be done with the buttonholes down the front of the shirt.

173

THAT CUSTOM-MADE LOOK
IN SLACKS AND SHORTS

Patterns for slacks and shorts are sold by waist sizes. Pick a pattern with the waist of your dress size—not of your own waistline. You may make additions at the sides to compensate for whatever difference exists between the pattern measurements and your own, just as you do when cutting the skirts of dresses and suits. Other figure problems will be taken care of during fitting, but two special ones are of note here.

IF YOU HAVE A LONG BODY AND SHORT LEGS   If this is your figure type, you probably have difficulty getting pants that will reach far enough up to the waistline; when you bend over your pants pull down in the back while the crotch cuts into your body. All you need do is add to the tops of the garment units. Thanks to the extra material, the crotch area is not thrown out of shape. (Fig. 84.) Be generous in the amount you add, since you can get rid of any excess depth during the fitting.

IF YOU HAVE A SHORT BODY AND LONG LEGS   If you are short from the waistline to the crotch, you may find that the seat of most ready-made pants droops on you. Make your own slacks and fit them perfectly by using the right pattern size and adding to the sides, while cutting the crotch the same depth as the pattern itself. Adjustments will be made later. If you carry most of your height in your legs, you may have to add to the bottom of your slacks. (Fig. 85.)

Assembling the parts of the slacks

Sew the center front and center back seams of the garment first, from the waistline to the bottom of crotch, and press them apart. Pin the inside seams of the legs together from the middle of the crotch down on each side and then sew them. Now you are ready to pin the pants together for fitting.

Pin the side edges with the wrong sides of the material together and

174

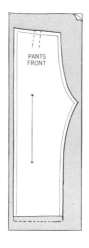

Figure 84   Figure 85

the pins inserted in vertical position on the outside, about 2 inches apart. Leave the left side open partway down to allow you to get into the garment. Once you have the pants on, pin the left side too. Move the pins near to the body for a closer fit or move them farther away toward the raw edges—for more room.

When *stretch* material is being used, and the stretch goes from side to side, you can take more liberties in the fitting because of the "give" of the material. But with ordinary material, it is important that the fit be easy enough so that the slacks or shorts will not be confining.

Tie a string around your waistline right over the tops of the pants. Then bend over as if picking up something from the floor; stoop down as if you were weeding your garden; and stretch your legs as if you were doing reducing exercises. What you are doing is drawing down below the string the right amount of material you need between the waistline and the seat of the pants for comfort.

If you are shorter than average from the waistline to the crotch, pull up the pants to bring the crotch where it belongs on you, and then do the bending, stooping, and leg stretching to give you the right amount extra you need.

Keep the string tied after you have moved around in the pants in order to check the side seams. It is just as important to have the side seams correctly aligned in your slacks and shorts as it is in your best skirt. If your tummy is large or your backside is flat, the side seams will fall forward. To correct this, pull up the back; this action will at the same time shorten the back crotch enough to make the garment more becoming. (Fig. 86.)

If your derrière is more pronounced than average, the seam will pull toward the back. To align it, pull up the front of the pants. (Fig.

175

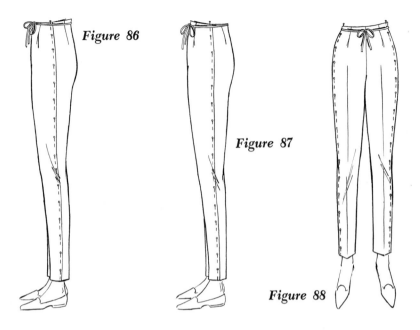

Figure 86

Figure 87

Figure 88

87.) When one side of the body is different than the other, either because the waistline is uneven or because the hip shapes are not alike, pull up on the side that is flat. You will thereby not only straighten out the side seams but also the draping of the legs of the pants against your own. (Fig. 88.)

Draw a chalk line around the waist at the string location. Remove the string, unpin the left side, and take off the pants. Trim away the fabric above the undulating chalk line, leaving ⅝ inch above the chalk line for seam allowance.

Chalk the wrong side of the side edges, and remove the pins from the outside of the garment. Next, sew the left seam together completely and press the seam apart before you start on the right-hand side. You can then rip enough of the stitching down from the waistline to insert a left-side zipper, just as you did in a skirt. Remember that if you sew the right-hand seam afterwards, the zipper job will be easier.

If the zipper opening is in the center back, insert it into the seam by ripping the seam down partway after you have chalked the waistline. The pressed seam will make it easier for you to set in the zipper, and the lapover will keep the zipper concealed at all times.

Linings for pants can be treated in different ways. The lining material can be incorporated into all the seams and darts, if the garment fabric is delicate and needs support, as in lounging clothes; underline each part of the pants, and treat the two fabrics as one. The lining can

176

also be made completely separate and joined only around the waistline; hand stitch it around the zipper.

The best way to avoid bulk while hemming the legs of heavy-cloth slacks is to catch-stitch the top edges without turning under any material. (Fig. 89.) With a knot tied in the thread, take a tiny stitch in the garment just above the top of the hem and then take one in the hem ½ inch to the right of your starting point, alternating from hem to garment at ½-inch intervals. If you are right-handed, proceed from left to right, but if you sew with your left hand, go in the opposite direction. Hold the hem upright as you sew.

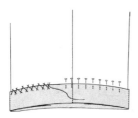

Figure 89

Pants with fly-front closings

The steps for constructing a garment with a fly front are a little different from those for a side closing. Make the preparation for fitting by sewing the center back of the crotch seam permanently, from the waist down, but sew the front seam with large machine stitches, as it will have to be ripped down after the fitting.

Pin the inside seams of the legs for the fitting of the pants. Insert the pins vertically, parallel with the seam edges, and then pin the outer seams of the legs. Put the pants on and pin yourself into them, the left-hand seam open just enough to let you get them on and off.

Tie a string around your waist and adjust the depth of the crotch; move the pins if necessary to get the garment to fit correctly. When you are satisfied, chalk the waistline and remove the pants. Now construct the fly closing after sewing from the bottom of the front crotch seam to the pattern dot which shows where the seam is to end and the fly closing is to begin. At this point, retrace your stitching line and sew right off the crotch seam through the line of stitching you've already done. (Fig. 90a.) Clip the seam inward from the start of the opening almost to the stitching line, and press the short seam open.

Cut a piece for the fly from your garment cloth, using the pattern to

177

get the right shape. Interface this piece with some cotton sheeting if the fabric is soft in texture to help keep the fly firm. Sew the fly piece, the right sides together, to the left of the pants front. (Fig. 90b.) Trim the seam down to ¼-inch width, and press the fly to the inside of the pants—but only enough to give it its proper shape. The pressed crease will be a guide when you sew the zipper into the opening.

Unfold the fly piece and bring it to the outside of the garment. Place the right side of the zipper flatly against the right side of the fly piece. Keep the zipper closed. Match the tops of the zipper tapes against the top of the fly piece and pin flat—one tape edge flush with the flattened out fold of the fly piece. Sew the edge nearest the raw edge of the fly piece through the fly piece. Withdraw the pins from the tape edge near the fold: they serve merely as a guide to the right amount of overlap needed to conceal the zipper. (Fig. 91.)

On the other side of the pants front, turn the seam edge under ⅝ inch and pin it right against the zipper teeth, starting at the bottom of the fly and proceeding upward. Stitch from the top of this front down, sewing as close to the edge of the fold and the zipper teeth as possible. Reinforce the bottom of the fly by stitching about ½ inch back and forth once or twice.

Now arrange the fly piece on the pants front just as you pressed it originally, and pin the outer edge of the fly piece against the wrong side of the pants. Then either sew around the outer edges of the fly piece, ⅝ inch in from the raw edges on the inside of the garment, or

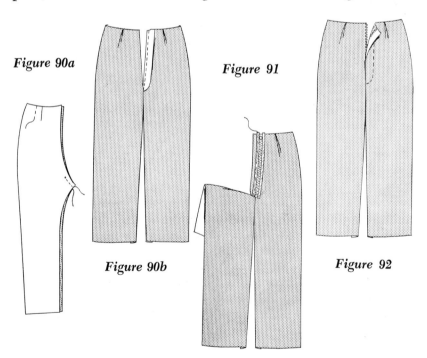

Figure 90a

Figure 91

Figure 90b

Figure 92

trace the stitching line onto the outer side of the pants from the pattern so that you can trim stitch by following the traced line. The stitching is, after all, more attractive right side up. (Fig. 92.)

From here on in, follow the directions for pants with side closings: sew the inside seams of the legs; fit the side seams; and hem the bottoms by hand.

How to make belt slides

It will add to the attractiveness of shorts if you make belt slides of the same material. There are different ways of attaching these slides. One of the popular ways is to make the slide from a 1-inch strip of the garment fabric in the following manner:

Fold a strip of cloth, 1 inch wide, right side out, with the edges meeting in the center, just the way flat folded bias binding is shown at notion counters. (Fig. 93a.) Then fold the strip again, this time with the edges completely out of sight, like double-folded bias binding. Machine stitch the double-folded edge first, then the single one close to the edges, and press. (Fig. 93b.) Cut each slide carefully, so that

Figure 93a

Figure 93b

Figure 94

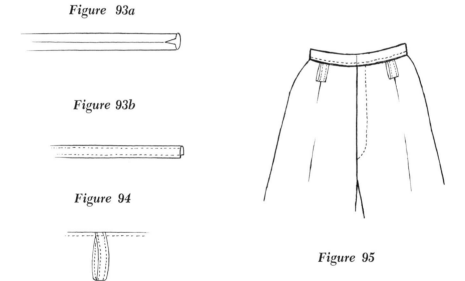

Figure 95

the belt will fit into the loops without being too loose or too tight. The loops are made by folding the strip end to end and pinning or stitching the ends to the top of the garment wherever desired. (Fig. 94.) Since the loops are decorative, it is a good idea to place one on each dart, both in the front and the back. This adds to the tailored effect. The loops are permanently sewn in with the waistband. (Fig. 95.)

ALL ABOUT NECKLINES

Necklines are always on exhibition, so give them proper consideration when choosing a style. The shape and style of a neckline have the same effect on the facial features as the styling lines have on the figure.

How to choose a becoming neckline

It is not always possible to find a pattern design that is completely right for you in every respect. The lines of the dress may be fine for your shape, but the neckline may be wrong for the contours of your face. Luckily, changing a neckline is a very simple matter when you make your own clothes. As a matter of fact, changing the lines of the neck is very much easier than changing the lines of the garment elsewhere.

So choose the design that will enhance your figure, and be prepared to substitute a more becoming neckline, if changing is needed.

If your face is narrow, the neckline must have the shape and details to create the illusion of roundness. Necklines with points, either in the shape of the neck itself or in collars with corners or points, would not be so becoming as those with curves. A narrow, long, pointed V-shaped neckline, for example, would not be so appealing as a round neck or a U-shaped neckline. However, this does not mean that all points and corners should be eliminated. A pointed neckline with curved lapels and collar would be perfectly suitable, as the lapels would broaden the appearance of the upper section of the figure, while their curved shape would give softness to the face. Even a V-shaped neckline could be used, provided the V was kept rather high and broad enough to extend beyond the contours of the face.

The round face can be made to look less round by introducing necklines with squares, points, and depth rather than width. Square necklines, pointed collars, pointed lapels, plunging V-shaped necklines: these would do flattering things to the round face. Curves should be

180

avoided wherever possible, although a closely fitted round neckline would be perfectly all right. It is the curved necklines that project out beyond the contours of the face that must be avoided, as these only add more to the roundness.

Is your chin square? If your chin is inclined to be a little wider than the average, avoid square necklines, double-breasted designs that button up high, and bows or other details that create horizontal lines across your chest, ending in line with or beyond the contours of your jaw line. Curves and angles are your best bets. If a bow is worn, place it to one side at a rakish angle. It'll be much snappier there, and will also divert the eye from the squareness of the chin.

Making a new neckline

Once you have decided on the neckline you wish to substitute for the one on your pattern, chalk the shape of it on the bodice. This is quite important, since cutting it free hand may result in the neckline being too large. You may be able to find a neckline in the style you want on another pattern, too. In that case, you can just lay the appropriate pieces of your new pattern on the bodice sections and pin or chalk the preferred neckline shape in its place.

You might also trace a pattern piece from one of your ready-made dresses that features the style you like. Or you could draw your own pattern, experimenting until you get the exact style and size you wish. When improvising a neckline in this way, bear in mind that the size of the neck opening will be larger when finished than it is in the cutting stage. Many times a neckline is found to be too large after completion, because the seam allowance was not considered when the neckline was planned. Seam allowance makes a tremendous difference in the size of the neck opening and should never be forgotten. It is easy enough to enlarge a faced neckline, even after it has been finished, but it is almost impossible to reduce it in size if it has been cut too large.

A faced square neck with a back opening

Naturally, when a neckline is being changed from its original shape, facings and other parts that go into finishing it become obsolete and must be replaced with facings to fit the new shape. It is advisable to use the improvised garment neck to cut the facing by, so that the two will be identical in shape and size. Cut the facings about 2 inches wide, making one for the front and one for the back, like the bodice pieces, and slash the opening down to the depth desired.

Sew the front and the back facings at the shoulder seams. The outer edge of the facing is then clean finished by turning under a ¼-inch edge

181

and machine stitching close to the fold. When the shoulder seams of bodice and facing have been pressed open, place the right sides together, and match them at the shoulders, front corners, and back slash. Sew them together with a ⅝-inch seam, holding the work with the dress on top and the facing underneath for more accurate stitching. The stitching along the slashed opening should be done only ⅛ inch away from the edge, to eliminate gapping at the bottom of the slash. Now clip the seam edges at the front corners to the stitching and the back edges every ⅜ inch apart. Clip the seam to the point at the bottom of the slash and the points at the top of the slash are clipped off diagonally. The seam itself need not be cut away. (Fig. 96.)

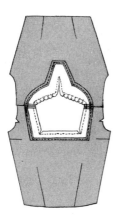

Figure 96

The facing is then turned over to the wrong side of the dress and the neck edge is basted around, close to the edge, and pressed. Hold the facing in place by hand tacking only at the shoulders and the center back directly below the slash. Take care not to stretch the neckline in pressing. One of the reasons for finishing the neckline whenever possible before the sides of the garment are sewn is to avoid this stretching.

A thread loop and a hook can be used for closing the back of the neck. If a zipper closing is desired, finish the neckline as outlined above, and then insert the zipper, stitching evenly on each side of the opening ¼ inch away from the edges. Several small buttons, with cloth or thread loops, can also be used for a closing.

When the neckline itself is generous in size, it is not always necessary to have a slash at the back or front. Only when the neckline is closely fitted is a slash needed. Never force a neckline over your head, as that will cause stretching. If it is not large enough to let your head through without a struggle, make an opening of some sort either in the front or the back.

Facing lapels on a center seam bodice

The lapels on a bodice with a center seam can be finished very easily if—contrary to pattern guide instructions—the facings are not joined at the bottom. The following system will give you fine results and a strong finish.

Sew the front center seam of the bodice from the bottom to the indicator shown on the pattern and then reinforce by sewing back about an inch. (Fig. 97.) Join the front and back facings together at the shoulders, but do not join the lower end of the front facings together: leave those free. Finish the outer edge of the facing in the way best suited for the weight of the fabric. If you are using lightweight cloth, interface the facing material with some cotton for support; treat the two layers, the dress fabric and the interfacing, as one at the joining seams. Run a line of machine stitching through the flat facing edge and pink close to the stitching line, or turn under a very narrow hem and machine stitch close to the fold. (Fig. 98.)

Pin the neckline of the garment and the facing right sides together, matching the shoulder seams. Next, pin the garment and facing edges down each side of the opening on the front, stopping at the end of the opening. Then sew, starting at the bottom of the opening on one side of the bodice, proceeding up and around the neckline and down on the opposite front edge, and stopping at the end of the opening there.

Figure 97   *Figure 98*

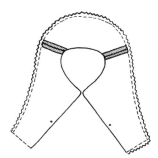

(Fig. 99.) Clip inward all around the neckline at ⅜-inch intervals so that the facing will not pucker when it is turned; clip off the corners of the lapels. Then turn the facing to the inside of the garment, rolling it with your fingers to bring the seam just inside of the neckline. Baste the edges around the neckline and down each front for pressing. After pressing, join the two loose ends of the facing to their respective sides of the front seam by hand.

If the garment fabric is bulky, the seams down the front and around the neckline should be graduated by trimming: the interfacing cut to the line of stitching; the middle layer trimmed to ¼ inch in width; and the third layer left the full width of the seam. Then clip in to the line of stitching.

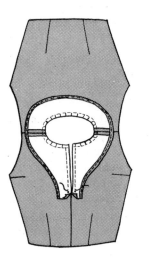

Figure 99

The bound neckline

Regardless of its shape, when a neckline is to be finished with a binding, part of which will show as a trimming feature on the right side of the garment, the binding must be cut on the true bias weave of the fabric. Unless it is cut on the true bias, it will not conform willingly and correctly to the shape onto which it must be sewn. To produce a true bias fold to guide the cutting of the strip, the cloth must be folded in this manner: Make a triangle by folding the cross weave of the fabric over the edge of the selvage. This produces a true bias fold. Cut through this fold and use the edges as guides by which to cut the necessary strips for the binding. (Fig. 100a & b.) The binding should be cut wide enough so that it can be used double. The doubled strip is not only prettier but much easier to handle than a single width.

There is no rule as to how wide the finished binding should be on the right side of the garment. It can be anywhere from ¼ inch to 1 inch in width, according to your wish. A very popular width for the finished binding on the right side of the garment is ¼ inch. To make it, cut the flat bias strip about 2 inches wide. Fold it right side out, and place the edges against the right side of the neck edge, starting on the right shoulder. (Fig. 101.) The raw end of the strip should be folded back from the right side of the garment at the starting point, so that it will

Figure 100a

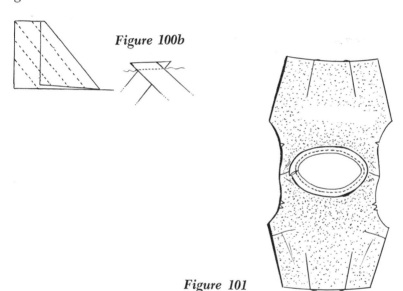

Figure 100b

Figure 101

be clean finished on the right side when done. Start stitching at this location with a ½-inch seam, stretching the bias strip slightly as you sew. The garment itself is not drawn at all during the stitching process.

This work is much more satisfactory when done free hand, not pinned or basted. Pinning and basting affect the free action of the bias weave and make it stubborn to handle. So just arrange and sew a few inches at a time until the neckline is completed. When you get to the part where you started sewing, overlap the binding about ¼ inch.

The raw edges of the binding, as well as the neck, are now trimmed off to an even ¼-inch width. The folded edge of the binding is then turned over the remaining edges to the inside of the neckline, allowing the part of the binding in which the raw edges were wrapped to remain on the surface of the garment.

Stitch on the right side of the garment, directly in the groove of the seam, right below the bindings. (Fig. 102.) The neck edge, as well as the binding edges, must be continuously kept in an upright position during the stitching process. This is done with the manipulation of the

Figure 102

left thumb, which forces the seam edges into their proper direction, while the thumb and forefinger of the right hand hold them in that position during the stitching. Arrange and sew only a few inches at a time until the complete neckline is finished.

No pressing is done on this neckline while it is being constructed. Press on the wrong side when the neckline is finished. During the pressing, the binding that is on the right side of the neckline will flatten out just enough to conceal the stitching directly below it, while the raw edges inside the binding will make a nice padded roll around the neckline.

When a wider bias finish is desired, the same procedure is followed. The binding can even be cut the same width as for the narrow finish. It is applied in the same way, except that the stitching is done farther away from the raw edge of the neck. The binding is then sewn by hand to the wrong side of the garment, attaching the folded edge to the stitching if it reaches that far, or to the underpart of the neck finish above the first row of stitching.

In binding the neckline of sheer fabrics the bias strip is still used double, but the width must be cut more exactly than when used on fabrics that are nontransparent, so that when it is turned over to the inside of the garment, the folded edge will just reach to the first row of stitching. It is then caught down by hand to the machine stitching. Any extra width in the binding would spoil the appearance of the neckline because it would show through the transparent material below the stitching line.

COLLARS, CUFFS, AND BELTS

Collars

There may be many times when you want to change the shape and size of the collar that is featured on the pattern to one that is more becoming. These changes do not involve any great dress-making knowledge as long as a few basic rules are understood. The changing of the collar will not alter the fit of the garment in any way, since in changing the shape of collars only the outer edges are changed. The neck edge is usually left in its original form, so that it will fit as well as the first design.

There are three different types of collars. The first and most common is the separate unit collar. This collar is constructed first and then set onto the garment with a facing, a bias strip, or by turning the top edge of the collar over the raw edges of the rest of the layers, including the neck edge, and blind stitching it to the neck by hand, just as was done in the sports shirt.

THE SCALLOPED EDGE   Scallops can easily be sketched with chalk onto the wrong side of the fabric, but make sure to leave enough edge at the top of the scallops for a narrow seam. The article is faced and the stitching is then done through the chalk line. Be sure not to make too sharp a point between the scallops, as that would make the V-shaped space between them pucker when turned over to the right side. The edge is then clipped straight to the stitching at the V between each curve, and the seam is trimmed to a ¼-inch edge. (Fig. 103.) The scalloped article is then turned over to the right side. Each scallop is pushed out to its utmost with the fingertips, basted close to the edge, and thoroughly pressed.

HOW TO STITCH A COLLAR WITH A BIAS STRIP   Pin the neck edge of the completed collar unit to the neck of the garment, the right side of the

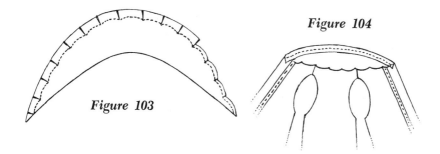

Figure 104

Figure 103

collar facing upward. Start pinning at the center back and work toward the fronts. Turn the front facings of the garment over so that their right sides are facing the right sides of the garment fronts. Then place a bias strip, cut about 1¼ inches wide and folded through the center, over the collar and neck edges, and sew from one front edge to the other in one operation. (Fig. 104.) Trim off the raw edges to about ¼ inch, and place the binding over the raw edges. Either hand sew it into place, or, if the collar is wide enough to cover the seam, stitch by machine.

HOW TO MAKE AND ATTACH A TAILORED SHIRT COLLAR WITH A NECKBAND
This severely tailored collar is usually found on men's shirts, although once in a great while it is featured on women's garments, too. Whether the garment is for you or the man of the house, the work on this type of collar is the same.

The collar is interfaced with preshrunk cotton. The interfacing is placed against the wrong side of the under-collar section. The right sides of the upper and under collars are then placed facing each other and stitched around the outer edges, leaving the lower edge open. (Fig. 105.) Trim the seams to ¼ inch and clip the corners diagonally to the stitching, and then turn the collar to the right side. Baste the outer edges, and press well.

The collar band (Fig. 106.) should now be attached to the collar.

Figure 105   Figure 106

The band, too, will be interfaced. It is very easy to confuse the edges of the collar band, since the edge that attaches to the collar is very similar to the edge that must be attached to the neck, so be sure to observe the matching notches in this following step.

Place one neckband on the outside of the upper collar and the other one on the outside of the under collar. The strip of interfacing is placed against the band that is going to be against the neck (the wrong side of the inner band). (Fig. 107.) Pin all the edges together and sew through all the thicknesses. Trim off the seam to ¼ inch and press in a downward position.

The inner neckband and the interfacing are now pinned to the inside of the garment neckline so that the raw edges of the seam will be on the right side when they have been joined to each other. The outer band is then turned under ¼ inch, placed over the raw edges, and sewn down close to the fold. (Fig. 108.)

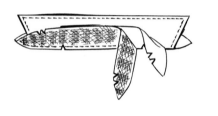

Figure 107

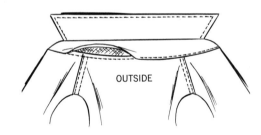

Figure 108

HOW TO CONSTRUCT A SHAWL COLLAR   There are many variations in the shape and size of the shawl collar but the construction is basically the same for all. The under collar in this style is cut all in one with the garment fronts. The upper section of the collar is cut all in one with the facing. This type of collar treatment is found in all kinds of wearing apparel: dresses, blouses, coats, and suits.

The center back seam of the collar is sewn (Fig. 109.) and pressed open. This collar should be interfaced with suitable material, depending upon the garment material. The interfacing is placed on the garment fabric, so that buttonholes can be made through it. Every pattern that features a shawl collar indicates how deep the clipping must be at the junction of the collar and the shoulder. This important clipping must be made right to the end of the clipping line, or else the cloth will pucker and ruin the looks of the collar. So when the pattern says "clip," clip!

Sew the shoulder seams and the under part of a shawl collar in one operation (Fig. 110.) without the use of pins. Do it this way: Place the right sides of the front and back shoulder lines against each other, with the front of the garment on the top. Start to sew at the outer end of the shoulder and continue toward the clipped corner, keeping the seam edges of the back and front shoulders even, until the clipped area has been reached. Here, continue to sew, aiming to reach the immediate left of the clipping point on the top piece. You should maintain the proper seam allowance, but only on the under part of the work, thus allowing the clipped part to spread itself out properly up to the pivoting point of the slash. When the point of the slash has been reached, leave the needle in the work, and with the presser foot lifted, turn the work so that the neck edge will be in a stitching position. Sew around the back of the neck, with the right amount of seam allowance, and pivot again in the same way when the opposite end of the neckline is reached, continuing on to the remaining shoulder seam. Check on the wrong side of the back of the garment to see if the shape of the shoulder and neckline is evenly outlined with the stitching that has just been done. This is the proof of whether the collar will set well around the neck or will pucker at the junctions.

Figure 109   *Figure 110*

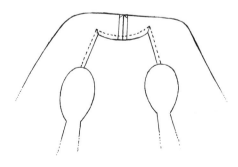

The facing, too, is cut in two pieces, so that the weave of the fabric will be the same as in the garment. The seam is joined together in the center back, and the outer edges are clean finished with ¼-inch edge turned and stitched by machine before attaching it to a dress, but left unturned in suits or coats. The right sides of the garment and facing are then placed against each other and pinned from the center back down on each side to the bottom. Stitch on the garment side of the work. Trim the seam to ¼-inch width, or in the customary staggered manner if the garment is interfaced. Turn the work right side out and baste the outer edge of the collar and fronts—rolling the edges so the seam won't show—and press well. The back of the collar is turned under ¼ inch and hand sewn to the neck edge of the garment (Fig. 111.) when there is no lining to cover this edge.

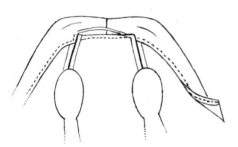

Figure 111

THE TUXEDO COLLAR   Here is another type of collar that is quite popular, especially on coats and suits. It resembles the shawl collar very closely in appearance, but the construction is quite different. The under section of this collar consists of two pieces cut on the bias so that they conform comfortably and becomingly to the shape of the neck. The pieces are sewn together in the center back, the seam pressed open. The under collar is usually interfaced, and joined to the neckline of the garment. The interfacing edge is completely trimmed off right to the seam around the neckline, both from the collar and the garment section as well. The neckline seams are clipped to the stitching, from the fronts to the shoulder seams, and these are pressed open. (Fig. 112.) The back part of the neckline and collar edge are allowed to remain in an upright position.

The facing and the upper collar are cut in one piece with a center back seam, just like the shawl collar. Sew the collar together in the center back and place it against the right side of the under collar after it has been pressed open. Pin from the center back toward each side. Then sew, holding the interfaced part or the garment side of the work on top so that the work will be kept smooth. Trim the seam edges in the customary staggered manner. Turn the work right side out. Roll and baste the edge of the fronts and the collar so that the seams won't show, and then press the edge well. The facing does not have to be turned under at the neckline of this type of collar when the garment is going to be lined, as the lining will cover the raw edges. If, however, the collar is for a dress or blouse, turn up the neck edge ¼ inch, and hand sew from shoulder to shoulder across the back.

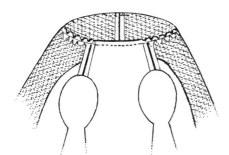

Figure 112

TRIMMING A COLLAR WITH VELVET   This type of detailing is very smart, whether the velvet or velveteen used is the same color as the garment cloth or a contrasting one. The velvet trim is applied by invisible hand stitching after the garment is finished and so does not affect the regular construction of the neckline. Fold the velvet on the bias, and cut it exactly the size of the original collar—using the garment pattern—even though it is going to be reduced in size later on. (Fig. 113.) Leave the

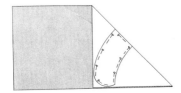

Figure 113

neck edge alone, but trim away ⅜-inch seam allowance on the other three edges. Now run a line of stitching around all four edges of the single layer of velvet, ⅜ inch from all four edges. The stitching will control the collar edges and keep them from getting out of shape; it is especially important if the edges are curved.

Turn the outer edges under through the line of stitching and hand baste flat on all edges. While basting, roll the collar edges a little to bring the machine stitching just underneath the collar. If the neck edge of the collar is curved, you may have to clip inward on the edge to make the material fall right. (Fig. 114.) But if the neck edge is straight,

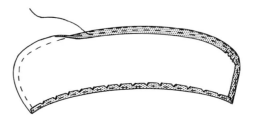

Figure 114

it is not necessary to clip. Corners, however, must be carefully folded and some of the velvet cut away to avoid bulk. (Fig. 115.)

Arrange the velvet collar on top of the garment collar, starting at the center of the neckline and working outward toward each end. Because ⅜ inch was trimmed from the outer edge of the velvet collar, and because an additional ⅜ inch was turned under, there will be a cloth border ⅜ inch wide surrounding the outer edge of the velvet, but the neck edge of the velvet will fit right up against the seamline that holds

Figure 115

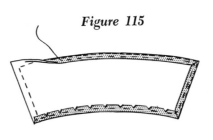

the original collar in place. Insert the pins as shown in Fig. 116. Hand sew the velvet collar with the "bridge stitch," keeping the stitches easy, lest they pull and cause puckers. Remove the basting stitches and press lightly with a dry iron on the under-collar side. Don't use moisture as it may come through to the velvet or velveteen and flatten the nap.

If you wish the entire collar to be covered with velvet, cut the collar

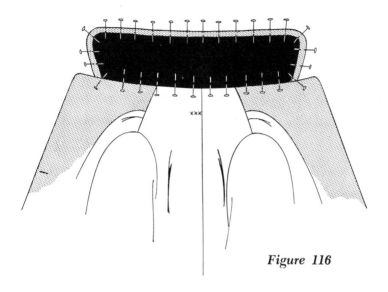

Figure 116

to the right size but don't trim off any of the edges. Instead, run a line of machine stitching around all sides ⅜ inch away from the raw edges, turn the edges under and baste them flat. Then mount the velvet on the cloth collar. Match the neckline edges first and then bring the outer edge of the velvet over to the edge of the cloth; pin, and bridge stitch into place letting the edge of the velvet overlap the edge of the cloth just enough so that the under collar is out of sight.

All about cuffs

There are just as many varieties of cuffs as there are collars. The shape and style of cuffs should bear a close relationship to those of the collar on the garment, if a collar is featured. If cuffs alone are featured, they can be made quite dramatic. They can even be the highlight of the design, if done in an outstanding fabric or designed along unusual lines.

THE STRAIGHT CUFF   To make straight cuffs that run continuously around the bottom of the sleeve, cut the fabric double the width of the finished cuff. For instance, if a 2-inch cuff is desired, the cuff will be cut 4 inches wide, plus seam allowance on both edges. The material is then sewn into the shape of a tube, and the seams are pressed open. Then slip the cuff over the right side of the sleeve, with the right side of the cuff facing the sleeve. The seams are matched evenly. Stitch them together with the regulation seam allowance. (Fig. 117.) The free edge of the cuff is then turned under about ½ inch, and the fold is placed over the raw edge of the first seam and either hand sewn or machine stitched. (Fig. 118.) Hand sewing is more suitable for silks and woolens, but machine stitching will hold better for cottons that get lots of wear and laundering. Because the machine stitching is done inside the sleeve, it does not detract from the appearance of the cuff.

When the straight cuff is used on suits and coats, it is constructed in the same manner as for an untailored garment. The only part of the work that is different is the attaching of the free edge of the cuff to the bottom of the sleeve. Where the free edge is turned in for clean finishing on a dress, and either hand or machine stitched into place, this edge remains raw on a suit or coat sleeve, to be covered by lining. The raw edge would be sewn with a large basting stitch, to keep it in place, just like the hem lines of jackets. The lining makes it more secure when it is stitched into the sleeve.

Figure 117   *Figure 118*

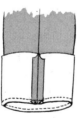

THE SHAPED OR SEPARATE UNIT CUFF   This cuff is constructed exactly like a collar, interfaced when necessary and attached to the sleeve with either a bias strip of garment material or a facing that is cut on the straight of the material to fit the shape of the bottom of the sleeve. Pin the finished cuff to the right side of the sleeve, matching notches so that the opened parts will be where they belong on the outside of the sleeves. Then place the bias strip over the top of the cuff edge and sew all the edges at once with the regulation seam allowance. The bias strip should be about 1¼ inches wide. The raw edge is trimmed off to ¼ inch and the strip is turned over the raw edges and sewn by hand or machine, depending on the garment. (Fig. 119.) When a fitted facing is used in place of the bias strip, cut the facing to the shape of the bottom of the sleeve and make a shallow tube of it by sewing the two

Figure 119

ends together. Then slip the tube over the cuff, which has already been pinned to the outside of the sleeve, and match the sleeve seam and the facing seam. This facing is usually cut about 1½ inches wide, or slightly wider. After stitching, trim the seam down to ¼ inch and direct the facing up the inside of the sleeve. If the garment is unlined, the edge of the facing is turned in and either hand or machine stitched into place. If this cuff is on a coat or suit, it is loosely stab stitched into position, without turning the edge under, to be caught down more securely later by the lining.

THE CONVERTIBLE CUFF The convertible cuff is very popular on garments where the sleeve length is changeable. It is particularly popular on cashmere and vicuña coats, because the convertible styling of the cuff eliminates the possibility of any part of the cuff becoming threadbare from constantly wearing the bottom of the sleeve at the same length. It is an excellent style when making anything from these luxurious bulky fabrics, because the sleeve, the cuff, and the cuff facing are all cut in one piece. Therefore, thick seams do not spoil the smoothness of the sleeve and cuff.

When the sleeve is cut, extra length is included to take care of the cuff and its facing. The extra length is then turned up on the inside of the sleeve and stab stitched into position. (Fig. 120.) Later the lining will be lapped over the edge.

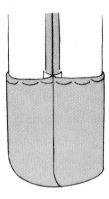

Figure 120

The cuff can also be made with the extended length added, if the yardage of material does not allow for cutting the cuff and facing all in one with the sleeve. Added material is also used in making a convertible cuff cut on the bias for design interest, as in the case of plaids or checks.

When interfacing is used in convertible cuffs, the canvas is stab stitched to the sleeve part of the cloth before the underarm seam of the sleeve is joined.

How to make a good-looking casual belt

Your best home-sewn silk and woolen dresses deserve beautiful commercially made belts to go with them. It is not always possible to make belts at home as good-looking as those that are made by concerns which specialize in such services as making belts and buttons. However, that does not mean that you can't make nice enough belts for your more casual cottons or your "at home" lounging things.

You can avoid an unattractive home-sewn look to your belt if you do not make it too wide. Narrow belts are generally more attractive and professional looking.

Cut the belt 3 inches wide and 3½ inches longer than your actual waist measurement. Fold the material wrong side out. Cut a piece of interfacing the same length as the belt material and the exact width of the folded fabric. Place one edge of the interfacing on the raw edges of the belt material, but leave the other edge free. Stitch all the raw edges at one time, and make a triangular stitching line at one end of the belt, sewing on the interfacing side of the work to keep the cloth from crawling. (Fig. 121.) The interfacing can be either shrunk unbleached muslin, horsehair canvas, synthetic interfacing fabric, or even self-material if the garment cloth is firm in texture.

198

Figure 121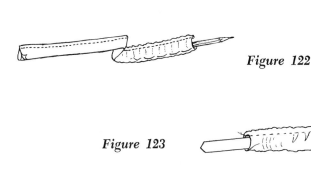

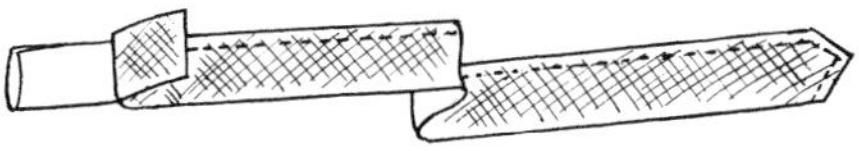

 **Figure 122**

Figure 123

Figure 124

TURNING THE BELT TO THE RIGHT SIDE Form a miniature pocket out of the finished end of the belt by tucking the triangular piece into the tubing, and then insert the rubber end of a full-length pencil into the little pocket. (Fig. 122 and Fig. 123.) Slide the belt onto the pencil until it has all been turned right side out, and shake the pencil out of the belt. Then hold the two ends of the belt and give it a couple of sudden yanks. This will straighten and flatten the interfacing inside the tubing. When the belt has been pressed, put trim stitching on the extreme edges, if desired, or leave it plain.

The belt should now be tried on for size, and the marks for snap fasteners should be made. There is extra length so that a piece is lapped over at the end. Finish off the end of the belt by hand with blind stitches, and then attach the snaps. A snap should be put at the end of the underlap section and another at the overlap end, about 1 inch away from the point of the triangle. Two little trim slides should then be made from a 1-inch strip of material, folded through the center, and refolded so that the raw edges are all concealed, just as was done for the belt slides on the Bermuda shorts. The slides should be machine stitched on each edge, and then cut to a length that fits easily around the closed belt. One of the slides should be placed over the snap on the front overlap, and the other on the underlap end, just where the snap fastener is sewn. (Fig. 124.) These trim slides are attached to the underside of the belt by hand, finishing the raw ends of the slides as neatly as possible.

199

Chain-stitch carriers to hold the belt at the proper location on the waistline can be made out of the mercerized thread that was used for stitching the dress. Several strands of thread should be used to make them secure and strong. The belt is worn with half its width above the waistline and the other half below. This is the way the carriers should also be made on the dress, using the belt for gauging the length of the chain. A few tiny stitches should be made into the side seam of the garment before the chain stitching is started, and then a few more stitches made at the finishing of the chain, so that the carriers do not pull off when putting the belt in and out of them.

Cloth carriers, similar to the trim slides, can be used instead of the thread carriers on garments that get lots of wear, such as bathrobes, house coats, children's clothes, or boys' belted coats. These are turned under and then top stitched at the two ends, with a slight slackness allowed in the carriers for easy fit of the belt.

Fancy cloth carriers are also used on certain types of sports dresses. These are usually in decorative shapes or are stitched several times with self-colored thread or contrasting colors.

HOW TO MAKE A CORD TIE BELT   Here is a belt that looks well on all types of dresses—tailored, semi-tailored, or dressy. It can be made from scraps of material if large pieces are not available. The strip for making this belt must be cut on the true bias. Many little bias pieces can be joined together, and if the seams are pressed well, they will never show in the finished product.

The width of the strip for the belt should be about 1¼ inches wide. The strip should be long enough to tie into two generous loops with ends. Make it between 1½ and 2 yards long, or even a bit longer. Fold the bias strip wrong side out, and stitch it ¼ inch away from the raw edges, stretching the strip to its utmost while you stitch so that the stitching will have the same suppleness as the material itself. If the strip is not stretched during stitching, the stitches will break when the strip is turned to the right side.

Insert a bobby pin into a generous portion of one of the ends of the bias tubing and use it as a bodkin by heading the opened end of the bobby pin into the tube and sliding it through from one end to the other. This will reverse the strip and turn it right side out. The empty tubing should then be filled with many strands of woolen yarn left over from your knitting. The yarn doesn't show, so any odd colors can be utilized for filling. The yarn strands can be looped over the bobby pin, which pulls them through easily. If at first you do not find the belt padded enough, more strands of yarn can be pulled through until the desired effect is achieved.

When cord belts are used on washable cotton dresses, nylon yarn can be substituted for the woolen yarn, so that no shrinkage will be encountered. It is not advisable to use yarns in colors darker than the fabric, as they may show through and make the belt look soiled.

Although cotton cable cording is often recommended as filler for belts of this kind, wool and nylon yarns are much softer and "crowd" inside a confined space more flexibly.

THE CONTOUR BELT   Belt-making kits, available at notion counters, have all the findings necessary for producing handsome contour-shaped belts, including buckles, stiffening, and easy instructions. Even when your pattern includes pieces for making your own contour belt, it is wiser and easier to use the belt-making kit instead, because of the good foundation furnished in the package.

WHAT YOU SHOULD KNOW
ABOUT SLEEVES

From time to time fashion decrees that one type of sleeve is more stylish than another. Of course one must keep in step with fashion, up to a certain point. But luckily no sleeve type is ever completely outmoded. Instead, it may be given a new look either by adding more fullness than was featured in the past, or vice versa.

Just as styling lines of a design either enhance or detract from your appearance, so it is with sleeve styles. Some will be much more becoming to you than others. Regardless of the fact that one type of sleeve may be considered more chic than another, there will always be patterns and ready-to-wear items that feature sleeve styles suitable for you. So if the latest cut is not your type, do the next best thing. Get the "new look" into the type of sleeve that you can wear becomingly.

The one-piece raglan sleeve

There are two types of raglan sleeves. One is made with a shoulder dart that controls the fullness at the top of the sleeve. The sleeve extends

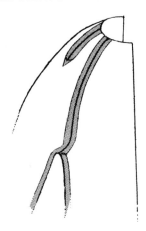

Figure 125

from the neckline of the garment and is cut to conform to the shape of the shoulder. The dart is sewn, slashed, and pressed open. The slashing is done to about ½ inch above the point. The front of the sleeve is joined to the front of the garment and the back of the sleeve to the back. (Fig. 125.) The seams can be pressed flat and left that way, or they can be detailed with a welt seam, which will be covered in the section on the two-piece raglan sleeve.

The underarm seam of the sleeve and the side seams of the garment are sewn in one continuous operation, from the bottom of the sleeve to the bottom of the garment.

The two-piece raglan sleeve with welt seams

This raglan sleeve is cut in two pieces with a seam running along the whole length of the top of the sleeve from the neck down, following the natural contours of the shoulder line. (Fig. 126a.) The back and the

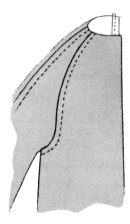

Figure 126a

front sleeve sections are joined to each other with the right sides placed against one another. The seam edge of the sleeve front is then trimmed off on the inside to ¼ inch. The untrimmed edge is then directed toward the front and pressed. The remaining seam edge is top stitched, either by machine or by hand picking with silk twist. The stitching is done about ½ inch or ⅜ inch away from the seam. If a wider welt is desired, you must remember to cut a wider seam for that purpose at the beginning, so that there will be sufficient under edge for the stitching to get caught to.

The front edges of the sleeves are now joined to the front armholes

203

of the garment, and treated in the same way as the center seam of the sleeves. The back-sleeve sections are joined to the back armholes of the garment and finished with a welt seam. The underarm seams of the sleeves and the side seams of the garment are sewn up in one operation, from the bottom of the sleeves to the bottom of the garment.

If the garment has a center back seam, that, too, is sewn with a welt seam, to tie in with the seaming on the sleeves and armholes. The welt should be uniform in width on all the seams of the garment. To welt seam the side seams is optional. (Fig. 126b.)

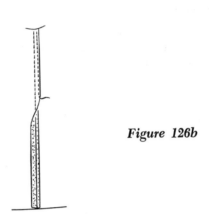

Figure 126b

The plain kimono sleeve

Kimono sleeves are cut all in one with the front and back of the garment. The shoulder and sleeve, being cut in one piece, are sewn with a continuous seam from the neckline to the bottom of the sleeve. The seam is pressed open carefully so as not to spoil the curved shape of the shoulder line. The underarm of the sleeve is sewn along with the underarm seam of the garment. The curved seams at the underarm sections, where the sleeve ends and the garment begins, must be clipped toward the stitching every ⅜ inch, so that the seam edge does not draw. (Fig. 127.) Clipping will prevent strain on the seam and will release more freedom for action. It is a good idea to sew this seam several times through the same line of stiching, for extra strength.

There are two kinds of kimono sleeves. The first is cut with sufficient draping under the arms so that the arms can be raised to a convenient height without straining the underarm seam. The other type requires

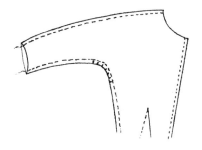

Figure 127

a gusset, or an extra piece of bias-cut material, which is inserted into the underarm section of the garment to give the necessary ease for raising the arms.

The fitted kimono sleeve with a gusset

This type of kimono sleeve has almost the smooth appearance and fit of a set-in sleeve. It is fitted more closely under the arms than the first type. It has very little or no draping under the arms and a gusset must be inserted there to give the garment freedom of movement. The reason why this kimono sleeve is so much smoother in appearance than the one without the gusset is because of the shape of the shoulders and sleeves. These sleeves have a downward angle and do not spread so much as the first type. The spread is what makes the difference. The pattern indicates where and how far to slash the garment pieces so that the gusset can be inserted properly. (Fig. 128.) Be sure to slash the garment right to the end of the indicating line, or you'll have trouble fitting the gusset into the space. Don't try to insert the gusset by fitting all four corners in one operation. Do it in two steps, like this: Mark each corner of the gusset on the right side with a seam allowance in the form

Figure 128

205

of a dot. Keeping right sides together, pin the point of the slash of
either the front or back section of the garment to the corresponding
mark on the gusset, holding the garment on top so you can see the slash.
Sew these together, matching the seam edges of the slash and the gusset
edges, and proceed toward the point of the slash, aiming to sew just to
the immediate left of the cut (Fig. 129.) Leave the needle in the work
at this point, and lift the presser foot to pivot. Now arrange the work
so you can sew on the opposite side of the slash and gusset. Although
the seam edge of the slash tapers to practically nothing by the time the
point of the slashing is reached, the seam allowance remains the same
width on the gusset edges.

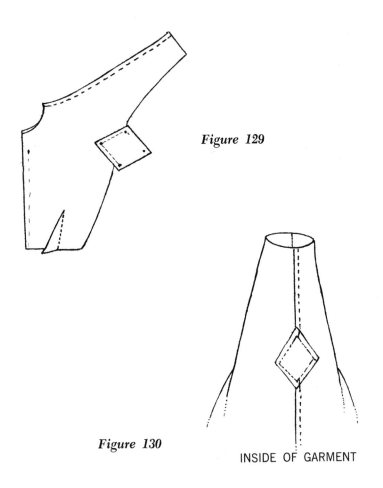

Figure 129

Figure 130

INSIDE OF GARMENT

The other side of the gusset is sewn as a continuation of the under-arm seam. Start sewing at the end of either the sleeve or the bottom of the garment, whichever way will put the slashed part of the garment on the top. Sew along with the regular seam allowance until the gusset section is reached. Here you will start tapering the seam allowance of the slash as was done in the first operation, to the immediate left of the cut. Pivot the work at that point, and continue to sew the rest of the seam to the end. When pressing the seam open, see to it that the gusset is flat and that the garment seams are turned over it. (Fig. 130.)

ALL ABOUT POCKETS

Anyone familiar with the basic steps for making bound buttonholes can make beautiful set-in pockets, since they are constructed with the same steps and precision workmanship. Different pocket styles can be produced through only slight variations, once the basic steps are thoroughly understood.

Pockets are often the focal points of the design, so their workmanship should be faultless. Pleasing optical illusions can be created by the location as well as the style of pockets. There may be times when you will want to substitute another style for the pocket featured on the pattern design, to enhance or disguise your figure. For example, a patch pocket or a flapped pocket located on the lower section of a suit jacket would not be suitable for a hip-heavy figure, because it would emphasize the hips and call attention to their size. However, a more subtle style, such as the bound or welt pocket, would be very nice, especially if inserted in a vertical or diagonal position.

When a new pocket is substituted for the one featured on the pattern design, nine times out of ten neither its placement nor its size is changed. But if the angle of its position needs to be changed, making the opening diagonal instead of vertical or horizontal, it can be done without running into any difficulty as long as the pocket is left the same distance from the side as originally planned.

You may find it necessary to raise or lower coat pockets if you are taller or shorter than average. By holding the pattern against you, you can find out whether a change is in order. Just move your hands as if you were inserting them into the pockets: if your elbows stand out too far from your body, lower the pockets a bit; if you have to make an effort to reach into the pockets, raise them a little. An inch in either direction can do a lot to make the pockets right without changing the appearance of the garment noticeably.

Fabric texture plays an important part in the way the finished pocket will look, and so a smart thing to do before inserting the pocket into the garment itself is to make a sample pocket in the garment fabric. With this you can judge the suitability of the material for the style, and analyze how it will look in the finished garment.

If you are making a coat of loosely woven material, it is wise to interface the parts where pockets will be inserted, because coat pockets receive much wear. For jackets and skirts, interfacing is optional, since the pockets are primarily decorative. To interface, stab stitch the canvas into position invisibly in the pocket area and mark the pocket on the canvas side with pencil, putting a dot at each end. Draw a short vertical line through each dot as a guide and then draw a horizontal line between the dots to show the length of the pocket. The symbol you make will resemble a goal post. Stitch through this symbol with long bright-colored thread to make the goal post visible on the outside of the garment, where the pocket will be started. Then choose your pocket.

The bound or buttonhole pocket

This is a favorite pocket style because of its versatility. It is suitable for any type of garment, in any kind of fabric, and is subtle enough in style and detail so that it can be used by all types of figures. It looks just as attractive on dressy things as it does on more casual items. It flatters that part of the figure on which it is located without emphasizing a figure fault. Making this pocket is just like making a great big buttonhole and then attaching a pocket to it.

Make the pocket welts any desired width. There is no rule in this matter, as there is when making buttonhole bindings. The welts are the trimming details of the pocket that appear on the right side of the garment, serving the same purpose as the bindings do on buttonholes. They can vary in width from ⅛ inch to 1 inch. The fabric is often a deciding factor in this matter, one texture being more pleasing in a narrow width, while another looks better wider. This is a place where making a sample pocket comes in handy, so that you can be sure that the width of the welt looks right. The welts can be made on either the straight or cross weave of the cloth. Bias weave is also used frequently, especially for added interest when the fabric is plaid or checked. The welt is folded right side out and stitched, let us assume, ¼ inch away from the fold. Then trim the raw edge to an exact ¼ inch to equal the width of the fold. (Fig. 131.) Cut the pair of welts generously long, about 1 inch or 1½ inches longer than the horizontal line of the goal post. Sew one welt above and the other below the symbol on the right side of the cloth, with the raw edges coming directly together over the horizontal line. (Fig. 132.) The threads should be left long at each end of the stitching, so that they can be caught in with the next sewing step for reinforcement. Now rip the goal-post carefully.

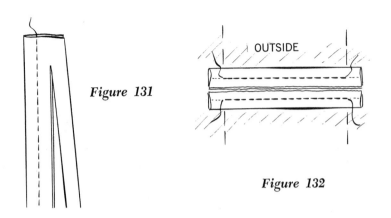

Figure 131

OUTSIDE

Figure 132

Now cut the pocket through from the wrong side of the cloth, slashing horizontally through the center of the space between the two rows of stitching, but stopping 1 inch away from each end. Here the cutting is continued at angles, coming right up to the very end stitch of each row of stitching. (Fig. 133.) Treat each end of the stitching in this manner. Then push the welts through the slash from the right side to the wrong side of the garment, and leave them until the pocket linings have been prepared.

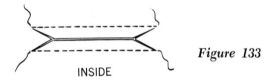

INSIDE

Figure 133

Cut two pieces of pocket linings from the lining cloth. They should be as long as the welts and about 3 or 4 inches deep, depending upon whether they will go on a coat or some other garment. Coats need fairly deep pockets. The figures above are approximate lengths and depths, because it is easier to construct a pocket when the linings are generous in size. They can be trimmed off to actual size after stitching. To the top of one of these linings attach a strip of garment cloth 1½ inches wide. Leave the other plain. (Fig. 134.)

Now attach the lining pieces to the welts on the wrong side of the material. Match the edges of the upper welt and the facing edge of the

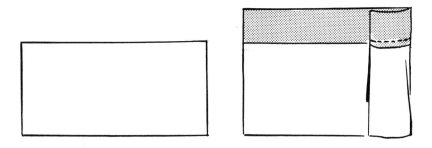

Figure 134

bigger lining piece, and stitch them together through the same rows of stitching that are already there from previous steps. Then attach the plain lining to the raw edges of the lower welt, and sew through the same rows of stitching that are already there. The ends of the welts are now sewn together with the triangular tab of the garment on top of them, just exactly as in the fourth step of making buttonholes. (Fig. 135.) The stitching is continued around the outer edge of the lining to

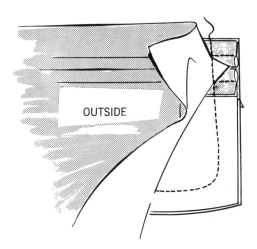

OUTSIDE

Figure 135

form the inside of the pocket, and ended at the opposite ends of the welts in like manner. The shape into which the lining is stitched is a matter of personal preference. Either square or round is correct. Trim the seam edges of the lining to about ⅜ inch or less.

It should be mentioned here that when the fabric is not heavy or bulky in texture, the lining piece that is attached to the upper welt may be completely made of the garment fabric, instead of just the narrow strip. This is true of all the following pockets.

The one-welt or set-in-welt pocket

This pocket is another favorite because its subtle styling makes it adaptable to everything and everyone. It has quite a close relationship to the first pocket in construction as well as appearance. The only difference between them is that this pocket has only one welt to do the job of detailing the pocket on the outside of the garment. This pocket is particularly attractive on garments made of fleecy and uneven-surfaced fabrics, although it is equally popular on other kinds of material.

The principles used in pocket construction are pretty much the same in all set-in types, but each one differs just enough from the others to make it necessary to apply the steps correctly and to see that the pocket parts have exact dimensions when sewn to the goal-post symbol, otherwise the finished results will be puzzling and disappointing. If you can make one set-in pocket, you can make them all.

Mark the goal-post symbol on the wrong side of the garment, or on the canvas, and sew it with long bright-colored stitching which will show on the outside. The welt can be made in any width desired, but 1 inch seems to be the most popular.

Make a welt by folding the fabric right side out and stitching 1 inch away from the fold. The raw edge is always just half of the width of the fold in this style of pocket, so cut the raw edge down to an exact ½-inch width. The welt is now placed BELOW the goal post on the right side of the garment, with the raw edges resting on the horizontal line, and sewn through the line of stitches that are already there, from post to post. (Fig. 136.) The threads should be left generously long so that they can be caught in with the next step for reinforcement.

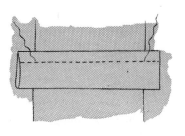

Figure 136

Cut two pieces of pocket linings from the lining material the length of the welt and about 3 or 4 inches deep, depending upon the type of garment the pockets will go in. One of the linings should have a 2-inch strip attached to it; the other is left plain. The extended end of the larger lining piece is placed above the goal post and stitched ½ inch away from the edge. (Fig. 137.) The stitching should be in line with that on the welt, and the right side of the lining should be facing the garment. Note how the distance between the two rows of stitching, that which holds the welt in place and that which holds the lining piece

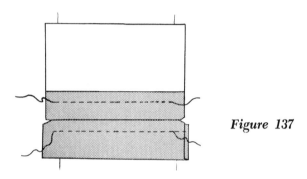

Figure 137

properly, is exactly the same as the width of the welt. The space and the welt must be equal in width, so that the outside features of this type of pocket will dovetail properly when the cutting has been done. Remove the goal-post stitches carefully.

Cut on the wrong side, exactly like a big wide buttonhole, except that the tabs are made 1 inch long; you start to cut angles toward the ends of the stitching 1 inch before the ends have been reached. The welt is then pulled through from the right to the wrong side, and the upper section of it is placed in an upright position to fit into the opened space provided for it. The lining piece is placed in a downward position on the inside of the garment. The remaining piece of lining is now attached to the raw edges of the welt, stitching through the same stitching that is already there. The triangular tab is then sewn down to the ends of the welt (Fig. 138) just as in making a buttonhole, but continuing the stitching around the outer edges of the lining and stitching the opposite triangular tab in the same manner over the remaining welt end. Trim the seam around the outer edge of the lining to about ⅝ inch or even less.

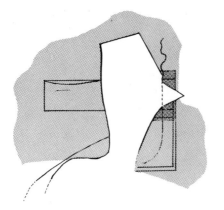

Figure 138

If you wish, this welt can be trimmed with stitches, running the rows close together parallel with the fold. Some fabrics are enhanced with trim stitching. Perfectly straight sewing is, of course, a "must" in such treatment. If you find that trim stitching is out of your line, forget it and stick with the nice untrimmed details.

The flap pocket

Although this handsome pocket is generally seen on men's attire, it is definitely suitable for ladies' clothes also. Nevertheless, some women would do well to choose another style, unless the part of the figure on which the pocket will be located is worthy of such attractive decoration. This pocket does not have the subtleness of some other styles. It is more outstanding and will certainly catch the eye.

Even though this is a fairly tailored pocket, it can be used on garments with a dressmaker feeling about them. If your fabric has a firmly woven texture, the flaps need not be interfaced. When the cloth is loosely woven or soft and flexible, it would be wise to use the same type of interfacing that is used in other parts of the garment, to keep the same amount of firmness in all interfaced parts. It is not necessary to stab stitch the interfacing to the garment fabric. Just stitch around the three outer edges, incorporating the interfacing into the stitching, and then trim the seams in the customary manner, because of the three layers. Corners and curves are treated in exactly the same manner as if these flaps were little miniature collars.

On some occasions the flaps are faced with lining material instead of the same fabric as the rest of the garment. This is necessary when a heavy garment cloth would make the flap too bulky if it were used. If you do this, be sure to cut the flap fabric slightly larger than the lining piece of the flap. Then, when you press the finished flap, after sewing and trimming the seams, the outer fabric can be generously rolled over the edge of the lining or facing part, and there will be no danger of the under section showing on the right side to spoil the appearance of the garment. Flaps must be faultlessly made and pressed. That is the only way they will contribute toward the appearance of the garment.

Mark the wrong side of the cloth or canvas with a goal-post symbol and sew through it with long, bright-colored stitching, so that the pocket placement can be seen on the right side. Then put the finished flap above the symbol, with its right side against the right side of the garment, and the raw edges resting on the horizontal line. Stitch it into position with a ¼-inch seam. Now make a welt from a strip folded right side out and stitched ½ inch away from the fold. Trim the raw edges to a ¼-inch width. This welt is then placed below the symbol, with the raw edges right up against the raw edges of the flap, and sewn from post to post with a ¼-inch seam directly through the first sewing. (Fig. 139.) Now rip the bright stitches carefully.

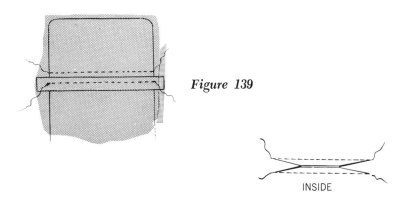

Figure 139

INSIDE

Figure 140

The pocket is now cut through from the wrong side of the cloth, slashing horizontally through the center of the space between the two rows of stitching, but stopping 1 inch away before reaching the ends of the stitching. Here the cutting is continued at angles, coming right up to the last stitch at the end of each row. (Fig. 140.) The welt is then pushed through gently from the right side to the wrong side of the

215

garment, and the flap is placed in a downward position on the right side.

Now cut two pieces of lining from the lining material the same length as the welt and about 3 or 4 inches deep. It is not necessary to attach a facing strip to the top of one of these lining pieces, as the flap covers the opening. But it can be included if you desire.

One of the pocket linings is now attached to the seam edge of the flap, on the wrong side of the cloth. Start this stitching at the extending edge of the lining piece, and then sew through the same stitching that is already on the flap edge, making sure to catch in the full ¼-inch seam width at the ends of the flap, where they have an inclination to slip away if not watched. The second piece of lining is attached to the raw edges of the welt in the usual manner, sewing through the original stitching.

With the pocket flap in a downward position, fold the cloth over at the end of the pocket, so that the triangular tab at the end, as well as the lining and welt pieces on the wrong side, are visible. Sew downward on these projecting parts (Fig. 141) but be sure to have the flap

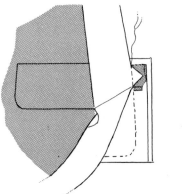

Figure 141

continuously in a downward position on the right side of the work during the complete sewing process. If the flap is directed in any other way, it will not lie in place properly on the right side of the garment. The seam around the outer edge of the lining can now be trimmed neatly away to about ⅜ inch, and the pocket is finished. Touch it up lightly with the iron on the wrong side of the cloth.

The flap pocket with feature stitching

On sports coats and jackets made of camel's-hair or other fleecy fabrics, the flap pocket is frequently seen with a double row of stitching encircling the outside shape of the pocket, even though it is a set-in type with the lining inside of the garment. The stitching is done either by hand or by machine, with the space between the rows about ⅜ inch. The flap is usually top stitched, too, when feature stitching is used, and the widths of the trim stitching match one another. The trim stitching on the flap should be done before it is sewn to the goal post.

The pocket is constructed just like the ordinary flap pocket. When the pocket is completed, the lining is pinned flat against the wrong side of the garment so that it can be caught in with the feature stitching.

The inner line for the feature stitching is drawn first, using chalk on the right side of the garment. Be sure to use only a chalk and a color that will rub off easily when the stitching is finished. The first line is drawn directly in line with the ends of the pockets, and the outer line ⅜ inch away from that. (Fig. 142.)

Figure 142

Start the first row of stitching at the top of the pocket opening, just below the welt under the flap, and continue around the marked line, ending at the opposite end of the pocket opening. Start the outer row at the center of the bottom line, so that the ending can be overlapped a stitch or two without being obvious.

The shaped welt or weskit pocket

This is a companion pocket to the one with a flap, the welt style being used on the upper section and the flapped pocket on the lower part of the garments. This pocket is seen on men's tailored or sports jackets as

217

well as on many types of ladies' apparel. Because of its unobtrusive character, the weskit pocket looks well on all types of figures, provided discretion is used as to where it is placed on the figure.

Although this is a companion pocket when used on men's wear, it does not have to be used that way on women's clothes. The shape of the welt can be varied, but the size must be comparable to the pocket featured on the pattern design. The location of the pocket also determines its size. For example, pockets on the lower section of the garment should be larger than those meant for the upper part.

This pocket is frequently seen on camel's-hair and tweed sports coats. The welt is often made out of one piece of fabric, cut wide enough so that it can be folded over and sewn at the two ends, thus eliminating a seam at the top edge of the finished welt. This can be done only when the welt has straight edges. When the shape is unusual or curved, the same techniques are used as when making a flap. Interfacing is used when needed for firmness. The welt should have three finished edges and one open edge. The difference between a flap and a welt of this kind is that flaps hang downward when in their normal position on the garment while welts stand upright.

Draw a goal-post symbol on the wrong side of the garment, or on the canvas which backs the pocket location, and sew through it with large bright stitches so the marking of the pocket will show on the outside. Place the welt *below* the goal post, with the raw edges up against the horizontal line, and sew with a ¼-inch seam. The lining should be cut in one piece for this pocket, instead of the usual two pieces, for the sake of getting acquainted with treating pocket linings in this manner. When pockets need not be too deep, as in ornamental pockets, this way of applying the lining is perfectly proper. Cut the pocket lining twice the necessary depth, using lining fabric, and cut it wide enough to extend about an inch beyond the welt ends. Then sew it above the horizontal line with a ¼-inch seam edge. The line of stitching on this part must be ½ inch shorter at each end than the stitching that appears on the welt. (Fig. 143.) Be sure to leave the ends of thread long enough to be caught in with the next step. Rip out the bright goal post now.

Cut in the center between the two rows of stitching, on the wrong side of the cloth, as in the previous pockets. One inch away from each end angle the cutting to the last stitch at each end of the rows. This will result in irregularly shaped tabs at the ends, instead of the usual triangular ones. (Fig. 144.) The lining is then pulled through from the right to the wrong side. The free end of the lining is now brought up and attached to the raw edges of the pocket welt on the wrong side of the garment. On the right side of the material, the welt is placed in an upright position, and the cloth at the end of the pocket is folded back, so that the lining on the inside of the garment is visible. (Fig. 145.)

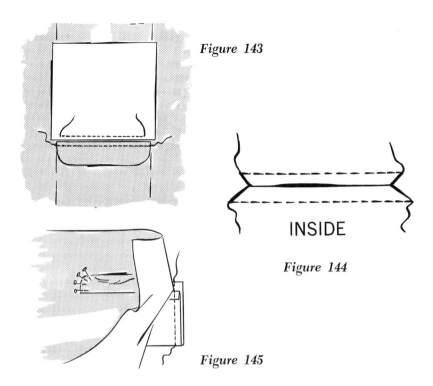

Figure 143

INSIDE

Figure 144

Figure 145

The tabs that are usually caught in with the stitching of the lining sides are not transferred to the wrong side of the cloth, but are allowed to remain on the surface of the right side, to be caught in with the stitching that will be done on the welt ends. (Fig. 146.) These ends can either be tacked invisibly by hand or sewn by machine very close to the edges, from the base to the tops. The ends of the thread are pulled through to the wrong side and tied. When hand sewing is used, it is done with the bridge stitch spaced closely so it will hold and yet be invisible. Leaving the tab on the surface of the fabric gives a

Figure 146

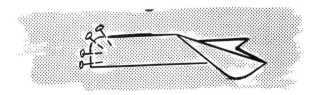

219

smoother base on which to sew the welt. If it were treated like the previous pockets, the sides of the welt would pucker. The little tab remains undisturbed inside of the pocket. Look inside a man's handkerchief pocket on a suit jacket, and you'll see the same type of tab.

The patch pocket

To make a good-looking patch pocket requires the same precision workmanship that is applied to any other style. Only then will it contribute to the good appearance of the garment. Although it is an easy pocket to make, the importance of perfect execution in its construction cannot be overemphasized. Unless each step is faultlessly done, this pocket can give more of a homemade appearance to the garment than any other style. Many an amateur sewer settles for a patch pocket because she feels that she can't go wrong with it, not realizing that unless she treats it with the same respect that she does any of the set-in styles, the results can be most disappointing.

There are a number of patch-pocket styles, but a very popular one, and the most basic in construction, is the plain patch pocket, lined with lining material. This pocket is suitable for most clothes except the very dressy styles. It is an excellent pocket to use on children's wear because it can take more punishment and hard usage than any of the set-in styles. Another reason this is a favorite pocket on clothes for growing children is that the young ones do not "outgrow" a patch pocket nearly so fast as the other kind. Last year's coat with a set-in welt pocket, for example, can look very short-waisted this year. But the depth of a patch pocket does much to counteract that appearance, even though the pocket is equally high on the garment. More optical illusions!

The size of the pocket depends on the kind of garment on which it will appear, and also on where it is located on the figure. Pockets above the waistline must be smaller than those on the hip section.

The pocket piece of garment fabric is cut about 1½ inches or 2 inches longer than the actual depth of the finished pocket. The extra length is allowed at the top of the pocket to act as a facing. The fold line, where the pocket ends and the facing begins, is identified with tiny clippings made in the edges of the pocket, about ¼ inch deep. The lining is then cut to the approximate depth of the pocket, or somewhat shorter, and sewn to the edge of the facing end, allowing a 1-inch space to remain unsewn in the center of the seam. (Fig. 147.)

The pocket is then folded through the fold line with the right sides together, and sewn around the three outer edges with the regular seam allowance. The sewing is done on the lining side. Control the slipping

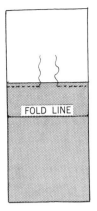

FOLD LINE

Figure 147

of the two fabrics as much as possible by placing your hands firmly on each side of the stitching.

Now turn the pocket right side out through the small opening in the center of the seam between pocket and lining. If the cloth is bulky, trim the facing edges on both sides of the pocket to a ¼-inch width, but not the pocket material itself. The corners must be trimmed away, both at the top and the bottom. (Fig. 148.) Baste the pocket all around the four edges, rolling the pocket material slightly over the edge of the lining, and then press thoroughly on the lining side. The little opening in the seam is sewn together by hand before the pocket is attached to the garment.

There are many attractive ways to attach the pocket to the garment. (Fig. 149.) It can be done with stitching right on the edge, or any distance away from the edge, either by hand picking or machine. When the stitching is done farther in than the extreme edge of the pocket, blind tack the loose fold after the actual sewing is done, so that it stays flat against the garment. This prevents the lining fabric from showing

Figure 148   *Figure 149*

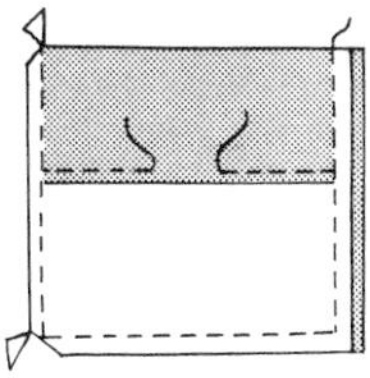

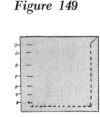

on the right side of the pocket. The pocket can also be completely blind stitched so that no outside sewing is visible. This is done with the bridge stitch about ⅛ inch in from the edge of the pocket. To do this, the edge is lifted up slightly so that the sewing can be done right underneath it. It can also be sewn through from the wrong side of the cloth, if the material is not too heavy. When the cloth is thick, there may be puckers under the pocket unless the work is done from the right side.

The patch pocket with all-in-one flap

A flap can easily be incorporated on the top of a patch pocket by cutting the cloth with additional length to allow for a flap of any desired depth, plus the flap facing and the additional pocket facing to which the lining will be attached. This is a minor mathematical problem, but it most certainly eliminates bulky edges and seams when making patch pockets with flaps, especially in heavy fabrics. The lining piece is attached to the facing edge of the pocket piece, with a part of the seam left open for turning the pocket right side out. (Fig. 150.) This is a very satisfactory way to make flapped patch pockets from napped cloth, because there is never confusion as to which way to cut the flaps in order to have the nap running in the same direction as the rest of the garment.

The pocket is folded through the fold line, with the right sides of the material together, and sewn around the three outer edges with the regular seam allowance. The sewing is done on the lining side, controlling the slipping of the fabrics by holding the hands on each side

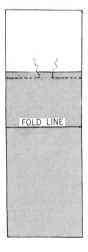

Figure 150

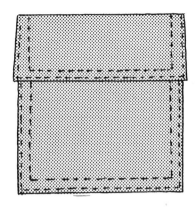

Figure 151

of the needle. Clip the corners in the usual way. Then turn the pocket to the right side, baste carefully around the edges, and press. The inch-wide opening is sewn by hand.

This pocket also can be sewn onto the garment in any way desired, by hand or machine. Any feature stitching on the flap should be done first. Then place the pocket onto the garment for stitching around the three outer edges (Fig. 151), continuing the rows of stitching where the ones on the flap ended, overlapping slightly for reinforcement.

The patch pocket with separate flap

This pocket is frequently found on sports shirts, although not confined to that type of apparel. It contains two entirely separate units, the pocket and the flap. The patch pocket is done in the same manner as the plain one, and the flap is made in exactly the same way as that for a set-in flap pocket. When these parts are completed, put them onto the garment in the following manner.

Mark a goal post on the garment. Place the flap above the symbol, with the raw edges on the horizontal line, and sew by machine with ¼-inch seam edge. (Fig. 152.) If the fabric edges are bulky, the top seam edge of the flap is cut off right to the stitching, and the under

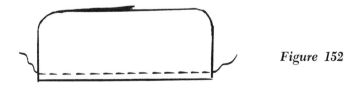

Figure 152

one is trimmed to ⅛ inch. The flap is then folded downward, and a row of pins placed horizontally across the top, about ¼ inch down from the upper part of the flap, so that the raw edges of the seam do not show when the flap is lifted. The under part of the flap is then hand sewn with the bridge stitch from one end to the other, just as close to the pinned line as possible, alternating from the flap to the garment about ¼ inch apart. (Fig. 153.) Then place the patch pocket under the flap, as close as it can go, and in a direct line with the flap on both edges. Pin it into place and sew it to the garment in any desired way. (Fig. 154.)

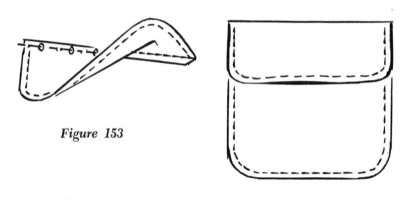

Figure 153

Figure 154

The side seam pocket

This pocket is very satisfactory when the design of the garment has sufficient softness in the styling to allow the cloth to drape across the tummy and hips so that the pocket won't draw or gap. (Fig. 155.) It is also suitable to insert into the side seams of slacks and shorts. Coats and jackets cut on straight boxy lines also feature this pocket style quite often, built right into the side seams between the front and back sections.

The seams into which the pockets are to be inserted are sewn together with part of the seam left open for the pocket opening. The ends of the stitching are reinforced by backtracking about ½ inch, so that the ends remain firm. Then cut two pieces of lining. One could be of garment fabric and the other of lining fabric. If desired, both pieces could be cut of lining cloth, with garment cloth facings, 1½ inches wide, attached to each one.

Figure 155

The piece of lining made of garment cloth is sewn to the back section of the garment edge, and the one cut of lining cloth is sewn to the edge of the front on the opened seam. (Fig. 156.) These pieces are then arranged so that the right sides face each other, and sewn from one end to the other on the outer edges. (Fig. 157.) Clip the seams at

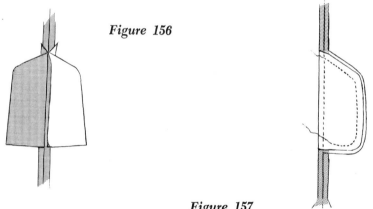

Figure 156

Figure 157

the top and bottom of the pocket, so that the seam edges can remain in an opened position, above and below the pocket.

Side seam pocket at a zipper closing

When side seam pockets are inserted into garments with center front or back closings, the procedure is the same as when the pocket is inserted into coats or jackets. But when there is a left-side zipper closing, the construction is somewhat different.

Let us assume that the side of the garment has been fitted, sewn, and pressed. The seam is then opened to the indicating mark, just as when a plain zipper job is to be done. The pocket linings are cut from the pattern pieces.

Attach one lining piece to the front of the garment with the right sides together, and stitch right through the fold appearing on the garment side. Then clip the garment seam edge right to the last stitch at the bottom of the stitching (Fig. 158), and flip the lining over to the

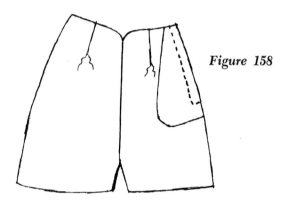

Figure 158

Figure 159

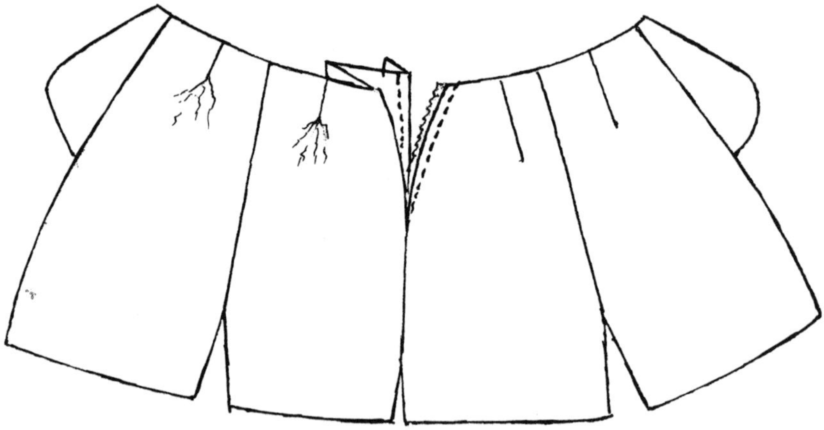

inside side of the garment. The second piece of lining is now placed against the first one, with the right sides facing each other, and sewn together all around the outer edges. The whole left pocket is now attached to the front of the garment. From here on the side seam of the garment is treated as if there were no pocket there at all, since the projecting seam edge of the last lining which was sewn serves the purpose of covering the front part of the zipper, just as though it were part of the garment front. (Fig. 159.) The pocket on the right-hand side is sewn in a continuous seam when the side seam is sewn, once the lining pieces have been joined to their respective parts.

Other types of pockets will come along from time to time which will be different in construction from the ones mentioned here. The lines of the design will determine their size and shapes, and the construction will take place at the same time as the garment is being constructed. These are called construction pockets, as they are cut right into the design, and form the styling of the garment. They will be thoroughly covered in the pattern construction sheet.

TRIMMING TRICKS

Cloth loops for closings and trimmings

Cloth loops, made from the garment fabric, add a professional touch to the finished product. They can be used on front and back closings, as well as on sleeves, and are suitable for all sorts of wearing apparel. The cording from which the loops are made can also be used for many decorative details, such as frogs, swirls, and looped scallops. They can be braided together and made into attractive belts. There is no limit to the uses to which self-cording can be put.

Cording is very easy to make if the strips of cloth are cut on the true bias weave. Bias fabric is flexible, whereas the straight or cross weave is firm, and flexibility is an essential in this cording.

In making the cording for loops, you don't need a large piece of cloth. Small pieces of cloth can be used, as they must be cut into short lengths anyway when applied to the edge of the garment. This is a good way to use up small scraps. Even in making cording for articles requiring longer lengths, the pieces can be sewn together and pressed flat. The seams will never show when properly handled.

Here's how the cording is made. Cut bias strips 1¼ inches wide. Fold the strip wrong side out and stitch ¼ inch away from the folded edge. Stretch the strip to its utmost during the stitching, so that the stitching will be as flexible as the cloth. Otherwise the stitching will break when the cording is turned over on the right side. At one end of the stitching of this bias strip flare out the seam, so that the tubing will be wide, in the shape of a funnel. This will make an easy job of turning the cording over to the right side.

A bobby pin makes an excellent gadget for turning bias tubing to the right side. Insert it into a generous portion of the wide-stitched end. Slide the bobby pin into position so that its open end heads toward the inside of the tube. Continue sliding the bobby pin through until it comes out at the opposite end, bringing the finished cording with it.

(Fig. 160 a & b.) Note that the raw edges of the bias strip were left untrimmed, to act as fillers, giving the finished cording a round, firm appearance. The raw edges are equally as effective as yarn for this purpose. The cording will be about ¼ inch thick.

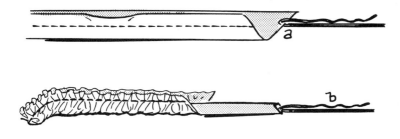

Figure 160

When making heavier cording, the strip of bias is cut the same as for the narrower, 1¼ inch wide. It is sewn farther away from the fold, depending on how thick a cording is desired. The raw edges are left on, and the strip is turned right side out with a bobby pin. Additional roundness is obtained by drawing several strands of woolen or nylon yarn into the tubing with the bobby pin. The number of strands needed depends upon the thickness of the yarn used. Be sure that the yarn is never darker in color than the material into which it is drawn, as the darker color will give the cording a soiled appearance.

When extra-heavy fabric is used for loops, it is necessary to cut off some of the raw edges after stitching. The heavier and harder the fabric texture, the less seam edge will go through the tubing without a struggle. Clip off a little at a time, testing it until you can pull the bobby pin easily. Fill with yarn if the cording is too soft or if it flattens out when formed into a loop. Coating fabrics and velveteen may have to be treated in this way.

Although it is not necessary to select the buttons before the loops are made, it is important that you have an idea of their general size. The approximate size is close enough, because buttons come in such a great variety of sizes and types that you will have no difficulty finding some to fit your loops.

It's not a bad idea to make a couple of practice loops first. This will give you an idea of how they will look when finished, and you can take the sample along when shopping for the buttons. Covered buttons can also be used with loops.

229

Cut the bias cording into short lengths, depending on the size of loop desired. Place the first loop ⅝ inch away from the top edge of the article, leaving enough edge for a seam at the top. The loops are placed on the right side of the fabric, at the right-hand side of the opening. The cording is made into a small arc, the distance between the two ends being the approximate diameter of the button you want to use. The cord should be placed on the garment with the seam facing up, so that when finished, the seamed side of the loop will be on the inside of the garment. Pin each end of the loop edge to edge with the opening, inserting the pins horizontally. (Fig. 161.) Place the loops one against the other, with no space between them. (There will be space only in the arcs.) When the loops are all arranged and pinned, stitch them. Only a ⅛-inch seam is taken along the edge of the opening, to avoid gapping at the bottom of the opening.

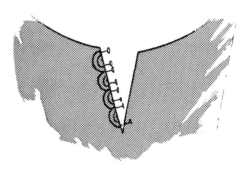

Figure 161

When loops are used in place of buttonholes on overlapped fronts of garments, as on a button-down-the-front blouse, the overlap that is allowed for the buttonholes must be removed. The part on which the loops are to be sewn is trimmed down first, leaving only ⅛ inch of seam beyond the center front, to which the loops can be joined. In this way the loops and the buttons will be located directly in the center of the garment. The side of the garment on which the buttons are to be sewn can be trimmed off also, if the garment is made of sheer cloth, but it can be left as is on opaque cloth, since the underlap will not show through.

The facing is then placed on the right side of the garment and pinned into position, over the loops and whatever part of the garment the facing must be joined to. Stitch on the garment side, through the exact row of stitching with which the loops were sewn. Trim the seam edges around the neck in the most satisfactory manner, depending on the features of the neckline. Clip off the corners to avoid bulk, and turn the facing to the inside of the garment. It is then basted into place and pressed well. If the loops are pressed on the wrong side with a heavy Turkish towel underneath them, they will remain nice and round, and retain their shape. Ball buttons, covered with the dress fabric, look well with loops and make a subtle but functional detail. (Fig. 162.)

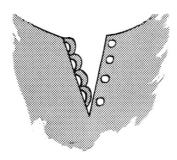

Figure 162

Bias cording can be used for many decorative trims around collars and collarless necklines. To make scallops of the cording around a round collar, you need only arrange the short pieces of the cording evenly around the outer edge of the upper collar on the right side of the cloth. (Fig. 163.) Pin the ends down in the same way as on the front opening and sew ⅛ inch from edge. The under collar is then placed over the scallops, right sides of the fabric together, and pinned for stitching. Stitch on the upper collar side, so that the row that stitched

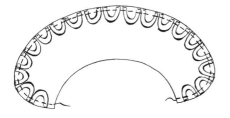

Figure 163

231

the bias pieces can be seen and used as a guide. Then turn the collar right side out and baste flat for pressing. (Fig. 164.)

This type of decoration is suitable for children's garments also. Picture the charm of a lark-colored cotton plaid dress with white piqué or linen collar outlined with cording made from the dress fabric.

Figure 164

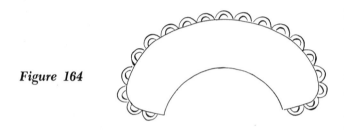

Here is another way to use loop trimming: Large collarless necklines can stand an interesting treatment, especially if the garment is cut on simple lines. Make two sets of cording loops, one long and one somewhat shorter. Arrange the longer pieces around the neckline first, forming them into arcs, one touching the other, with the ends of the cording even with the neck edge. The cording arcs, of course, are arranged on the right side of the material with the seamed side of the cording facing out. When the large arcs have been sewn into place, the little ones are arranged inside of them. (Fig. 165.) They are pinned into

Figure 165

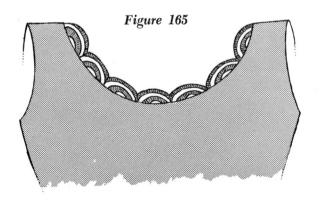

position and sewn with the machine. The facing is placed on the right side of the neck edge, pinned into position, and sewn from the garment side, so that the same row of stitching can be followed as that which holds the bias cordings in place. Press on the wrong side, using a heavy towel for padding.

Still another version of this neck trimming is done in the following manner: Arrange the longer cordings on the right side of the neckline, matching the ends of the cordings on the raw edges of the neckline. Pin into position and then stitch into place. Arrange the shorter cordings inside of the large arcs, and pin them into place for stitching. When they have been sewn, cut a bias strip of fabric 1½ inches wide. Fold it through the center and then sew it to the right side of the neckline with a ½-inch seam, pulling the binding slightly while stitching, so that it will hug the neckline when finished. Trim all edges of the neckline evenly and turn the folded edge over to the wrong side of the garment, allowing ¼ inch of it to remain on the right side for trim. Sew the inside of the binding by hand to the rows of stitching that are visible inside the garment. (Fig. 166.)

This type of trimming is also smart on sweaters, either in self-tone or one of a harmonizing hue. Picture how smart satin trim in self-color would be on a cashmere. Countless ideas can be carried out using bias cording trim. Shoestring straps, used singly or in several strands, can hold up the bodice of an evening gown very effectively. A pair of straps can be sewn into any strapless blouse or gown. You can conceal them inside the garment on the occasions when you don't want to use them.

Bias cording can also be used for braided belts. Use all one color, or one strand each for each color in a printed fabric, or make a multicolor belt from the fabrics of several dresses, so that the belt is suitable

Figure 166

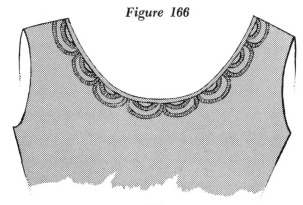

233

to wear with each one. Or if you don't want to wear a belt but object to the seam joining a bodice and skirt, you can use a strip of spaghetti to conceal the seamline: Complete the garment first; place the seam of the cording against the seam on the garment; and then sew the cording around the waistline with bridge stitching. Tuck the ends of the cording in neatly and finish them by hand, or bring them together with a tiny snap or hook and eye. In this easy way you will get the same effect as if you had sewn a special piece of cording between the bodice and the skirt. (Fig. 167.)

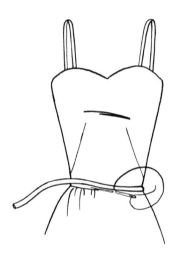

Figure 167

How to make frogs

Frogs made of garment material are also effective decorations, and are easily made. They can be used for functional purposes or for decoration only. On neck closings, use them singly, or in pairs or more, depending on their size. If they are large, too many will look over-elaborate. Experimenting with a strip of bias cording will prove how easy it is to produce unusual frog designs.

Here is how one interesting arrangement is done: Make a strip of cording about 12 inches long. Fold it through the middle and roll the two ends upward on the outside of the folded cord until the loop is the desired size. The little rolls are pinned through, and then sewn here and there by hand on the wrong side of the fabric. (Fig. 168 a & b.) Frogs are usually used in pairs, one for the left side and one for the right.

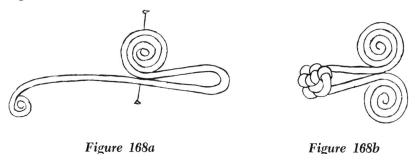

Figure 168a

Figure 168b

An additional little roll, made from a shorter piece of cording, will give the frog an even fancier appearance when placed between the two rolled-up ends and tacked by hand to the rest of the frog. Buttons to be used with frogs can be covered with the same material as the garment. Or you might prefer to purchase bone or composition buttons to harmonize with the fabric. The button is sewn into the loop of the frog on the left-hand side of the garment, and the loop on the right is used as if it were a buttonhole.

If you wish to produce a Chinese effect, build a knot button into one of the frogs. Make the strip for this half of the frog pair longer than the one for the loop, as the knot button requires extra material. Build the knot button into the center of the bias cording and then make the design of the frog in the shape of the opposite side of the pair. Again, the frog with the button is used on the left-hand side of the garment and the one with the loop on it is used on the right. (Fig. 169.)

Figure 169

How to make and apply welt cording

Cable cording in different thicknesses is sold by the yard at most notion counters. It has many interesting uses. One of them is for making novelty belts for casual clothes which have a nautical flavor about them. The cording is also used for drawstrings on play clothes and bathings suits, as well as a filler for making welt trimming for all types of wearing apparel. It can be used in this way for neck and sleeve detailing, sewn between the outer fabric and the facings. It resembles the bound neckline, but is rounder and more pronounced.

Welt cording is made by cutting cloth strips on the true bias, 1½ inches wide, and joining the pieces inconspicuously. This, of course, is done by thorough pressing. The cable cording is then wrapped in the bias strip, with the material facing right side out, and stitched as close as possible to the cord. (Fig. 170a & b.) Use a cording foot on your

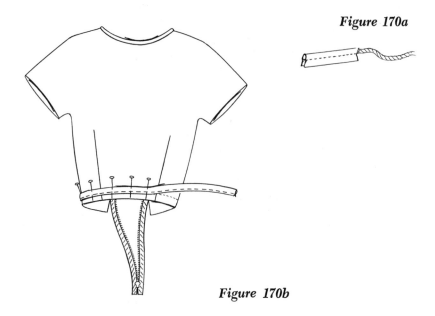

Figure 170a

Figure 170b

sewing machine for this purpose. Stretch the cloth slightly as the cording is being sewn. This welt cord is comparable to the welting that is used in making slip covers, only the cording used in clothing is much firmer and finer. It is also pure white, where the other is natural.

Welt cording is often used around the waistline in place of a belt, both in adults' and children's clothes. It is used in casual as well as more formal types of clothes. For example, a taffeta or peau de soie evening dress looks very well with just cording between the fitted bodice and the bouffant skirt.

When cording is inserted between the bodice and the skirt, the construction procedure is different from that used for a simple seam. The bodice pieces are assembled and fitted, and the sides sewn together. The skirt sections are completely assembled, sides joined, with the exception of the side that will have the zipper closing. This is true of the bodice also. Leave the left side open if the closing is located there, or the center back, on a back-closing garment.

The welt cording is then placed on the right side of the fabric of the bodice section, with the raw edges of the cording flush with the raw edges of the bottom of the bodice. The cording is then sewn with the cording foot, so that the stitching can be done close to the cording. The skirt is then pinned and stitched with the right sides facing the bodice, through the row of stitching that holds the cording in place, so that it can be used as a guide. (Fig. 171.)

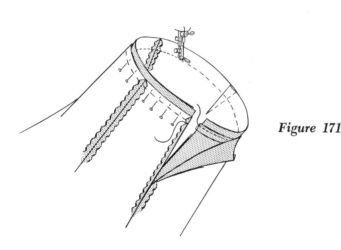

Figure 171

When inserting a zipper in a garment with welt cording around the waist, it is advisable to remove some of the cording from the opened edges so that when the opening is folded over to cover the zipper, only one layer of cording remains in the welt. This avoids bulk. This rule applies to any section of a garment where cording has to be folded. The underpart of the cording can be easily removed.

When applying welt cording around a neckline that is large enough so that no opening is necessary, start the cording at one of the shoulder seams so that it will not show. If the neckline has an opening, however, start the cording there. Welt cording can be made of contrasting or harmonizing color to bring out one of the colors of a print just as well as it can be made of the garment fabric itself. In applying it to any part of the garment, always draw it slightly in the first stitching, so that it goes on smoothly. If it is not held rather taut at this point, it may come out a little looser than desired.

Cording could also be used like any other type of trim around collars and cuffs. Another effective use for this trim is in outlining the edges of jackets, especially blazers.

Slot seams

An ordinary construction seam in any part of the styling area of a garment can be turned into a decorative detail with slot seaming. (Fig. 172.) Materials of all textures can be treated in this way to give your garment added interest. Here is how slot seams are made:

Figure 172

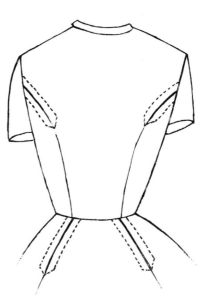

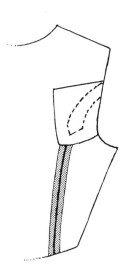

Figure 173

Whatever part of the seam is to be detailed as a slot seam will be sewn with the largest machine stitching. You can treat the complete seam in this manner, or only a section, like the design illustrated here. The stitching gauge is adjusted to sew with the large stitch up to a specific place, and then readjusted to regular-sized stitching for the continuation of the seam. The seams are then pressed open. The last big stitch in the seam, where the detailing will end, should be clipped with the point of the scissors on both sides of the seam. A stay or under-lay of fabric is then placed underneath the slot seam part of the gar-ment. The stay is cut on the same weave of the cloth as the fabric in the location of the slot seam, and it must be large enough so that it will cover the raw edges of the seams. (Fig. 173.) Pin the underlay smoothly to the wrong side of the garment, and then trim stitch on the right side of the cloth in any way desired, keeping within the seam width on the wrong side of the cloth, of course. The stay is now trimmed off to the size of the other seam edges and the large machine stitching is pulled out. This will not disturb the rest of the seam because of the previous clipping of the thread on both sides of the raw edges at the bottom of the large stitch. A contrasting colored stay can be used if desired. This is a good way to introduce another color in a subtle way. The seam opens just enough to allow a peek at the underlay. It is an attractive detail whether the color of the stay is self-tone or contrasting.

Italian quilting or trapunto work

Your lack of drawing talent need not limit your ability to enhance a

239

simple dress with attractive designs worked out in Italian quilting. Trapunto work, whether simple or elaborate, will give your wearing apparel a truly individual touch. (Fig. 174.)

Dramatized simplicity is always a good choice for fashion appeal, and trapunto is the answer. If you are handy with blackboard chalk, you can draw a spray here or a vine there on the garment you wish to detail: the chalk will rub off after you have completed your stitching. A trapunto monogram or initial makes a handsome touch on the bodice of a dress or the pocket of a blouse. The letters will be raised enough to produce especially subtle detail. Or you can trace things from children's coloring books: you will be surprised at the designs you can find in them.

Your more elaborate sketching can be done on lightweight cotton—perhaps organdy—put underneath the part of the garment to be decorated. Pin or baste the fabric with the drawing into position, so that it will stay in place while you machine-trace it onto the garment piece. The design must be reversed on the inside of the garment so that it will come through right on the outside.

Machine stitch the outlines of the design either in the color of the garment or in a contrasting one. The closely sewn lines form channels through which the yarns will be drawn; the designs will seem raised or quilted. When you do trapunto on washable materials, use nylon yarns for filling the channels; woolen yarns look best on garments that will be dry cleaned. Cotton yarns are not resilient enough: they would cause the design to be stiff.

Figure 174

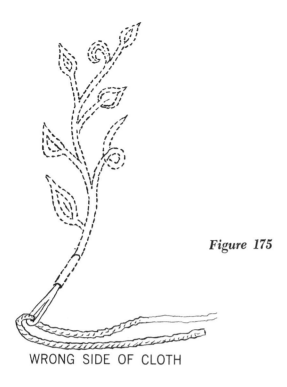

Figure 175

WRONG SIDE OF CLOTH

Thread the yarn through a darning needle with a large eye. Working from the wrong side of the garment, head the needle through the channels to pull the yarn into the design. (Fig. 175.) When you reach a point or corner, puncture the backing material with the needle point, draw the needle out of the design, and then reinsert it in the same hole but at a new angle. Some parts of the design may need to be packed more than others. Additional strands of wool can be inserted until the outside of the design is pleasing. The more puff there is, the more effective the design will be. Do not hesitate to withdraw the needle if the going gets rough in some sections of the design. Cut the yarn and start all over again as often as necessary. Cut the ends of the yarn off close to the backing. When the complete design has been filled with the yarn, press the quilting on the wrong side of the work with a moistened pressing cloth, using a heavy towel underneath so that the design will be more pronounced. If there are any loose stitching threads where the thread was broken to start a new angle on the channels, pull them through to the wrong side of the garment, and tie them.

Another very simple quilting idea that would add lots of interest to a tailored garment is done with several rows of stitching around the neckline, after the facing has been attached. The yarn is then drawn

241

Figure 176

between the facing and the outer material, padding the spaces between the rows of stitching. The corrugated appearance that results will net many admiring glances. (Fig. 176.)

Quilting can be done on collars, yokes, belts, or wherever your fancy deems it pleasing. When used on collars or around necklines, there is no need to interface that part of the garment, as the quilting gives the necessary firmness. On the other hand, if a belt is quilted, use interfacing also to obtain the maximum firmness.

Italian quilting with a transfer pattern

Many beautiful transfer patterns are found in the fancywork catalogues at pattern counters in department stores. They are grouped for special uses, as well as general use. For example, there will be special designs suitable for beading, quilting, smocking, and other types of handwork.

When one of these transfer patterns is used for the trapunto design, the pattern is transferred to the backing material and not to the garment itself. The backing is then placed on the part of the garment where the design will be featured, pinned to the wrong side of the cloth, and basted in place. The printed design is faced away from the inside of the garment, so that it will be visible to work on. Machine stitch on the backing, following the lines of the transfer carefully. Then proceed as in the free-hand design, with yarn filling to the desired roundness.

Fringe made from garment fabric

Very effective fringe trimming can be made from strips of the garment fabric cut on the horizontal weave. This trimming can be used on collars, cuffs, pocket flaps, yoke edges, and even down the fronts of garments. (Fig. 177.) It is an effective way to coordinate two items of wearing apparel, thus tying them into an ensemble.

242

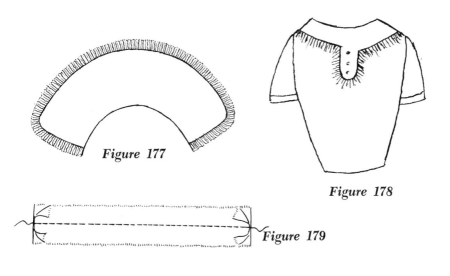

Figure 177

Figure 178

Figure 179

Figure 180

For instance, fringe made from the tweed of a skirt can outline the neckline of a blouse made in harmonizing jersey. (Fig. 178.) A sweater may be trimmed with fringe made from the suiting fabric with which it is worn. A natural linen collar, outlined with fringe made from Black Watch gingham, can dress up a little girl's Black Watch gingham dress.

Most fabrics woven from firmly twisted yarns, either natural or synthetic, can be used for fringe. Cottons and woolens are particularly satisfactory. It is easy to test the suitability of cloth for this purpose by fraying some of the horizontal yarns and judging from the appearance of the vertical ones.

A very nice fringe suitable in width for most trimming, is made from strips cut 1½ inches wide on the true horizontal weave of the fabric. In cutting the strip for the fringe, make sure to follow the true weave from one selvage edge to the other. If a thread can be drawn to mark a straight line, it will help a lot. If the cloth is woven of fine yarns, such as gingham, percale, sheer wool, it would be wise to incorporate two or three strips, so that the fringe will be rich and full. When the yarns are heavy, one strip will be enough.

Place the strips of fabric one on top of the other and run a row of stitching directly through the center so that they will stay in place. (Fig. 179.) The strip is then folded through the stitching and another row of stitching is made through the fold, ⅛ inch away from the edge. The layers of material are then converted into fluffy fringe just by fraying the horizontal yarns from one end of the strip to the other. (Fig. 180.) Start to pull out the yarns on the bottoms of the strips, and work

243

toward the stitched fold. When each layer of fabric has been thus treated, the fringe is ready to apply to any part of the garment. The machine stitching controls the fraying, and should be done even when the fringe is made from single fabric, down the front or side front of garments, as in kilts. If the single layer of garment fabric does not make the fringe sufficiently thick, additional strips of cloth can be placed underneath the surface piece and machine stitched in place.

The fringe is inserted between the upper and under collar in the same way as for any other trimming edge. The stitching at the edge of the fringe is placed on the stitching line on the right side of the upper collar, and sewn to it. The under collar is then placed against the upper one, and sewn through the same row of stitching, so as not to disrupt the even width of the fringe.

When fringe is used to outline yokes of any type of garments, it is first sewn to the outer edge of the yoke, before the yoke is attached to the rest of the unit. The row of stitching is then used as a guide for stitching the yoke and the lower section to each other. In this way the fringe is not disturbed.

If the fringe becomes matted after the garment is laundered, comb it out with a wet comb. This will separate the yarns and restore them to their original condition.

Hand picking and saddle stitching

Coats and suits made of soft-textured fabrics, such as camel's hair, cashmere, vicuña, as well as other materials of like appearance, are greatly enriched when hand sewing, beautifully done, is featured on the edges of fronts, collars, cuffs, or outlining some of the important construction seams. Single-strand buttonhole twist is most satisfactory for this type of work. Use it in the color closest to that of the garment fabric, or slightly darker.

Complete the garment before doing this work. Although hand picking appears to be done through the complete thickness of the front of the garment and the facing, it is really done through only part of these layers. First it is done on the garment side, catching only some of the cloth underneath the top fabric. Then a completely separate operation is done on the facing side. Make sure that the stitches do not come through on either one of these operations.

HAND PICKING Without knotting the thread, start the stitching by inserting the needle into the material at the preferred distance from the edge, and bring the thread through to the surface far enough away from the starting point to lose the end of the thread inside of the work. This eliminates the need for knots and keeps the stitches from getting

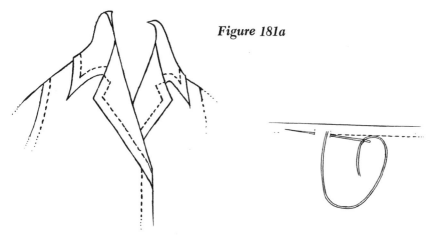

Figure 181a

Figure 181b

loose at the ends. Insert the needle ¼ inch to the right of where it came through, and bring it back to the surface ½ inch to the left of where it came through. This is a little ¼-inch backstitch. You go back ¼ inch but go forward ½ inch, and the distance between the little backstitches is ¼ inch, just the same as the length of the stitches themselves. (Fig. 181a & b.) The stitches are taken through the outer material only and some of the cloth immediately underneath it, but do not go through to the right side of the facing. The facing is done in the exact same manner as the top fabric. On a collar, the stitching could be done only on the outer side. A collar that is worn turned up, however, would look best with hand picking done on the under section also. The same rule applies to cuffs.

When hand picking is done on construction seams, the width should be comparable to that which is used on the garment edges. One of the reasons why hand picking is such a favorite on garments of luxurious fibers is that the edges thus finished remain supple while at the same time the outer fabric and the facing are held together in a very decorative way.

SADDLE STITCHING There is a similarity in the appearance of saddle stitching and hand picking, but the saddle stitch is a running stitch, rather than a backstitch. This trim is very effective on casual clothes, especially dresses and blouses. Although only one row of saddle stitching can be used to good effect, two or more rows are also very decorative. Embroidery floss in contrasting or self-color can be used for this purpose. The stitches may be any desired length, although about ¼ inch showing and ¼ inch concealed is a good choice. When several rows are used, the stitches can either be lined up with one another on each row, or staggered. (Fig. 182.) Both ways are effective and smart. Saddle stitching can be done with woolen yarn on garments made of wool.

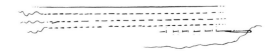

Figure 182

Embroidered arrowheads

Arrowheads at the ends of slashed pockets, at the top of pleats, or at the beginning of a slit at the bottom of skirts, not only add to the attractiveness of the garment but at the same time reinforce that part of the detail. The arrows are made with firmly twisted embroidery cotton or silk, or with buttonhole twist. Buttonhole twist, usually made of pure silk fibers, comes in most popular and fashionable colors. It is used for hand-embroidered buttonholes as well as for hand picking, saddle stitching, and any other details that come under the heading of tailored embroidery, of which the arrowhead is one.

Mark a triangle on the article with pointed chalk, making a dot for each corner, and holding the arrow so that it points in an upward direction. Mark the dots No. 1 for the one on the left, No. 2 for the one on the peak, and No. 3 for the dot on the righthand side. Proceed to work as follows: Use a single thread strand of twist. Knot the end and bring the thread through to the right side of the cloth directly through the middle of dot No. 1. Take a tiny stitch at No. 2, and pull the thread through so that the thread from No. 1 and No. 2 lies flat at an angle on the surface of the cloth. (Fig. 183a, b, & c.) Then insert the needle down through the middle of dot No. 3, and point it back to the surface at the immediate left of dot No. 1. You are now back at the starting point and you need only repeat the steps. Each time a stitch is taken at point No. 2 the needle is inserted on the outside of the triangle, and each time the needle is inserted down at dot No. 3 it is done inside the base of the triangle, to the left of the stitch and dot No. 3 and brought back to the surface of the cloth to the right of the last stitch at dot No. 1. When the space between dot No. 3 and No. 1 is filled, the arrowhead is finished. The thread is transferred to the wrong side of the arrowhead and secured with a knot. The thread in

246

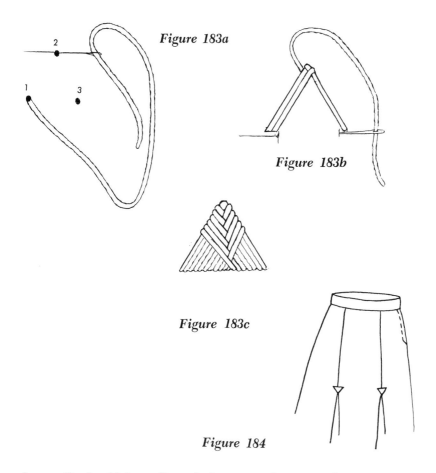

Figure 183a

Figure 183b

Figure 183c

Figure 184

the needle should be sufficiently long to make a complete arrowhead from start to finish.

Arrowheads placed just above the pleats not only enhance the appearance of a garment but also prevent strain on the ends of the seams over the pleats. And they help to hold the pleats in place since some of their stitches go through to the underlay of the pleats. (Fig. 184.)

With fashions constantly changing, new features and details will pop up in your sewing ventures all the time. No one book can cover all phases of sewing for all time, but if the fundamental principles of constructing clothes and details are understood thoroughly, the work involved in new fashions will be easy. Your knowledge will expand as time goes on. Each sewing venture will help toward the success of the next one.

With the basic knowledge derived from this text you will find unlimited vistas opened to you. Experiment now and then, discover short cuts of your own. It's fun, and stimulating. Good luck!

INDEX

251